ADDITIONAL PRAISE FOR *GLOBAL NEGOTIATION:*

"I have been a consumer of Dr. Graham's numerous publications on international negotiations since my first business trip to Japan over two decades ago. His latest work, *Global Negotiation: The New Rules,* with William Hernández Requejo, both reinforces culturally-based negotiating principles that remain fundamentally stable over time, and provides valuable insight into emerging negotiating trends and approaches. Microsoft does business in over 100 countries. We have possibly the broadest set of diverse customers ranging from government to corporations to end consumers. It is possible that the importance of consistently negotiating mutually beneficial outcomes around the world is only eclipsed by our imperative to build world-class software and services. *Global Negotiation* is a great guide to driving thoughtful, productive negotiations across borders."

—Michael Delman, Corporate Vice President,
Microsoft Corporation

"In an ever-shrinking and fiercely competitive world, this book provides the reader with up-to-date rules of engagement for success."

—Manuel Junco, Senior Vice President,
Downstream Business Line, Fluor-Daniel

"For many American businessmen, learning and understanding the principles of successful international negotiations is a daunting and seemingly impossible challenge. This book is helpful in providing useful insights and guidelines. It will become an important resource tool for not only beginners but also for experienced veterans in dealing with the cultural and strategic nuances in cross-border negotiations. It is a must read."

—Dean Yoost, retired Senior Partner,
PricewaterhouseCoopers

GLOBAL NEGOTIATION

The New Rules

William Hernández Requejo
and John L. Graham

Requejo and Graham

palgrave
macmillan

GLOBAL NEGOTIATION
Copyright © William Hernández Requejo and John L. Graham, 2008.
All rights reserved. No part of this book may be used or reproduced in any
manner whatsoever without written permission except in the case of brief
quotations embodied in critical articles or reviews.

First published in 2008 by
PALGRAVE MACMILLAN™
175 Fifth Avenue, New York, N.Y. 10010 and
Houndmills, Basingstoke, Hampshire, England RG21 6XS.
Companies and representatives throughout the world.

PALGRAVE MACMILLAN is the global academic imprint of the Palgrave
Macmillan division of St. Martin's Press, LLC and of Palgrave Macmillan
Ltd. Macmillan® is a registered trademark in the United States, United
Kingdom and other countries. Palgrave is a registered trademark in the
European Union and other countries.

ISBN-13: 978-1-4039-8493-7
ISBN-10: 1-4039-8493-X

Library of Congress Cataloging-in-Publication Data
Graham, John L.
    Global negotiation : the new rules / John Graham and William
Hernández Requejo.
        p.   cm.
    Includes bibliographical references and index.
    ISBN 1-4039-8493-X
    1. Negotiation in business.   2. Cultural awareness.   3. International
business enterprises—Management.   4. International trade—Social
aspects.   I. Requejo, William Hernández.   II. Title.
HD58.6.G69   2008
658.4'052—dc22

                                                                2007036155

A catalogue record of the book is available from the British Library.

Unless otherwise noted, quotations are from private, confidential
interviews with the authors.

Design by Letra Libre, Inc.

First edition: March 2008

10 9 8 7 6 5 4 3 2 1

Printed in the United States of America.

CONTENTS

ACKNOWLEDGEMENTS

This book contains the insights, ideas, and words of our teachers, co-authors, and research collaborators. We are deeply indebted. They are:

Nancy Adler, Rob Allerheiligen, Doug Andrews, Cathy Anterasian, Yao Apasu, Richard Bagozzi, Bill Bishop, Rich Brahm, Nigel Campbell, Jennifer Chandler, George Devos, Gabriel Esteban, Leonid Evenko, Paul Garb, John Gerretsen, Mary Gilly, Kjell Gronhaug, John Gumperz, Ned Hall, Jim Hodgson, Dick Holton, Rika Houston, Shigeru Ichikawa, Runtian Jing, Wes Johnston, Alain Jolibert, Mike Jones, Mike Kamins, Dong Ki Kim, Tina Klein, Kam-hon Lee, C. Y. Lin, Hans-Gunter Meissner, Taylor Meloan, Alma Mintu-Wimsatt, Bruce Money, Joyce Neu, Alena Ockova, Mahesh Rajan, Mike Robinson, Wayne Rodgers, Teddy Schwarz, Dave Stewart, Sara Tang, Rajeev Tyagi, Joel West, Tom Wotruba, and Guang Yang. We owe special thanks to Roy Herberger, Yoshihiro Sano, Philip Cateora, Mark Lam, and Lynda Lawrence for their contributions to our book.

The optimism and negotiation skills of Jill Marsal and Sandra Dijkstra at the Sandra Dijkstra Literary Agency have literally (no pun intended) made this book possible. We also want to thank everyone at Palgrave Macmillan that helped us turn our ideas into pages—they are Airié Stuart, Aaron Javsicas, Chris Chappell, Marie Ostby, Donna Cherry, Erin Igoe, and Dylan Moulton. Finally, at the Merage School, both Lindsey Lambert and Gail Ho provided crucial support as well.

WILLIAM'S ACKNOWLEDGEMENTS

Gov. Bill Richardson, Mark Stevens, Alonso Perezmartinez, Robert Reich, Steven Johnson, Victor M. Cueto, and the many unknown, unrecognized negotiators that have made this world a better place.

WILLIAM'S DEDICATION

For "Maqui" (my Wife, for her love and faith), for Hortensia (my Mom, need I say more?), for Helen, (for her many years of wisdom) and for my grandfather, Fidel Requejo (for true civility).

JOHN'S DEDICATION

For my role models: Of course, my father, John M. Graham, then Manuel Casagrande, Jerry Spolter, Jim Gleckler, Tom Lawson, Tom Wotruba, Ned Hall, Rick Bagozzi, Roy Herberger, Philip Cateora, and Lionel Gilly.

THE NEW FOCUS ON KNOWLEDGE, COMMUNICATION, AND CREATIVITY

Give a man a fish . . .

In our experience, we've often been witness to global negotiations that have yielded wonderfully creative outcomes. Indeed, that's the fundamental idea—international commerce works best (and delivers human progress) when knowledgeable businesspeople meet, communicate effectively, and concoct creative business arrangements that make sense for all parties involved. Usually achieving success is not easy because the diversity of international meetings makes communication and relationship building difficult. But the diversity of international meetings can also produce new ideas and new perspectives on those ideas that can be exploited for mutual benefit by patient and creative negotiators on both sides of the table.

Despite our best advice, over the years we have also been witness to global negotiation disasters. Below, with some pain, we describe two of those. First, we focus on a single meeting between Americans and Koreans. Second, we briefly describe the complexities of a huge South American energy project. The first case involved millions of dollars and the second, billions. In both cases, opportunities were lost for all involved.

FILLETED IN SEOUL[1]

He must have practiced it. The chair cartwheeled through the air, impaling itself into the wall, all four legs at equal depth. The flying chair was a real conversation stopper. Everyone at the table, both the Americans and the chair chucker's fellow Koreans, just stared at the chair in awe. There was a brief, uncomfortable silence, and no one moved. Then the lead American negotiator stuffed his notes into his briefcase, stood up, and announced, "We're done."

The sales team of a U.S. semiconductor manufacturer was in heated negotiations over the ever-decreasing profit margins of their wireless semiconductors sold to their Korean customers. The negotiations were always tough, but ever since the decline in U.S. cell phone purchases, the negotiations had become even more difficult. Faced with decreasing sales and a long-term economic downturn, the American team was in a difficult position. But the Korean cell phone makers were in dire straits as well.

The Korean company was inextricably linked to the U.S. market by both its semiconductor purchases and its consumer sales. With the U.S. slowdown, inventories of phones and associated component parts were mounting quickly. The only path out of disaster was to continue the series of innovations that would help maintain their lead in the new features war with their global competitors. Although highly efficient in the manufacture of silicon chips, the Koreans didn't possess the requisite design capabilities. "Features" had become key. The Americans provided those design features in their chips.

The Korean contingent represented three levels of their business community. The eldest member was in his 60s and proudly "old school." He served as the authority figure and decision maker. Two others, both in their mid-40s, were experts in the technological and financial aspects of the transaction, respectively. They represented the generation that understands their elders, but they were brought up in a much more Westernized way than the eldest member of the contingent. The last Korean negotiator was an up-and-coming business manager in his early 30s with an MBA from a top American university. The last had thrown the chair.

The U.S. team had been quickly thrown together and included a business manager, a project technician, and a Korean-American project director. The three hadn't worked together often, and none had much in the way of international experience. As usually happens within the information technology (IT) sector, given the complexity of the products and services offered, an "international team" is usually composed of "engineer-types" that have shown some propensity toward the "soft-skills area." Training is almost always nil. Thus, the performance of such negotiation teams varies dramatically based upon the circumstance into which they're thrown.

And these circumstances were tough. After an 18-hour flight, which included a four-hour layover in Tokyo, the U.S. team was fighting serious jet lag. Further, all still suffered from the national angst associated with the still-recent September 11 terrorist attacks on the World Trade Center in New York.

Moreover, the political background music was loud for the Koreans as well. Their cousins to the north were ramping up their nuclear weapons program in direct response to President Bush's most recent "axis of evil" appellation. This unhealthy mix of circumstance and inexperience had tensions running high. Suspicion, distrust, and fear were part of the brew. Because tensions are often contagious, the ambiance had turned brutally brittle. That's when the chair hit the wall.

The Americans should have headed for the door at "We're done." But, a fatal hesitation let the senior Korean take command. He ordered his "unruly" minion out of the room. He profusely apologized for his "unprofessional" behavior. He explained how important this project was to the entire company, as exemplified by the younger executive's "inexcusable" anger. He entreated the Americans to continue. *And,* he left the chair fixed in the wall. The rattled Americans stayed and talked, and gave things away.

Tossed into such a situation, it was not surprising that the American team balked. Unable to comprehend the event, they fell into a depressed, reactionary position. Unable to quantify the chair toss and afraid that the deal would be lost, they acquiesced to most of the Korean demands. The already slim profit margins the product generated for the American company disappeared.

What the U.S. team did not know was that the Korean team had planned the event. Indeed, it was just part of a carefully orchestrated negotiation gambit involving all three levels of Korean managers and careful timing of the show-stopping flying chair. As it remained lodged in the wall, the Americans remained overwhelmed by the emotional outburst. The Koreans were able to extract from the Americans huge concessions, and the young Korean became a hero. Thus, the seemingly irrational Korean behavior turned out to be actually quite rational.

The youngest Korean had been thoroughly trained in American negotiation techniques. All four Koreans had traveled many times to the

United States to receive cultural training and negotiations training specifically. The Koreans had worked together several times before and had conducted multiple rehearsal sessions. Their regimented skills development process successively placed them in increasingly more complex and difficult negotiation situations. Furthermore, the actual composition of the negotiating team was such that virtually all management levels were represented, from senior level to that of an "apprentice." The elder member of the team had an ongoing relationship with American senior management back in the United States. The younger Korean negotiators interacted in a more Westernized manner with the Americans. The "chair launcher" was not only a highly qualified engineer but, as mentioned, he had an MBA from a major American university, spoke English fluently, and understood the unique culture of the U.S. manufacturer, having done an internship with them during his time in the United States.

Only two of the Americans had worked in Korea before, but even they had only four visits between them. Also, they had only the briefest chance to review the past efforts of previous teams. Although the Korean American manager understood many of the cultural issues involved, he was not trained as a negotiator. All the Americans had been very successful with domestic clients. They and their superiors at headquarters simply assumed that they would be talking English the entire time, and that they were walking onto a relatively level playing field.

Without the proper skill set, the U.S. team had fallen prey to a typical American IT sector cultural flaw. Within the hard sciences/engineering world of high tech, "soft skills" such as sales, marketing, public relations, corporate diplomacy, and relationship building are woefully, even dangerously undervalued. The Koreans had successfully addressed this fundamental flaw in the training they underwent and preparations they made for their meeting with the Americans. Most simply stated, the Americans had (1) not understood cultural differences, (2) made no adjustments based on cultural differences, and (3) carelessly composed their negotiation team. Ouch!

When the largest market in the world is not your own, international expansion requires complete knowledge of that market. The Koreans had done their homework. The Americans, behaving true to form, assumed that they would be able to *reason* with the Koreans. It was precisely this American cultural proclivity to resort to reason that the Koreans had focused on and used to their advantage. The power of reason gave way to the power of "dramatic irrationality." The chair worked, and indeed, the youngest member of the Korean team had practiced throwing it.

Finally, there is a much more fundamental lesson here. One might conclude that the Koreans won this negotiation. But in reality no one *wins* negotiations. Business negotiations are not a competitive activity. They are a creative activity if done well. Yes, they may have done the (price) cutting, but the Koreans were also filleted in Seoul on this one because no one asked the question, "How can we better manage the inherent volatility in our industry for our mutual benefit in our ongoing business relationship?" No one asked, "What options are we ignoring by our razor thin focus on prices in this particular deal?" No one asked, "How can we leverage the complexity of supplying a global market from two very different business systems, Korea and the United States?" No one asked questions.

RIO URUBAMBA (HEADWATERS OF THE AMAZON), PERU

Flying chairs and supposedly angry Koreans are not the only hazards involved in international business negotiations. Indeed, it's time to get really worried when your guide says, "Make sure you don't touch the water, especially if you have a cut or scrape." Even the toughest American can't beat up a potent virus. Yes, a "dirty" river did slow progress, but other kinds of corruption also interfered in one of the biggest commercial projects in Latin American history. The global negotiation over the production of natural gas, discovered deep in the Amazon jungle in the early 1980s, was really not concluded even with the initial flow of gas some 700 km across the Andes to Lima in 2004. Still today, circa 2008, contracted prices for oil and gas produced in South America continue to be in a state of flux, immersed in the rapids of the continent's contentious politics. Compared to the ten minutes of interaction in Seoul described above, our story of the Camisea pipelines demonstrates the daunting complexity, and thus the creative opportunities, of global commerce at the extreme.

As part of a multi-country infrastructure energy development project proposed by Royal Dutch Shell to the Peruvian government, a group of engineering and construction companies had been asked to submit bids and designs for one of the largest energy projects in South American history. Building the bid required engineers and commercial folks to reconnoiter the sites involved in the project—all the way from the proposed spigot in Lima to the source of the gas some 700 kilometers to the east, over the Andes and into the steaming jungle of the Urubamba River valley. And, as the local guide had chided, that river contained some dangerous bugs for any antiseptic American in the area.

Back in the 1980s a group of Shell explorers had discovered some 13 trillion cubic feet of natural gas in Peru just west of the Andes. In "collaboration" with President Alberto Fujimori's government, Shell sought to tap that resource and pipe it over the Andes to Lima for distribution to the needy populace. The project was revolutionary in more than one respect and monumental in every aspect.

A decade later, the development of the site was estimated to be worth $2.7 billion to the engineering/construction firm winning the contract, approximately $11 billion to the large oil and gas multinational involved, and similarly many billions of dollars to the Peruvian government. The potential for even larger long-term revenue streams was there as well. Maintenance, operations, royalties, and derivative opportunities associated with such a project were inestimable. The project entailed a complete restructuring of Peruvian energy policy. Peru would go from being a nineteenth-century diesel-burning economy to a modern, clean-energy, gas-burning economy over a period of just six years. Within this period, all the necessary infrastructure developments had to take place, including new gas distribution and regulatory systems, new appliances that would have to be purchased by consumers, and so on. Finally, globally important and fragile ecosystems were included in the area to be developed. Thus, the stakes were exceedingly high, indeed global, with respect to economics, cultures, and natural environments.

In an attempt to manage such complexity, Shell established a design competition. Two of the largest American engineering/construction companies were invited to participate. Shell challenged Fluor-Daniel and Bechtel to propose how all these multifaceted interests might be addressed through the development of the project. The best design, the best bid, won the billion-plus-dollar award. Both firms went to work on a so-called win/win/win/win commercial structure.

Sadly, the complexity of the project that might have been exploited instead proved to be beyond the comprehension and capabilities of even these great multinational firms. Both American firms had on their corresponding Boards of Directors ex-State Department and/or ex-Central Intelligence Agency members who could have participated more comprehensively in the design. It was not a lack of information, but rather the use of the information that proved to be the major stumbling block.

The long-term strategic analysis entailed the coordination of Shell's technical and commercial specifications, the Peruvian politicians' national and personal interests, the demands of the various NGOs and corresponding environmental interests—including those of the indigenous people, the particular technical needs of the engineering and construction companies, and perhaps most importantly, the needs of that ubiquitous concept known as "the people of Peru."

The first critical factor was the interests of the Peruvian government. During this period, the Fujimori administration had tremendous influence and power over all transactions within the country. Political issues were everywhere to be found and within them, corresponding levels of complexity. From a practical perspective, Shell was larger than the entire Peruvian economy, yet the natural resources were on Peruvian soil. The temptations and threats of graft and corruption were great. And, since American firms were interacting with foreign governmental officials, the Foreign Corrupt Practices Act (FCPA) pertained, making illegal the otherwise unethical bribes seemingly expected by the Peruvian officials involved.

As it turned out, Shell was unable to work effectively with the Fujimori administration, and because of "various conflicts with the government," they dropped out of the project in 1998. Shell and its partner, Mobil Oil, literally walked away from the $250 million and the long years they had invested in the project. The Fujimori government then sought to revive the project, seeking proposals from other companies. Ironically, following the collapse of Fujimori's regime and his flight to Japan to avoid corruption charges in late 2000, the contract for continued development was signed by the interim president, Valentin Paniagua. Led by the Argentine Plus-Petrol, a global consortium of companies (South Korean, Belgian, and Hunt Oil of Dallas, Texas) won the contract to develop the gas field and pipeline project, offering a 37.4 percent royalty to the Peruvian government. They in turn built the pipeline with Grana y Montero and Techint, the Peruvian construction company and Argentine pipe layer, respectively, which were original members of the Fluor-Daniel consortium. The foreign companies invested $1.6 billion in the project. Finally on August 6, 2004, the Lima natural gas spigot was turned on, some 20 years after the initial discovery of the field. Since then, the pipeline has ruptured five times, but it remains in production.

PlusPetrol, Grana y Montero, and Techint were able to participate in the project ultimately by exploiting advantages Shell and the American engineering/construction firms lacked. The South American companies had a profound understanding of Peruvian culture, and they exercised patience. Indeed, ethnocentrism and impatience are often the cause of Americans' failures in global negotiations. Moreover, the global diversity of the PlusPetrol-led consortium yielded a new level of creativity in the negotiations.

Why did the Shell-led initiative fail? Could things have been structured in such a way so as to avoid these results? Who should have taken the lead in the negotiations? The "dirty river" metaphor is apt. That is, the potential for corruption proved hazardous in at least three ways: Graft in the Fujimori government, environmental damage to the rain forest, and diseases spread across the cultural interfaces in both directions (don't touch the water). Why weren't these events foreseen and better managed by the Shell development team? When is it time to walk away from a negotiation?

Looking back, one executive involved explained to us recently, "My own interpretation has always been that while Shell was being very straight and 'technical' with the government, the government thought that such a powerful global company must be playing some kind of game to get the better of the poor Peruvians. So, the government played that game, thinking Shell was playing it, and Shell didn't understand that the government supposed it was playing a game. Neither of the two parties actually 'walked away,' as both were expecting the other to call the bluff in the very last minute. It didn't happen and both sides were surprised with no project. This was a classic case of not understanding one another's hand."

So perhaps the daunting complexity really boiled down to a simple, but fundamental cross-cultural misunderstanding. How might Shell have more clearly communicated its intentions? What might Shell have done to better understand their customer? Where were the crucial creative thinking and international discussions that transform complexity into viable options for mutual gain? The answers to these questions and many others are the focus of this book.

THE NEW RULES

We have developed *Global Negotiation: The New Rules* to serve as a systematic guide to efficient and creative international commercial negotiations. Our purpose is to help negotiators everywhere in the world, including Americans, avoid making the kinds of mistakes we described above. But, even more than avoiding such mistakes, the new rules we delineate and describe here are intended to transform international negotiations from traditional competitive and/or problem-solving activities into truly creative and innovative processes. The new rules are simply stated:

#1. Accept only creative outcomes.
#2. Understand cultures, especially your own.
#3. Don't just adjust to cultural differences, exploit them as well.
#4. Gather intelligence and reconnoiter the terrain.
#5. Design the information flow.
#6. Invest in personal relationships.
#7. Persuade with questions.
#8. Make no concessions until the end.
#9. Use techniques of creativity.
#10. Continue creativity after negotiations.

But, the effective application of these ten simple rules requires the deeper understanding of the international negotiation processes we think of as a protocol, or road map, for global negotiations. While most readers around the world will find many novel ideas here, Japanese readers, for the reasons described below, might wonder what the fuss is all about. The Japanese approach to international business negotiations includes these rules already, by nature.

Indeed, we acknowledge that successful executives (not only Japanese ones) around the world are now moving toward a new global code of conduct for commercial negotiations, that is, a new set of rules, an etiquette, or a protocol for commercial diplomacy. A primary purpose of our book is to expedite the acceptance of these new rules and to demonstrate the usefulness of the code. You will see that the bases of the new rules are the integrated use of knowledge, communication, and creativity toward building commercial arrangements that deliver mutual prosperity around the world.

The new rules are applied in the context of a global negotiation process. The blueprint for this process is perhaps best represented as the skeleton of a fish (see exhibit I.1): When infused with the concepts of knowledge, communications, and creativity, this diagram represents the structural framework for our book. The metaphor of the fish works for us in several ways. Our students and clients have told us that the figure looks like a fish, so we know it works as a visual mnemonic for them. And, in a sense, negotiations follow the pattern depicted. Like a fish's tail, the

THE GLOBAL NEGOTIATION PROCESS

"The Fish"

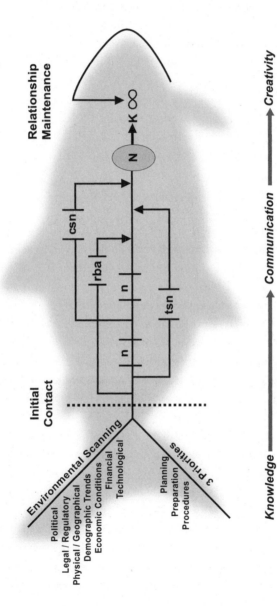

Knowledge ➝ Communication ➝ Creativity

N = formal negotiations
n = informal negotiations
K = contract/definitive agreement
rba = relationship building activities
tsn = technical side bar negotiations
csn = creative side bar negotiations

Exhibit I.1   The Global Negotiation Process: "The Fish"

knowledge gained through environmental scanning, planning, and preparations powers the entire process, including relationship-building activities, technical and creative sidebar negotiations, and formal and informal meetings. The main body of the fish, then, is comprised of the *communications* among partners. Finally, the head of the fish includes the *creativity* of agreement, the vision reflected in the contract, and the view of the future manifest in the ongoing relationship.

And, there's more to this fish metaphor. First, it reminds us of our favorite book title ever, *Dolphins and Sharks,* a book about Russians and Americans and business negotiations. Of course, the title begs the question, who's who? Are the Russians the sharks? Or, is it the Americans? The book's author, Peter Shikirev, our Russian colleague, sagely points out in his Cyrillic-spattered pages that there are sharks (competitive negotiators) and dolphins (creative negotiators) in both countries, and you would be wise to figure out pretty quickly what kind of fish you are swimming with.

And more. The Dutch were the first to dominate trade in Europe through their fishing fleets in the North Sea. You see, the marketing of fish involves the most difficult negotiation circumstance—bargaining over a perishable. That is, if you don't reach a timely agreement, then the focus of the interaction is destroyed. Fish rot, and quickly. A boatload of rotten fish is the opposite of a creative outcome. For our friends in Korea, it wasn't fish rotting, it was chips, the fast-obsolescing silicon kind. The Americans should have recognized that both sides were in a hurry and equally vulnerable. Yes, a hold full of fish requires expert negotiations; thus, the Dutch have developed a culture that depends on excellent international trading skills.

The best fishermen on the planet? Of course, it's the Japanese. It's no coincidence that they're also among the best international negotiators. Even the Dutch attest to Japanese prowess at the negotiation table, as we'll detail in the next chapter. It's also no coincidence that the greatest fish market on the planet is the Tsukigi in Tokyo. The per capita consumption of fish in Japan is among the highest in the world. The global price is set for seafood in this "New York Stock Exchange" of fish. A big bluefin tuna caught in the Atlantic, iced and shipped by air to Tokyo, can bring $10,000 at auction, and then be shipped by air back to Boston for hungry sushi consumers. Moreover, the symbolic association of fish in Japan parallels their consumption. Fish represent well-being, happiness, and freedom in Japan. The fish is one of the Eight Auspicious Symbols used in Japanese Buddhism. For Buddhists, it symbolizes living in a state of fearlessness, without danger of drowning in the ocean of sufferings, and migrating freely from place to place. *Koninobori* (paper carp) are flown all over Japan in early May, celebrating the birth of the culturally preferred boys. Finally, dried fish are also part of the Shinto ceremony associated with opening a new business, among others.

By now you're either ready to go out for sushi or just plain tired of the long-winded mnemonic we just served up. But it is important to note that throughout the book we will make reference to the Japanese negotiation style as a multifaceted example of best practices. Their historical intimacy with this most perishable product has honed their negotiation skills in a very deep cultural way. But back to basis of our book.

Because we firmly believe that all negotiating, whether in the domestic or international environment, is both science and art, the new rules must work in multiple ways. At a primary level, the new rules (along with the fish) serve as a template for managers to set up the process by which they will structure upcoming negotiations; painting by numbers, if you will.

At this first level, the fish model helps to identify the areas of research, preparation, planning, and procedures. It proceeds to establish the critical timeline and the initial point of contact where relationship building commences. It further distinguishes between formal and informal, creative, and technical sidebar negotiations by recognizing those sets of events that, in turn, lead to the contract. It also projects into the future by anticipating the need for relationship maintenance. This level works well to introduce the novice negotiator to the various stages and issues implicit in global negotiations. It begins to inform and organize the multidisciplinary nature of the subject into manageable working units.

At a secondary level, and when further integrated with the concepts of knowledge and communications, the new rules provide an organizational development component for the generation and training of negotiation teams. When coupled with the fields of knowledge management and communications, the new rules establish the process by which future negotiators are developed. They assume a systematic approach by which a corresponding higher level of responsibility is given to the various members of a negotiation team. It also anticipates continuity, which is so critical within relationship building. The knowledge obtained in the pre-negotiation stages is subsequently translated into a greater responsiveness at the negotiation stages. This continuity is maintained in the post-negotiation stage so critical for any potential dispute resolution.

The second level also presents the more complex nature of culture within an organizational as well as individual setting. Whereas at the first level the correct emphasis was on the national culture, at this next level as we shall see, more focus is given to the organizational and psychological aspects of the transaction. Through an apprenticeship at these various stages, the development of future negotiators is more strategically defined. Here, the transaction and the organization become the canvas upon which negotiation strategies will be further developed. A master artist may have associated apprentices; each painting a section of the canvas under her watchful eye.

The ability to work in this cohesive manner is directly linked to the successful use of modern communications channels within a global environment. At this second level, communications competence and flexibility are critical. Whether e-mail, voice over Internet protocol (VoIP), instant messaging, telephone, teleconferencing, or face-to-face communications, the use of these channels at this level is addressed herein and their corresponding appropriateness is considered.

Only when the two previous levels of understanding have been mastered do the new rules obtain their most creative expression. At this point the fish may change into an arrow or a circle or a scheme that more accurately reflects the particular demands of an organization and its management. The organization may be said to acquire a "style," one honed and perfected through the previous two stages. This evolution is premised on the structure of the learning organization, the dissemination and communication of knowledge, and an ability to create.

Only after Picasso had clearly demonstrated his ability to mimic the masters did he gain the freedom to explore in the abstract style. In very much the same way, the new rules become the best expression of the demands and concerns of the organization that acquired them. The rules engender a style intrinsic to the organization. Here, what may have been simply regarded as a negotiation development program now becomes part of the overall corporate culture. It becomes one more tool that the learning organization has in its belt.

But it is precisely this freedom to evolve that permits *Global Negotiation: The New Rules* to transcend the traditionally limited scope of international business negotiations to potentially serve as a framework for global negotiations and networks. If further developed, the new rules have the ability to create the means by which buyers and sellers, companies, countries, regions, and cultures can begin to understand each other on the road toward mutual prosperity. Indeed, these are *The New Rules* of international commerce.

PLAN OF THE BOOK

The remainder of the book is divided into four parts: Part I addresses cultural differences, the most salient aspect of international business negotiations. Indeed, culture is to humankind what water is to fish. That is, culture sustains us, but we don't usually notice that it's there. In Part II, we detail our ideas about the application of the new rules, that is, the Fish from tail to head. We provide specific advice about preparations, creative negotiation processes, and the development and maintenance of long-term global commercial relationships. Part III includes specific details and advice for negotiating with partners in three foreign countries that are among America's major trading partners—India, Mexico, and China. Our associated website, www.GlobalNegotiationBook.com, includes similar information on all the world's major trading countries. In Part IV of the book we conclude with ideas on how to integrate a culture of creative international negotiations into your company or organization. That is, we endeavor to show you how to teach your associates *how to fish!*

> *Give a man a fish, and he can eat for a day.*
> *Teach a man to fish, and he's never hungry again.*
> —Chinese proverb

PART I

YES, CULTURE MATTERS

I n chapters 1–5, we linger on the crucial topic of cultural differences and their impact on global negotiation. Understanding cultural differences are not only key to avoiding most of the pitfalls in global negotiation; they are also key to the creativity inherent in global commerce. Thus, the first three rules apply:

#1.   Accept only creative outcomes.
#2.   Understand cultures, especially your own.
#3.   Don't just adjust to cultural differences, exploit them as well.

CHAPTER 1

ADAM SMITH, JOHN WAYNE, AND THE AMERICAN NEGOTIATION STYLE[1]

He fishes well who uses a golden hook.

—Latin proverb

W e fully appreciate that not everyone reading this book is an American. Indeed, we trust our topic truly has global implications, so we expect many of you are not. Our fundamental advice here, Rule #2, still applies whether you're Indian, Mexican, or Chinese. You still need to understand your own culture to be an effective international negotiator. Indeed, we provide help in this regard for many people on the planet in Part III of the book and on our associated website—www.GlobalNegotiationBook.com. Therein we provide summaries of the cultures and negotiation styles we have observed around the world. Even if you are not American, reading this chapter will help you work with your American colleagues, clients, and customers.

Before we address the origins of cultural differences (chapter 2), their impact on business systems (chapter 3) and negotiation styles around the world (chapter 4), and the influences of personality and background on negotiation behaviors (chapter 5), we need to first address the unique style of business negotiations that comes natural to most Americans. Our story starts in New Jersey.

THE IMPORTANCE OF CULTURE (NEW JERSEY)

Some years ago John Graham attended a conference on international business alliances sponsored by the Rutgers and Wharton business schools. Now, New Yorkers reading this probably see a Jersey joke coming (culture in New Jersey?), but the keynote speaker at the conference started out a bit differently.

"You've all heard the story about the invention of copper wire—two Dutchmen got a hold of a penny." This bit of anecdotage was served up during a dinner speech by the American president of a joint venture owned by AT&T and Philips. At one level, the story is a friendly gibe, although the professor from the Netherlands sitting at our table didn't appreciate the American's remarks in general nor the ethnic joke in particular. Indeed, at another level, the story is stereotyping of the worst sort.

However, at an even deeper level there is an important lesson here for all managers of international commercial relationships. Culture can get in the way. The American president was in his "humorous" way attributing part of the friction between him and his Dutch associates to differences in cultural values. (As an aside, humor often works poorly across cultures.) He might have blamed personality differences or clashing "corporate" cultures, but instead he identified national cultural barriers to be a major difficulty in managing his joint venture. Although we do not appreciate his humor, we certainly agree that cultural differences between business partners can cause divisive, even decisive problems.

Kathryn Harrigan at the Columbia University School of Business once suggested that a crucial aspect of international commercial relationships is the negotiation of the original agreement. The seeds of success or failure are often sown face-to-face at the negotiation table, where not only the financial and legal details are agreed to but also, and perhaps more importantly, the ambience of cooperation is established. Indeed, as Harrigan indicates, the legal details and the structure of international business ventures are almost always modified over time, and usually through negotiations. But either the initial atmosphere of cooperation established face-to-face at the negotiation table persists, or the venture fails.

THE DUTCH VIEW OF THE AMERICAN
NEGOTIATION STYLE (SPAIN)

This chapter is not about American bashing. You don't need us for that. There are more objective sources. We ran across this quote in *Expansion*, a Spanish newspaper: "Los mejores negociadores son los japoneses, capaces de pasare dias intentando conocer a su oponente. Los peores, los norteamericanos, que piensan que las cosas funcionan igual que en su país en todas partes."[2] Roughly translated, this says, "The best negotiators in the world are the Japanese because they will spend days trying to get to know their opponents. The worst are the Americans because they think everything works in foreign countries as it does in the USA."

Part of the reason we've included this quote is it balances out the aforementioned "penny-stretching crack." That is, Samfrits Le Poole, the much quoted author of *How to Negotiate with Success,* is Dutch. And, we've learned to always listen to what our Dutch associates have to say about international business. As we mentioned in the introduction, as a people, they are among the great traders of the world. The Netherlands is located strategically at the mouths of the three great rivers—the Maas, the Waal, and the Rhine—that both feed and divide (the Protestant north from the Catholic south) Western Europe. Many Dutch seem to know about five languages, and seem to have lived in as many different countries.

Certainly there are some Americans that are very effective in international business negotiations. And in some circumstances, the best prescription might be something we call an American approach. However, in the pages to follow we must be critical at times, because the secondary purpose of this chapter is to get you to change your behavior. But usually meaningful changes in behavior take both time and many contacts with your foreign counterparts. In fact, the best way to learn to behave appropriately in a foreign country is by letting yourself unconsciously imitate those with whom you interact frequently. A penchant for careful observation is also crucial. Hopefully, this chapter and those that follow will help to sharpen your observation skills.

The primary purpose of this chapter, then, is to make you aware of the multiple ways cultural differences in values and communication styles can cause serious misunderstandings between otherwise positively disposed business partners. And many of these problems manifest themselves in face-to-face meetings at the international negotiation table. For example, a silent Japanese individual doesn't necessarily mean reticence, and a Spaniard's frequent interruptions shouldn't communicate rudeness to you. Are there places where American humor works? Do all Chinese reopen closed issues? When should business be brought up in Brazil? How important are foreign language skills these days? How do you tell it's time to walk away from a deal in Peru? And what does it mean to be kissed by your Russian business partner?

We cannot answer all of these questions here. Clearly, after you've finished this chapter, even this book, you'll still have more work to do. It will be your responsibility to deepen your understanding of cultural differences by asking your clients and partners directly about the "strange" things they do that aren't mentioned in our book. Such informal interactions in a friendly way will in the long run be more important than any chapter or book or course on this subject, including ours!

Now we turn directly to a brief discussion of the essence of the American negotiation style. Indeed, as Socrates said some 2,500 years ago, "know thyself."

THE JOHN WAYNE STYLE

Picture if you will the closing scenes of John Wayne's Academy Award-winning performance in *True Grit*. Sheriff Rooster Cogburn sits astride his chestnut mare, a Colt .45 in one hand, a Winchester .73 in the other, whiskey on his breath, reins in his teeth, stampeding across the Arkansas prairie straight into the sights of villains' guns. A face-to-face shootout with four bad guys, and sure enough, the John Wayne character comes through again.

Great entertainment, yes! We know it's all fantasy. We know that in real life Sheriff Rooster Cogburn would have ended up facedown in a pool of blood in the dust, alongside his dead horse. But it's more fun to see the fantasy nonetheless.

Such scenes from movies (think Clint Eastwood in *Unforgiven,* Daniel Day-Lewis in *Last of the Mohicans,* or even Uma Thurman in *Kill Bill*), television, and books influence our everyday behavior in subtle, yet powerful ways. We tend to model our behavior after such John Wayne figures. And when everyone else plays the same game, the bluff and bravado often work. But such behavior becomes a problem when we sit face-to-face across a negotiation table with business executives who haven't grown up on a steady diet of American action heroes. Our minds play out the familiar scenes. But instead of six-guns, flintlocks, or samurai swords, our weapons are words, questions, threats and promises, laughter, and confrontation. We anticipate victory, despite the odds—four against one is no problem. But we are often disappointed to find it's not like the movies. It's a real-life business negotiation. At stake are the profits of our companies, not to mention our own compensation and reputation. And like a real-life sheriff, we lose.

This scenario repeats itself with increasing frequency as American enterprise becomes more global. The cowboy bargaining style, which has served us well in conference rooms across the country, does us a great disservice in conference rooms across the sea.

Probably no single statement better summarizes the American negotiation style than "Shoot first, ask questions later," a phrase straight out of an old Saturday-matinee Western. But the roots of the American negotiation style run much deeper than movies and television reruns. To understand the American approach to bargaining, we must consider more basic aspects of our cultural background—in particular, the seeds of Western thought, our immigrant heritage, our frontier history, the fundamental competitiveness of our social and business systems, and finally, much of the training in our present-day business and law schools.

THE ROOTS OF AMERICAN CULTURE

Culture starts with geography.[3] Our ancestors adapted social systems and thinking processes to the problems and opportunities their environments presented them. The cradle of ancient Western civilization is Greece 500 BC. Look at a map and you'll see thousands of islands. That's the prominent geographical feature of Greece. Islands allow for individualism, and isolation—indeed, the word isolation comes from the French *isola*, or island. If you got mad at your neighbor you could always move to another island, particularly when the seas are Aegean calm. You didn't need his or her help to cast your net. In fact, you couldn't fit many folks into your boat anyway. Of course, boats did get bigger and trade brought a flood of new ideas from all over the Mediterranean. Most would agree that personal freedom, individuality, objective thought, and even democracy have deep roots in this ancient island realm.

Now fast forward two millennia. Throughout its history, the United States has been a nation influenced by its immigrants. Certainly the continuous mixing of ideas and perspectives brought from across the seas has enriched all our experiences. Every newcomer has had to work hard to succeed; thus the powerful American work ethic. Another quality of our immigrant forefathers was a fierce individualism and independence—characteristics necessary for survival in the wide open spaces. Indeed, The Declaration of Independence both coincided with and seeded our history and national identity.[4] But independence often does us disservice at the negotiation table. Negotiation is by definition a situation of interdependence—a situation that Americans have never handled well.

We inherit more of this island/individualistic mentality from our frontier history. "Move out West where there's elbow room," ran the conventional wisdom of the first 150 years of our nation's existence. Americans as a group haven't had much practice negotiating because they have always been able to go elsewhere if conflicts arose.

The long distances between people allowed a social system to develop with not only fewer negotiations but also shorter ones. A day-long horseback ride to the general store or stockyard didn't favor long, drawn-out negotiations. It was important to settle things quickly and leave no loose ends to the bargain. "Tell me yes, or tell me no—but give me a straight answer." Candor, laying your cards on the table, was highly valued and expected in the Old West. And it still is today in our boardrooms and classrooms.

We must also recognize the uniqueness of the fundamental driving forces behind our social and business systems. Adam Smith in his *Wealth of Nations,* published in 1776, well justified their emphasis in perhaps the most important sentence ever written in English: "By pursuing his own interest he frequently[5] promotes that of the society more effectually than when he really intends to promote it." In a stroke of his pen, Smith solved the age-old conundrum of group versus individual interests. And, through his co-author, one Benjamin Franklin, he inseminated the philosophy and structure of the most dynamic social system ever devised by humankind. Thus, in no other country on the planet are individualism and competitiveness more highly valued.

Of course, our educational system also reflects Adam Smith's profundity. And, what goes on in the classrooms in our business and law schools in turn has a strong influence on Americans' negotiation style. Throughout the American educational system we are taught to compete, both academically and on the sporting field. Adversarial relationships and winning are essential themes of the American socialization process. But nowhere in the American educational system are competition and winning more important than in case discussions in our law and business school classrooms.[6] Those who make the best arguments, marshal the best evidence, or demolish the opponents' arguments win both the respect of classmates and high marks. Such skills will be important at the negotiation table, but the most important global negotiation skills aren't taught or, at best, are shamefully underemphasized in both business and legal train-ing.[7] We don't teach our students how to ask questions, how to get infor-mation, how to listen, or how to use questioning as a powerful persuasive strategy. In fact, few of us realize that in most places in the world, the one who asks the questions controls the process of negotiation and thereby ac-complishes more in bargaining situations.

THE TEN TRAITS OF THE AMERICAN NEGOTIATION STYLE

A combination of attitudes, expectations, and habitual behaviors consti-tutes the John Wayne negotiation style. Each characteristic is discussed separately below, but it should be understood that each factor is con-nected to the others to form the complex foundation of a series of ne-gotiation strategies and tactics that are typically American. We hope it is clear that what we are talking about is the typical or dominant behavior of American negotiators. Obviously not every American executive is im-patient, a poor listener, or argumentative. Nor does every American man-ager encounter difficulties during international negotiations. But many do, particularly when compared with businesspeople from other coun-tries. Finally, you will also notice that almost all of the ten traits of the American negotiation style listed below ignore the new rules and the basic best practices of negotiations we described in the last chapter—knowledge, communication, and creativity.

I Can Go It Alone

Most American executives feel they should be able to handle any negotia-tion situation by themselves. "Four Russians versus one American is no problem. I don't need any help. I can think and talk fast enough to get what I want, what the company needs." So goes the John Wayne rational-ization. And there's an economic justification: "Why take more people than I need?" Another more subtle reason might be, "Why not take full credit for success? Why split the commission?" Often, then, the American side is outnumbered when it shows up for business discussions.

Being outnumbered or, worse yet, being alone is a severe disadvan-tage in any negotiation situation. Several things are going on at once—talking, listening, preparing arguments and explanations, formulating questions, and seeking approval. Numbers help in obvious ways with most of the above. Indeed, on a Chinese negotiation team one member may be assigned the task of carefully listening with no speaking responsibilities at all. Consider for a moment how carefully you might listen to a speaker if you didn't have to think up a response to his or her next question. But perhaps the most important reason for having greater, or at least equal, numbers on your side is the powerful, subtle influence of nodding heads and positive facial expressions. Negotiation is very much a social activity, and the approval and agreement of others (friend and foe) can have critical effects on negotiation outcomes. Numbers can also be a subtle indicator of the seriousness and commitment of both parties to a negotiation. Clearly American negotiators are at a communications disadvantage when "going it alone."

Just Call Me Mary

Americans more than any other cultural group[8] value informality and equality in human relations. The emphasis on first names is only the tip of the iceberg. We go out of our way to make our clients feel comfortable by playing down status distinctions such as titles and by eliminating unnecessary formalities such as lengthy introductions. But all too often we succeed in making only ourselves feel comfortable, while our international clients are often uneasy or even annoyed.

In many countries, interpersonal relationships are vertical; that is, in almost all two-person relationships, a difference in status exists. The basis for this status distinction may be any of several factors, including age, sex, place and level of education, position in a firm, which firm, or even one's industry of employment. For example, the president of the number one firm in an industry holds a higher status position than the president of the number two firm in the same industry. The Japanese, in particular, are very much aware of such distinctions and of their positions in the hierarchy. And for good reason: Knowledge of their status positions dictates how they will act during interpersonal interactions. Thus, it is easy to understand the importance of exchanging business cards in Japan; such a ritual clearly establishes the status relationships and lets each person know which role to play. The roles of the higher status position and lower status position are very different, even to the extent that different words are used to express the same idea, depending on which person makes the statement.

Such rules for conducting business discussions are difficult for Americans to understand. We can perhaps get by with our informal, egalitarian style when we're dealing with foreigners in the United States. And, creativity can be enhanced in more egalitarian contexts—more ideas tend to be put on the table when status distinctions are minimized. However, we often also make things difficult for ourselves and our companies by asking executives in Shanghai, Tokyo, Paris, or London to "just call me Mary (or John)."

Pardon My French

Our biggest communications disadvantage is the weakness of our foreign-language skills. Often we aren't even apologetic about it. We rightly argue that English is the international language, particularly with regard to technology, science, and commerce. Wherever we go, we expect to find someone who speaks English. Often we do; but when we don't, we are left to the mercy of third-party translators.

Having to bargain in English puts a second, very powerful negotiation tool in the hands of our opponents. On the face of it, bargaining in our first language should be an advantage, but even the most powerful argument fizzles when the other side responds, "Sorry, I'm not sure I understand. Can you repeat that please?" Bargainers listening in a second language have more freedom to use the tactic of selective understanding. It also works when they speak. Previous commitments are more easily dissolved with the excuse, "That isn't exactly what I meant."

A third disadvantage concerns our assumptions about those who speak English well. When facing a group of foreign executives, it is a surprisingly common mistake to assume that the one who speaks English best is also the most intelligent and influential in the group. This is seldom the case in foreign business negotiations. Yet, we often direct our persuasive appeals and attention toward the one who speaks the best English, and thus we accomplish little.

Check with the Home Office

It is not always easy to identify the key decision maker in international business negotiations. Indeed, American bargainers become very upset when halfway through a negotiation the other side says, "I'll have to check with the home office," thus making it known that the decision makers aren't even at the negotiation table. In such a situation, Americans feel they've wasted time or even been misled.

Having limited authority at the negotiation table is a common circumstance overseas and can be a useful bargaining tactic. In reality, the foreign executive is saying, "In order to get me to compromise you have to convince not only me, but also my boss who is 7,000 miles away." Thus, your arguments must be most persuasive. Additionally, such a bargaining tactic helps to maintain harmony at the negotiation table by letting the home office take the blame for saying no.

But such tactics go against the grain of the American bargaining style. Americans pride themselves in having full authority to make a deal. After all, John Wayne never had to check with the home office! Thus, knowledge about authority limits on the other side of the negotiation table will often be crucial.

Get to the Point

As mentioned earlier, Americans don't like to beat around the bush, but prefer to get to the heart of the matter as quickly as possible. Unfortunately, what is considered the heart of the matter in a business negotiation varies across cultures. In every country we have studied, we have found business negotiations to proceed in the following four stages:

1. Non-task sounding
2. Task-related exchange of information
3. Persuasion
4. Concessions and agreement

The first stage includes all those activities that help establish rapport. It does not include information related to the business of the meeting. The information exchanged in the second stage of business negotiations has to do with the parties' needs and preferences. The third stage involves their attempts to change each other's mind through the use of various persuasive tactics. The final stage is the consummation of an agreement, which is often the summation of a series of concessions or smaller agreements.

From the American point of view, the heart of the matter is the third stage—persuasion. We have a tendency to go through the first two stages quickly. We do talk about golf or the weather or family, but relative to other cultures, we spend little time doing so. We state our needs and preferences, and we're quick about that, too. We tend to be more interested in logical arguments than in the people with whom we're negotiating.

In many other countries the heart of the matter, that is, the key knowledge pertains not so much to information and persuasion as to the people involved. In Saudi Arabia, much time is spent getting to know one another. Since the Saudis would prefer not to depend on a legal system to iron out conflicts, a strong relationship of trust must be established before business can begin. Americans new to the Saudi way are particularly susceptible to what we call the "wristwatch syndrome." In the United States, looking at your watch usually gets things moving along. In Saudi Arabia, such impatience signals apprehension and thus necessitates even longer periods of non-task sounding.

We must also add that international negotiators can disagree about what stage their negotiations are actually in. Take, for example, the comments of two top trade negotiators during a television interview:[9]

CLYDE PRESTOWITZ (former U.S. Trade Representative): One of the weakness of many American negotiators is they do want to be liked, and there's a tendency of some American negotiators to separate themselves from their own team and approach the Japanese on the basis of "I really understand you, and my team may be asking too much, but I'm the one you can deal with." And the Japanese just love that, because then they know they can drive a wedge down the middle of the American side and they know they've won the negotiation.

TAIZO WATANABE (Japanese trade official): Sometimes we like to find that sort of person not really intending to put the wedge between the members of the American delegation, but we'd like to do the Japanese way. That is, formal negotiations are one thing, but it is also important to have a kind of confirmation of the basic understanding about what this meeting is intended to be. That kind of process of confirmation does not necessarily take the formal table, but social sort of occasions and we would like to sort of have dinner together and drinking together, especially in Japan, and just try to establish the fundamental basis of communication.

Apparently Mr. Prestowitz thought the persuasion process had started, when Mr. Watanabe was still working on gathering information. Also, notice Prestowitz's comments about "winning" the negotiation—competitive thinking at its worst.

Lay Your Cards on the Table

Americans expect honest information at the negotiation table. When we don't get it, negotiations often end abruptly. We also understand that, like dollars, information must be traded. "You tell me what you want and I'll tell you what we want." And there is an uncommon urgency to this request for reciprocity. Compared to the negotiation styles of managers in the 20 other cultures we have studied, Americans expect information in return almost instantly. We begin to feel very uncomfortable if something is not given in return that day. Reciprocity is important in all cultures, but because relationships tend to last longer elsewhere, foreign negotiators are willing to wait until later to see their partner's cards and they are therefore more patient communicators. Moreover, the Watanabe interview provides evidence that the Japanese don't typically lay their cards on the table, nor do they expect Americans to do so. Thus, they see it as necessary to gather information at both the negotiation table and the dinner table.

Don't Just Sit There, Speak Up

Americans are uncomfortable with silence during negotiations. This may seem a minor point, but we have often witnessed Americans getting themselves into trouble by filling silent periods. Such subtleties in the communication styles of our foreign counterparts are often missed.

The American style of conversation consists of few long silent periods—that is, any pause of ten seconds or greater. Alternatively, in some parts of Asia, the conversational style includes occasional long periods of silence, often in response to an impasse. We have found that American negotiators react to Thai or Japanese silence in one of two ways. Either they make some kind of a concession or they fill the gap in the conversation with a persuasive appeal. The latter tactic has two counterproductive results: (1) the American does most of the talking, and (2) he or she learns little about the others' point of view.

Don't Take No for an Answer

Persistence is highly valued by Americans. We are taught from the earliest age to never give up. In sports, classrooms, or boardrooms, we are taught to be aggressive and to win. Subsequently, we view a negotiation as something to be won. We expect a negotiation to have a definite conclusion, a signed contract. Moreover, we are dissatisfied and distressed if we don't get the bigger piece of the pie. But even worse than losing a negotiation is not concluding a negotiation. We can take a loss—consoling ourselves that we'll do better next time—but not the ambiguity of no outcome.

Although we will see that persistence is important in many parts of the world, the American competitive, adversarial "persistence pays" view of negotiation is not necessarily shared by our foreign clients and vendors. Negotiations are viewed in many countries as a means of establishing long-term commercial relations, which have no definite conclusions. Negotiations are considered a cooperative effort through which interdependence is manifest and each side tries to add to the pie, to be creative.

Take the situation in Japan as a good example. The correct strategy for Americans negotiating there is a Japanese strategy: ask questions. When you think you understand, ask more questions. Carefully feel for pressure points. If an impasse is reached, don't pressure. Suggest a recess or another meeting. Large concessions by the Japanese side at the negotiation table are unlikely. Most Japanese executives see negotiations as a ritual in which harmony is foremost. In Japan, minds are changed behind the scenes.

One Thing at a Time

Another factor hurting creativity is the American tendency to attack a complex negotiation task sequentially. That is, they separate the issues and settle them one at a time. For example, we have heard American bargainers say, "Let's settle the quantity first and then discuss price." Thus, in an American negotiation, the final agreement is a sum of several concessions made on individual issues, and progress can be measured easily: "We're halfway done when we're through half the issues." However, in other countries, particularly Eastern cultures, concessions tend to be made only at the end of a negotiation. All issues are discussed using a holistic approach, and nothing is settled until the end.

American executives often interpret this holistic approach as though "the other side cannot commit to anything," and therefore feel that little progress is being made. Agreements are often unexpected and often follow unnecessary concessions by American bargainers.

A Deal Is a Deal

When an American makes an agreement, he or she is expected to honor the agreement no matter what the circumstances. But agreements are viewed differently in other parts of the world. International law scholar W. H. Newman put it well:

> In some parts of the world it is impolite to openly refuse to do something that has been requested by another person. What a Westerner takes as a commitment may be little more than friendly conversation. In some societies, it is understood that today's commitment may be superseded by a conflicting request received tomorrow, especially if that request comes from a highly influential person. In still other situations, agreements merely signify intention and have little relation to capacity to perform; as long as the person tries to perform he feels no pangs of conscience, and he makes no special effort, if he is unable to fulfill the agreement. Obviously, such circumstances make business dealings much more uncertain, especially for new undertakings.[10]

Indeed, deals sealed by iron-clad contracts often work against creative adjustments to unforeseen circumstances and opportunities. For example, such iron-clad contracts with several Latin American governments are at the time of this writing being toughly tested by $95-a-barrel oil and generally escalating energy prices. But, it's quite difficult for litigation-inured Americans to find advantage in flexible agreements.

I Am What I Am

Most Americans take pride in determination, not changing one's mind even during difficult circumstances. John Wayne's character and behavior were constant and predictable. He treated everyone and every situation with an action-oriented, forthright style. John Wayne could never be accused of being a chameleon—changing colors with changing environments.

Many American bargainers take the same determined attitudes with them to the negotiation table: competition, persistence, and determination no matter what. But during international business negotiations, inflexibility can be a fatal flaw. The first part of Rule #3 pertains—adjust to cultural differences. Inflexibility can damage creativity. There simply isn't a strategy or tactic that always works. Different countries, different personalities, and different circumstances require different approaches.

FINAL COMMENTS

Most Americans are not aware of a native negotiation style. We tend to perceive bargaining behavior in terms of personality: the Texas "good ole boy" approach, that of the Wall Street "city slicker," or the "laid-back" Californian. But when viewed through the eyes of our foreign clients and partners, we Americans have an approach to bargaining all our own. And this distinct flavor we bring to the bargaining table, this John Wayne style, is the source of many problems overseas. Much of our American style works against our gaining knowledge, communicating accurately, and creating value for all partners to negotiations. We must learn to look beyond "golden hooks" and "copper wire" and other simple bromides. We must adjust our behavior and gain an appreciation for subtler forms of negotiation that often work quite well around the world.

CHAPTER 2

WHAT'S SO DIFFERENT ABOUT CULTURES ANYWAY?

*Many go fishing all their lives without knowing
that it is not fish they are after.*

—Henry David Thoreau

A s the New England author/philosopher Henry David Thoreau observed, much of human behavior is unconscious. Culture operates in much the same way. That is, we often do not consciously notice its pertinence or importance. Instead, we often ascribe uncomfortable differences in international encounters to the other's personality, incompetence, and such.

For example: Having a big fish on the end of the line can be quite exciting. It can also be a lot of work—back-breaking, muscle-cramping exasperation. The worst is when you've finally maneuvered that trophy close to the boat, and again your fishing reel begins to sing. There he goes again, down with your monofilament line paying out through the eyes of your arching pole to the dark blue depths. Once again, you'll have to begin the exhausting tedium of bringing him back to the boat.

We've seen this drama played out in a boat off Baja. We've also seen this drama played out in an office tower in Rio de Janeiro. In the latter case, the role of the fisherman was played by a young vice president of a major East Coast bank, and the role of the big fish was enacted by his Brazilian client.

It was a hot afternoon in February and all three executives were sweating because the air conditioning had gone out. Two representatives of

BankBoston were calling on the Brazilian financial manager of the local office of Solar Turbines (a Division of Caterpillar Tractor Co.).

The American bankers were in Brazil to present a new set of financial services developed specifically for the branch offices of American companies in other countries. The junior BankBoston executive had been in Rio for more than two years. She spoke some Portuguese and had called on the client previously. Their relationship seemed quite positive. The vice president, having recently been made responsible for the Rio de Janeiro branch, had come to Brazil for the first time to meet the clients and to convey some of the particulars of the "new product and service offerings" to potential customers and his staff.

Because of the heat, the senior American refused the offered cup of coffee. We would be the first to agree that Brazilian coffee is a killer. More than one small espresso-sized cup and both your collar and shoes begin to feel too tight. In fact, Brazilians who visit the United States call our strongest, blackest brew "tea." Refusing the coffee was only the banker's first mistake. There would be others.

Introductions were made. The talk began with the usual how-do-you-like-Rio questions: "Have you been to Ipanema, Copacabana, Corcovado . . . ?" They also talked about the flight down from New York: "Did you stop in Bahia?" After about five minutes of this chatting, the senior American quite conspicuously glanced at this watch, and then asked his client what he knew about the bank's new services.

"A little," responded the Brazilian. The senior American whipped a brochure out of his briefcase, opened it on the desk in front of the client, and began his sales pitch.

After about three minutes of "fewer forms, online transfers, and reducing accounts receivables," the Brazilian jumped back in, "Yes, that should make us more competitive . . . . and competition is important here in Brazil . . . in fact, have you been following the World Cup *futbol* (soccer) matches recently, great games. . . ." And so the reel began to whir, paying out more monofilament, right there in that hot high-rise office.

Given a few minutes' dissertation on the local *futbol* teams, Pelé, and why *futbol* wasn't tremendously popular in the United States, the American started to try to crank the Brazilian back in. The first signal of this renewed effort was the long look at his watch, then the interruption, "Perhaps we can get back to the new services we have to offer."

The Brazilian did get reeled back into the subject of the sale for a couple of minutes, but then the reel stated to sing yet again. This time, he went from efficient banking transactions to the nuances of the Brazilian financial system to the Brazilian economy. Pretty soon, the three were all talking about the world economy and making predictions about the U.S. presidential elections.

Another look at his Rolex, and the American started this little "sport fishing" ritual all over again. He never did get to page two of his brochure. The Brazilian just wasn't interested in talking business with someone he didn't know pretty well.

Our guess is that the local American bank representative had told her boss that the best you can expect to accomplish in a first meeting with Brazilians is to establish good rapport. Maybe this can be done in five minutes in the United States, but it takes much longer in most other countries, especially Brazil. The time it takes to sip that first canister of caffeine is the bare minimum. Then you should really forget about technical business talk at the first meeting.

Probably the VP actually heard the advice. Perhaps he really didn't understand its importance and he really didn't appreciate how rude this American "let's-get-down-to-business" attitude can appear to foreigners. Or more likely, even if he was trying to adapt to Brazilian customs, it's not so easy to *not* "act naturally." That's because much of our "acting" in such interpersonal situations is unconscious.

That Brazilian financial manager never did get close to the boat, and it was not clear that the local rep could fix things after the VP returned to Boston. When the two of them left, the Brazilian summed up the meeting for one of the Americans in his office, "Some of these Americans are unbelievable! At least most of the people I work with in this company know how things work outside the States." The Brazilian attributed the banker's bad behavior to his incompetence. But, more likely, Thoreau's comments apply. You may recall from the last chapter that according to Dutch negotiations expert Samfrits LePoole, "thinking everything works everywhere just like in the States" is actually attributable to American culture.

YES, CULTURE MATTERS AND IT CAN BE MEASURED

There are many influences on negotiators' behaviors. Personality, education, experience, training, and intelligence (that is, commercial, technical, and/or emotional) all affect how executives behave at the negotiation table. We'll get to these other important topics in chapter 5. When negotiations are between folks from similar cultural backgrounds, we tend not to notice the importance of cultural differences. But at the international negotiation table, culture is perhaps the most important factor to consider. Certainly, cultural differences were the major obstacle for the aforementioned bankers in Brazil. Our presentation in this chapter is primarily meant to provide an in-depth understanding of the hidden elements of culture as they vary around the world. An important secondary purpose is to give you some tools with which to roughly calculate the significance of the problems you may face, that is, the depth of the cultural thicket you are likely to encounter in any particular country. In chapters 3 and 4, we will narrow our focus to culture's influence on business systems and negotiation styles, respectively.

There are many ways to think about culture. Dutch management professor Geert Hofstede refers to culture as the "software of the mind" and argues that it provides a guide for humans on how to think and behave; it is a problem-solving tool.[1] Anthropologist and business consultant Edward T. Hall provides a definition of culture that is even more relevant to international negotiators: "The people we were advising kept bumping their heads against an invisible barrier. . . . We knew that what they were up against was a completely different way of organizing life, of thinking, and of conceiving the underlying assumptions about the family and the state, the economic system, and even Man himself."[2] The salient points in Hall's comments are that cultural differences are often invisible (as water is to fish), and that if managers and negotiators ignore them such an oversight often hurts both their companies and their careers. For a case of the U.S. government "bumping its head" on culture recently, see exhibit 2.1 regarding Iraq. We've included it here because it not only demonstrates the costs of ignoring cultural differences, but it also suggests the opportunities that cultural differences can deliver.

Finally, James Day Hodgson, former U.S. Ambassador to Japan, describes culture as a "thicket."[3] This last metaphor holds hope for struggling global negotiators. According to the ambassador, thickets are tough to get through, but effort and patience often do lead to successes.

Most traditional definitions of culture center around the notion that culture is the sum of the *values, rituals, symbols, beliefs, and thought processes* that are *learned* and *shared* by a group of people, and *transmitted* from generation to generation. So, culture resides in the individual's mind. But the expression "a culture" recognizes that large collectives of people, including business executives, can, to a great degree, be like-minded. For the engineers among our readers we've provided a schematic (see exhibit 2.2, page 39) of the origins and impacts of culture. Let us briefly explain.

Exhibit 2.1

A version of John L. Graham's op-ed was published in the October 21, 2005 edition of the *Orange County Register.*

Exiting Iraq

The primary lesson in international relations of the last 50 years is that culture trumps politics. When the British gave up control of India, the "nation" divided into three based on religion and languages. The Israelis recreated their own country. China took Tibet and the Koreas divided; but angst remains in both cases because political borders defy culture. Colonially designed sub-Saharan Africa continues to writhe in tribal (read cultural) conflicts. Parsed Vietnams and Germanys have been stitched back together. The Czechs and Slovaks have gotten a divorce. Even Canada periodically contemplates a divide. The Brits and the Portuguese returned Hong Kong and Macao, respectively. The Soviet Union and Yugoslavia disintegrated. And, now we have colonially designed Iraq in its death throes.

Contrary to the Bush administration's plan for a democratic state, what will evolve there whether we like it or not is three states—one Shiite in the south, one Kurdish in the north, and a Sunni state in the middle. Indeed, the civil war has already commenced there. The civil war there is also killing and wounding thousands of our young men and women and wrecking our economy here. Following is a proposed exit strategy that specifically takes into account culture as the defining element of organization on the planet. As national borders around the world fade with the new globalization, cultural borders take on new salience. Ignoring this simple fact of international, or better intercultural, relations will only continue the catastrophe in Iraq.

After World War I, the British arbitrarily composed Iraq. The British held it intact until the Sunnis took over—the most recent incarnate was, of course, Saddam Hussein. For the Sunnis, control of the country (even using poison gas on the Kurds) has been important because they lack oil in the center. The main oil reserves are located in the Shiite south and the Kurdish north. So, as the Sunnis are losing control of their "wealth" with the new constitution, they fight to defeat it, yielding the current carnage.

Iraq should be at least temporarily divided into Sunni, Shiite, and Kurdish regions, and should be administered by three different countries. After things calm down, if they wish, if there remains an Iraqi cultural pull, if economics drive cooperation, then it is easy to reunite peacefully. Of course, reunification by force à la Hussein and Kuwait, or China and Tibet, makes no sense. Instead, think the European Union or NAFTA, and peaceful integration.

The Japanese and the Norwegians should be immediately entreated to participate in the pacification and economic redevelopment in the Kurdish north and Shiite south, respectively. Both countries produce some of the best negotiators in the world and both know the petroleum business well enough to earn back their investments of personnel and capital. For example, the Norwegian-brokered peace plan is finally being implemented in the Israeli/Palestinian conflict.

A separate Kurdish state will be seen as a threat to both Turkey and Iran with their own Kurdish minorities. Efficient borders, managed, organized, and financed initially by the Japanese, will let commerce flow and ease the urge to expand to a larger Kurdistan. By the way, the Japanese have a cultural advantage in negotiations with the Turks–both their languages have the same roots, Altaic ones. Finally, both the Norwegians and the Japanese owe us on the international relations tally sheet. You may remember the damage done to our defenses by Toshiba and Kongsberg milling machines producing quieter propellers for Soviet subs during the 1980s. It's time to call in that chit.

That leaves the Sunni Triangle to us and the tough job of pacification of the former ruling minority, now deprived of oil revenues. I propose that USAID help the people of Baghdad rebuild the city and the Sunni Triangle as the educational center of the Middle East. And the University of California system, not Halliburton, should be invited to help in a long-term, systematic way. Indeed, look around the world–oil revenues never guarantee wealth. The lesson of the twenty-first century global economy is that education is the only truly precious product. Or, just take a look at the development of Irvine. The Irvine Company gave the land away to the UC Regents, dramatically increasing the value of their surrounding land for commercial and residential development. Indeed, perhaps the Regents should have charged a fee to the Company to accept the gift. But, the point is that education attracts civilization.

There's a final interesting irony associated with the University of California helping out in Baghdad. Regular readers of these pages may recall an article of mine from 1998 (October 18) that describes the origin of the word "California." Rather than the story about a mythical Princess Calafia, etc. told most recently by Kevin Starr in his tome on the history of the state, or by Whoopi Goldberg at Disney's California Adventure, or in your kid's current fourth-grade text book, the name California actually appears first in the eleventh-century French epic poem, the *Song of Roland*. Most Roland scholars agree that in the poem, the meaning of the term *Califerne* is "the Caliph's domain." Cortez and his fellow Spanish explorers initially believed Mexico was India, and northwest of India was the Muslim Middle East of the time. So, perhaps blue-state Californians from the University of the "Caliph's domain" will be especially welcome because of this strange cultural artifact based on the old Spaniards' geographical mistake.

Implementation of this culturally nuanced plan would allow for troop withdrawals to commence almost immediately and to be completed by March 1, 2007, that is, four years after the invasion commenced.

Japanese negotiators are known for their polite and indirect manner. Where does this aspect of their negotiation style come from? The mountainous islands of Japan have always been the most crowded places on the planet with regard to arable land (*geography*). The Japanese have lived closer together in big cities longer than anyone else (*history and political economy*). This observation led anthropologist John Pfeiffer to once describe the Japanese as "the most civilized society, by definition." So, over the millennia, the Japanese have *adapted* to their crowded environment by developing manners of speaking and organization that tend to reduce confrontation. You can see this reflected in their *social institutions* such as *schools*. All classroom behavior is *ritualistic*—think of our pledge of alle-

Exhibit 2.2 How Culture Works

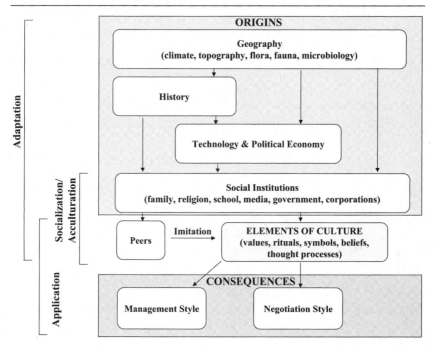

giance as a parallel to their morning song. The Japanese children are *socialized* and *acculturated* in their classrooms to be nonconfrontational. They also *imitate* the older students in their schools. Thus, Japanese students don't question their teachers, they just sit and listen. And, indeed, you can see these culturally determined ways of interacting being *applied* in their international negotiations. Indeed, many of you have.

For the fun of it we suggest you work through this little chart beginning with the wide-open spaces of historical (actually, also present-day) America, and ending with what Georgetown University linguist Deborah Tannen[4] has called our *Argument Culture.* That is, Americans' conversational style is aggressive compared to most around the world. See if you can find the connections. You'll understand yourself better from the exercise.

ELEMENTS OF CULTURE

Just above, we attempted to define culture by listing its five elements: values, rituals, symbols, beliefs, and thought processes. International negotiators must plan for and conduct their interactions with managers from other countries with due consideration of each of the five.

Values

Underlying the cultural diversity that exists among business systems around the world are fundamental differences in cultural values. The most useful information on how cultural values influence various types of business and market behavior comes from seminal work by Geert Hofstede. Studying over 100,000 IBM employees in 66 countries, he found that the cultures of the nations studied differed along four primary dimensions. Subsequently, he and hundreds of other researchers have determined that a wide variety of business behavior patterns are associated with two of those four dimensions: the Individualism/Collective Index (IDV), which focuses on self-orientation, and the Power Distance Index (PDI), which focuses on authority orientation. The Individualism/Collectivism dimension has proven the most useful of the dimensions, justifying entire books on the subject.[5] Indeed, Professor Hofstede has provided us all with perhaps the single most useful tools for evaluating and predicting the extent of cultural differences in international commerce. There are a few more to come, but please see Hofstede's scores listed in exhibit 2.3.

Individualism/Collectivism Index (IDV). The Individualism/Collective Index refers to the preference for behavior that promotes one's self-interest. Cultures that score high in IDV reflect an "I" mentality and tend to reward and accept individual initiative, whereas those low in individualism reflect a "we" mentality and generally subjugate the individual to the group. This does not mean that individuals fail to identify with groups when a culture scores high on IDV, but rather that personal initiative and independence are accepted and endorsed. Individualism pertains to societies in which the ties between individuals are loose; everyone is expected to look after himself or herself and his or her immediate family. The United States and the Netherlands are good examples. Collectivism, as its opposite, pertains to societies in which people from birth onward are integrated into strong, cohesive groups, which throughout people's lifetimes continue to protect them in exchange for unquestioning loyalty. Think China or Russia here.

Power Distance Index (PDI). The Power Distance Index measures the tolerance for social inequality, that is, power inequality between superiors

Exhibit 2.3 Culture Quantified: Index Scores for Countries and Regions

Country	Individualism/ Collectivism	Power Distance	Primary Language	Distance from English
United States	91	40	English	0
Australia (total)	90	36	English	0
Australian (Aborigines only)	89	80	Australian	7
Great Britain	89	35	English	0
Canada (total)	80	39	English	0
Hungary	80	46	Hungarian	4
Netherlands	80	38	Dutch	1
New Zealand	79	22	English	0
Belgium (Dutch speakers only)	78	61	Dutch	1
Italy	76	50	Italian	3
Belgium (total)	75	65	Dutch	1
Denmark	74	18	Danish	1
Canada (French speakers only)	73	54	French	3
Belgium (French speakers only)	72	67	French	3
France	71	68	French	3
Sweden	71	31	Swedish	1
Ireland	70	28	English	0
Norway	69	31	Norwegian	1
Switzerland (German speakers only)	69	26	German	1
Switzerland (total)	68	34	German	1
Germany	67	35	German	1
South Africa	65	49	Afrikaans	1
Switzerland (French speakers only)	64	70	French	3
Finland	63	33	Finnish	4
Estonia	60	40	Estonian	4

(continues)

Exhibit 2.3 (continued)

Country	Individualism/ Collectivism	Power Distance	Primary Language	Distance from English
Luxembourg	60	40	Luxembourgish	1
Poland	60	68	Polish	3
Malta	59	56	Maltese	5
Czech Republic	58	57	Czech	3
Austria	55	11	German	1
Israel	54	13	Hebrew	5
Slovakia	52	104	Slovak	3
Spain	51	57	Spanish	3
India	48	77	Dravidian	3
Surinam	47	85	Dutch	1
Argentina	46	49	Spanish	3
Japan	46	54	Japanese	4
Morocco	46	70	Arabic	5
Iran	41	58	Farsi	3
Jamaica	39	45	English	0
Russia	39	93	Russian	3
Brazil	38	69	Portuguese	3
Arab countries	38	80	Arabic	5
Turkey	37	66	Turkish	4
Uruguay	36	61	Spanish	3
Greece	35	60	Greek	3
Croatia (Zagreb)	33	73	Serbo-Croatian	3
Philippines	32	94	Tagalog	7
Bulgaria	30	70	Bulgarian	3
Mexico	30	81	Spanish	3
Romania	30	90	Romanian	3
Portugal	27	63	Portuguese	3
Slovenia (Ljubljana)	27	71	Slovene	3
East Africa	27	64		8
Malaysia	26	104	Malay	7
Hong Kong	25	68	Cantonese	6
Serbia (Belgrade)	25	86	Serbo-Croatian	3
Chile	23	63	Spanish	3
Bangladesh	20	80	Bengali	3
China	20	80	Mandarin	6
Singapore	20	74	Mandarin	6
Thailand	20	64	Thai	7
Vietnam	20	70	Vietnamese	7
West Africa	20	77		8
El Salvador	19	66	Spanish	3
Korea (South)	18	60	Korean	4

(continues)

Exhibit 2.3   (continued)

Country	Individualism/ Collectivism	Power Distance	Primary Language	Distance from English
Taiwan	17	58	Taiwanese	6
Peru	16	64	Spanish	3
Trinidad	16	47	English	0
Costa Rica	15	35	Spanish	3
Indonesia	14	78	Bahasa	7
Pakistan	14	55	Urdu	3
Colombia	13	67	Spanish	3
Venezuela	12	81	Spanish	3
Panama	11	95	Spanish	3
Ecuador	8	78	Spanish	3
Guatemala	6	95	Spanish	3

Source: Geert Hofstede, *Culture's Consequences,* 2nd edition (Thousand Oaks, CA: Sage, 2001)

and subordinates within a social system. Cultures with high PDI scores tend to be hierarchical, with members citing social role, manipulation, and inheritance as sources of power and social status. Mexico and Malaysia are good examples. Those with low scores, on the other hand, tend to value equality and cite knowledge and respect as sources of power. Think Australia and Norway here. People from cultures with high PDI scores are more apt to have a general distrust of others (not in their groups) because power is seen to rest with individuals and is coercive rather than legitimate. High PDI scores tend to indicate a perception of differences between superior and subordinate and a belief that those who hold power are entitled to privileges. A low score reflects more egalitarian views.

Rituals

Life is filled with rituals, that is, patterns of behavior and interaction that are learned and repeated. The most obvious ones are associated with major events in life. Marriage ceremonies, funerals, and graduations are good examples. Very often these rituals differ across cultures. One good way to learn about the different rituals across cultures is to watch how these rituals are depicted in film. *Monsoon Wedding* is perhaps the best example of this for Western audiences who are not generally exposed to the images of the grooms on white horses and edible flowers that can be a part of the ceremony for high-income folks in New Delhi. Learning about the rituals in other cultures can be invaluable, as we learned at a cross-cultural wedding in the United States that had the reception before the ceremony.

Life is also filled with little rituals such as dinner at a restaurant or a visit to a department store, or even grooming before heading off to work in the morning. In a nice restaurant in Madrid, dinner often starts at about midnight, the entire process can be a three-hour affair, and the check won't come until you ask for it. Walking into a department store in the United States often yields a search for an employee to answer questions. Not so in Japan, where employees bow at the door as you walk in. Visit a doctor in the United States and a 30-minute wait in a cold exam room with nothing on but a paper gown is typical, followed by a brief appearance of the production-line oriented doctor. In Spain, the exams are often done in the doctor's office, thus the doctor has more time to know his/her patients. There's no waiting because you find the doctor sitting at his/her desk. Rituals are important. They coordinate everyday interactions and special occasions. They let people know what to expect.

Business negotiations are perhaps the most fundamental of business rituals. All the to-be-discussed differences in business customs and culture come into play more frequently and more obviously in the negotiating process than in any other aspect of business. The basic elements of business negotiations are the same in any country: They relate to the product, its price and terms, services associated with the product, and finally, friendship between business partners or between vendors and customers. But, it is important to remember that the negotiating process is complicated, and the risk of misunderstanding increases when negotiating with someone from another culture.

Attitudes brought to the negotiating table by each party are affected by many cultural factors and customs often unknown to the other participants and perhaps unrecognized by the individuals themselves. Each negotiator's cultural background conditions his/her understanding and interpretation of what transpires in negotiating sessions. The possibility of offending one another or misinterpreting each other's motives is especially high when one's own values, experiences, and knowledge are the principal bases for assessing a situation. Such ethnocentrism, whether conscious or not, is the prime enemy of international negotiators. One standard rule in negotiating is "know thyself" first, and second, "know your counterpart." Knowledge about the people, *on both sides of the table,* is indeed our Rule #2.

Symbols

Anthropologist Edward T. Hall tells us that culture is communication. In his seminal article about cultural differences in business settings, he examines the "languages" of time, space, things, friendships, and agreements.[6] Indeed, learning to interpret correctly the symbols that surround us is a key part of socialization. And, this learning begins immediately after birth as we begin to hear the language spoken, see the facial expressions, feel the touch, and taste the milk of our mothers.[7] We begin our discussion of symbolic systems with language, the most obvious part, and the one that most often involves conscious communication.

Language

We should mention that for some around the world language is itself thought of as not just a symbolic system, but also as a social institution that often bears political importance. Certainly, the French go to extreme lengths and expense to preserve the purity of their *Française*. In Canada, the national language has been the focus of political disputes, including the secession of Quebec, although things seem to have calmed down most recently. At the same time, the English/Spanish controversy looms larger in the United States and Mexican immigration affects political policy in several states as well as at the federal level. Unfortunately, as the number of spoken languages continues to decline worldwide, so does the interesting cultural diversity of the planet.

The importance of understanding the language of a country cannot be overestimated, particularly if you're negotiating in France! Just as idiomatic meanings vary across English-speaking countries and regions, they do as well across Arabic-, Chinese-, and Spanish-speaking countries and regions. For example, *tambo* means a roadside inn in Bolivia, Colombia, Ecuador, and Peru; a dairy farm in Argentina and Uruguay; and a brothel in Chile.

The relationship between language and business systems and negotiations is important in another way. Recent studies indicate that a new concept, *linguistic distance,* is proving useful in understanding differences in values across countries. Linguistic distance has been shown to be an important factor in determining the amount of trade between countries. The idea is that crossing "wider" language differences increases transaction costs and makes trade and negotiations less efficient (see exhibit 2.3).

Over the years, linguists have determined that languages around the world conform to family trees based on the similarity of their forms and development. For example, Spanish, Italian, French, and Portuguese are all classified as Romance languages because of their common roots in Latin. Distances between languages can be measured on these linguistic trees. If we take English as our starting point, German is one branch away, Danish two, Spanish three, Japanese four, Hebrew five, Chinese six, and Thai seven. These "distance from English" scores are listed for a sampling of cultures in exhibit 2.3.

Other work in the area is demonstrating a direct influence of language on cultural values, expectations, and even conceptions of time. For example, as linguistic distance from English increases, individualism decreases.[8] These studies are the first in this genre, and much more work needs to be done. However, the notion of linguistic distance appears to hold promise for better understanding and anticipation of cultural differences in negotiators' values, expectations, and behaviors.

Moreover, the relationship between language spoken and cultural values holds deeper implications. That is, as English spreads around the world via school systems and the Internet, cultural values of individualism and egalitarianism are spreading with it. For example, both Chinese Mandarin speakers and Spanish speakers must learn two words for "you" (*ni* and *nin,* and *tú* and *Usted,* respectively). The proper usage of the two depends completely on knowledge of the social context of the conversation. Respect for status is communicated by the use of *nin* and *Usted.* In English, there is only one form for "you."[9] Speakers can ignore social context and status and still speak correctly. It's easier, and social status becomes less important. Française beware!

Aesthetics as Symbols

Art communicates. Indeed, Confucius is reputed to have opined, "A picture is worth a thousand words." And, of course, so is a dance or a song. As we acquire our culture, we learn the meaning of the wonderful symbolic system aesthetics represents; that is, the arts, folklore, music, drama, and dance. Executives everywhere respond to images, myths, and metaphors that help them define their personal and national identities and relationships within the contexts of culture and business systems. The uniqueness of a culture can be spotted quickly in symbols having distinct meanings. Think about the subtle earth tones of the typical Japanese restaurant compared with the bright reds and yellows in the décor of ethnic Chinese restaurants.

One author has suggested that understanding different cultures' metaphors is a key doorway to success. Maryland management professor Martin Gannon[10] has identified metaphors that represent cultures around the world. In the fascinating text he compares "American Football" (with its individualism, competitive specialization, huddling, and ceremonial celebration of perfection) to the "Spanish Bullfight" (with its pompous entrance parade, audience participation, and the ritual of the fight) to the "Indian Dance of the Shiva" (with its cycles of life, family, and social interaction). One might argue with the details of his ideas, but empirical evidence is beginning to accumulate supporting the notion that metaphors matter.

Beliefs

Of course, much of what we learn to believe comes from religious training. And it is certainly impossible to adequately consider matters of true faith and spirituality here. Moreover, the relationship between superstition and religion is not at all clear. For example, one explanation of the origin of the Western aversion to the number 13 has to do with the Christian story of Jesus sitting with his 12 disciples at the Last Supper, and that Judas Iscariot, the disciple who betrayed Jesus, was the thirteenth at the table.

However, many beliefs around the world are secular in nature. What Westerners often call superstition may play quite a large role in a society's belief system in some parts of the world. For example, in parts of Asia, ghosts, fortune telling, palmistry, blood types, head-bump reading, phases of the moon, faith healers, demons, and soothsayers can all be integral elements of society. Surveys of advertisements in Greater China show a preference for an "8" as the last digit in listed prices—the number connotes "prosperity" in Chinese culture. Some Japanese negotiators will believe your B blood type is what makes you individualistic and creative, not your American culture.

It's called art, science, philosophy, or superstition, depending on who is talking, but the Chinese practice of feng shui is an important ancient belief held by Chinese, among others. Feng shui is the process that links humans and the universe to *ch'i,* the energy that sustains life and flows through our bodies and surroundings, in and around our homes and workplaces. The idea is to harness this *ch'i* to enhance good luck, prosperity, good health, and honor for the owner of a premise and to minimize the negative force, *sha ch'i,* and its effect. Feng shui requires engaging the services of a feng shui master to determine the positive orientation of a building in relation to either the owner's horoscope, the date of establishment of the business, or the shape of the land and building. It is not a look or a style, and it is more than aesthetics: Feng shui is a strong belief in establishing a harmonious environment through the design and placement of furnishings and the avoidance of buildings facing northwest, the "devil's entrance," and southwest, the "devil's backdoor." Indeed, even Disney designed all its new rides in Hong Kong Disneyland according to the principles of feng shui.

Too often, one person's beliefs are another person's funny story. It is a mistake to discount the importance of myths, superstitions, or other cultural beliefs, however strange they may appear, because they are an important part of the cultural fabric of a society and influence all manner of behavior. For the negotiator, it can be an expensive mistake to make light of superstitions in other cultures when doing business there. Making a fuss about being born in the right year under the right phase of the moon or relying heavily on handwriting and palm-reading experts, as is the tradition in some countries, can be difficult to comprehend for a Westerner who refuses to walk under a ladder, worries about the next seven years after breaking a mirror, buys a one-dollar lottery ticket, or seldom sees a thirteenth floor in a building.

Thought Processes

We are now learning in much more detail the degree to which ways of thinking vary across cultures. Richard Nisbett broadly discusses differences in "Asian and Western" thinking in his wonderful book, *The Geography of Thought*.[11] He starts with Confucius and Aristotle and develops his arguments through consideration of historical and philosophical writings and findings from more recent behavioral science research including his own social-psychological experiments. While he acknowledges the dangers surrounding generalizations about Japanese, Chinese, and Korean cultures on the one hand, and European and American cultures on the other, many of his conclusions are consistent with our own work related to international negotiations, cultural values, and linguistic distance.

A good metaphor for his views involves going back to Confucius's aforementioned picture. Asians tend to see the whole picture and can report details about the background and foreground. Westerners alternatively focus on the foreground and can provide great detail about central figures, but notice relatively little in the background. This difference in perception—big picture versus focus—is associated with a wide variety of differences in values, preferences, and expectations about future events. Nisbett's book is essential reading for anyone negotiating internationally. His insights are pertinent to Japanese bargaining in Boston or Belgians in Beijing.

Culture, particularly the one you are immersed in, is hard to see. Culture's strong currents generally operate below the surface of human consciousness. In the next two chapters we focus specifically on how deeply culture influences both management and negotiation styles. In closing we are quite encouraged by the publication of the important book *Culture Matters*.[12] We obviously agree with the sentiment of the title, and hope that the book will help rekindle the interest in culture's pervasive influences that Max Weber and others initiated so long ago.

CHAPTER 3

CULTURE'S INFLUENCE ON MANAGEMENT STYLE AND BUSINESS SYSTEMS

Catch a man a fish, and you can sell it to him.
Teach a man to fish, and you ruin a wonderful business opportunity.

—Karl Marx

That culture profoundly affects management style and overall business systems is not a new idea. Another influential German, sociologist Max Weber, made the first strong case back in 1930[1] in his discussion of the connections between the Protestant work ethic and capitalism. Culture not only establishes the criteria for day-to-day business behavior but also forms general patterns of values and motivations. Executives are largely captives of their heritages and cannot totally escape the elements of culture they learned while growing up.

In the United States, for example, the historical perspective of individualism and "winning the West" seems to be manifest in individual wealth or corporate profit being dominant measures of success. Japan's lack of space and natural resources and its dependence on trade have focused individual and corporate success criteria on uniformity, subordination to the group, and society's ability to maintain high levels of employment. The feudal background of southern Europe tends to emphasize maintenance of both individual and corporate power and authority while blending those feudal traits with paternalistic concern for minimal welfare for workers and other members of society. Various studies identify North Americans as individualists, the Japanese as consensus-oriented and committed to the group, and central and southern Europeans as elitist and rank-conscious. Although these descriptions are stereotypical and at best represent national averages, they illustrate cultural differences that are often manifested in business behavior and practices. Such differences also coincide quite well with Hofstede's scores listed in exhibit 2.3 on page xx. Knowledge of the *management style*—that is, the business culture, management values, and business methods and behaviors—existing in a country and a willingness to accommodate the differences are important to success in any international venture.

AUTHORITY AND DECISION MAKING

The very strong belief in the United States that business decisions are based on *objective analysis* and that managers strive to be scientific has a profound effect on the U.S. manager's attitudes toward objectivity in decision making and accuracy of data. While judgment and intuition are important criteria for making decisions, most U.S. managers believe decisions must be supported and based on accurate and relevant information. Thus, in U.S. business, great emphasis is placed on the collection and free flow of information to all levels within the organization and on frankness of expression in the evaluation of business opinions or decisions. In other cultures, such factual and rational support for decisions is not as important; the accuracy of data and even the proper reporting of data are not prime prerequisites. Further, existing data frequently are for the eyes of a select few. The frankness of expression and openness in dealing with data characteristic of U.S. businesses does not fit easily into some cultures.

Characteristics such as enterprise size, ownership, public accountability, and cultural values that determine the prominence of status and position (PDI) combine to influence the authority structure of business. In high-PDI countries such as Peru or Pakistan, understanding the rank and status of clients and business partners is much more important than in more egalitarian (low PDI) societies such as Denmark and Israel. In high-PDI countries, subordinates are not likely to contradict bosses, but in low-PDI countries they often do. Although the international businessperson is confronted with a variety of authority patterns, most are a variation of three typical patterns: top-level management decisions, decentralized decisions, and committee or group decisions.

Top-level management decision making is generally found in those situations where family or close ownership gives absolute control to owners and where businesses are small enough to make such centralized decision making possible. In many European businesses, such as those in France, decision-making authority is guarded jealously by a few at the top, who exercise tight control. In other countries, such as Mexico and Venezuela, where a semi-feudal, land-equals-power heritage exists, management styles are characterized as autocratic and paternalistic. Decision-making participation by middle management tends to be de-emphasized; dominant family members make decisions that tend to please the family members more than to increase productivity. This is also true for government-owned companies where professional managers have to follow decisions made by politicians, who generally lack any working knowledge about management. In Middle Eastern countries, the top man makes all decisions and prefers to deal only with other executives with decision-making powers. There, one always does business with an individual per se rather than an office or title.

As businesses grow and professional management develops, there is generally a shift toward decentralized management decision making. Decentralized decision making allows executives at different levels of management to exercise authority over their own functions. As mentioned above, this is typical of large-scale businesses with highly developed management systems such as those found in the United States.

Committee decision making is by group or consensus. Committees may operate on a centralized or decentralized basis, but the concept of committee management implies something quite different from the individualized functioning of the top management and decentralized decision-making arrangements just discussed. Because Asian cultures and religions tend to emphasize harmony and collectivism, it is not surprising that group decision making predominates there. Despite the emphasis on rank and hierarchy in Japanese social structure, business emphasizes group participation, group harmony, and group decision making—even at the top management level.

The demands of these three types of authority systems on a negotiator's ingenuity and adaptability are evident. In the case of the authoritative and delegated societies, the chief problem is to identify the individual with authority. In the committee decision setup, it is necessary that every committee member be convinced of the merits of the proposition or product in question. The negotiator's approach to each of these situations differs.

MANAGEMENT OBJECTIVES AND ASPIRATIONS

The training and background (i.e., cultural environment) of managers significantly affect their personal and business outlooks. Society as a whole establishes the social rank or status of management, and cultural background dictates patterns of aspirations and objectives among businesspeople. These cultural influences affect the attitude of managers toward innovation, new products, and conducting business with foreigners. To fully understand another's management style, one must appreciate the goals of the business organization and the practices that prevail within the company. In dealing with foreign business, a negotiator must be particularly aware of the varying objectives and aspirations of management.

Security and Mobility

Personal security and job mobility relate directly to basic human motivation and therefore have widespread economic and social implications. The word *security* is somewhat ambiguous, and this very ambiguity provides some clues to managerial variation. To some, security means a big paycheck and the training and ability required to move from company to company within the business hierarchy; for others, it means the security of lifetime positions with their companies; to still others, it means adequate retirement plans and other welfare benefits. In European companies, particularly in the more relationship-oriented countries, such as France and Italy, there is a strong paternalistic orientation, and it is assumed that individuals will work for one company for the majority of their lives. For example, in Britain managers place great importance on individual achievement and autonomy, whereas French managers place great importance on competent supervision, sound company policies, fringe benefits, security, and comfortable working conditions. There is much less mobility among French managers than British.

Personal Life

For many individuals, a good personal and/or family life takes priority over profit, security, or any other goal. In his worldwide study of individual aspirations, David McClelland[2] discovered that the cultures of some countries stressed the virtue of a good personal life as being far more important than profit or achievement. The hedonistic outlook of ancient Greeks explicitly included work as an undesirable factor that got in the way of the search for pleasure or a good personal life. Alternatively, according to Max Weber, at least part of the standard of living that we enjoy in the United States today can be attributed to the hard-working Protestant ethic from which we derive much of our business heritage.

To the Japanese, personal life is company life. Many Japanese workers regard their work as the most important part of their overall lives. The Japanese work ethic—maintenance of a sense of purpose—derives from company loyalty and frequently results in the Japanese employee maintaining identity with the corporation. Although this notion continues to be true for the majority, there is strong evidence that the long languishing Japanese economy has moved the position of the Japanese "salary man" from that of one of Japan's business elite to one that is ridiculed. Japan's business culture is gradually shifting away from the lifelong employment that led to the intense company loyalty.

We can get some measure of the work-personal life tradeoff made in different cultures with reference to exhibit 3.1. As a point of reference, 40 hours per week of work times 50 weeks equals 2,000 hours annually of work. The Americans appear to fall in the middle of hours worked, far above the Europeans and below the Southeast Asians, when comparing such numbers worldwide. Most Americans are getting about two weeks of paid vacation, while in Europe they are taking between four and six weeks. In Singapore and Hong Kong, Saturday is a workday. However, the scariest datum isn't in the table. While hours worked are decreasing almost

Exhibit 3.1 Annual Hours Worked

Singapore	2,307
Hong Kong	2,287
United States	1,979
Japan	1,842
Canada	1,776
Britain	1,719
Germany	1,480
Norway	1,399

Source: International Labor Organization, 2004

everywhere, in the United States the numbers are increasing, up 36 hours from 1990. Even better, considering our favorite fishing fable related in exhibit 3.2.

Affiliation and Social Acceptance

In some countries, acceptance by neighbors and fellow workers appears to be a predominant goal within business. The Asian outlook is reflected in the group decision making so important in Japan, and the Japanese place high importance on fitting in with their group. Group identification is so strong in Japan that when a worker is asked what he does for a

Exhibit 3.2   The American Tourist and the Mexican Fisherman

An American tourist was at the pier of a small coastal Mexican village when a small boat with just one fisherman docked. Inside the small boat were several large yellowfin tuna. The tourist complimented the Mexican on the quality of the fish and asked how long it took to catch them.

The Mexican replied, "Only a little while."

The tourist then asked, "Why didn't you stay out longer and catch more fish?"

The Mexican replied, "With this I have enough to support my family's needs."

The tourist then asked, "But what do you do with the rest of your time?"

The Mexican fisherman said, "I sleep late, fish a little, play with my children, take a siesta with my wife, Maria, stroll into the village each evening where I sip wine and play guitar with my amigos. I have a full and busy life."

The tourist scoffed, "I can help you. You should spend more time fishing and with the proceeds, buy a bigger boat. With the proceeds from the bigger boat you could buy several boats. Eventually you would have a fleet of fishing boats. Instead of selling your catch to a middleman, you could sell directly to the processor, eventually opening your own cannery. You would control the product, processing, and distribution. You could leave this small village and move to Mexico City, then Los Angeles, and eventually to New York City where you could run your ever-expanding enterprise."

The Mexican fisherman asked, "But, how long will this take?"

The tourist replied, "15 to 20 years."

"But what then?" asked the Mexican.

The tourist laughed and said, "That's the best part. When the time is right you would sell your company stock to the public and become very rich, you would make millions."

"Millions? . . . Then what?"

The American said, "Then you would retire. Move to a small coastal fishing village where you would sleep late, fish a little, play with your grandkids, take a siesta with your wife, stroll to the village in the evenings where you could sip wine and play your guitar with your amigos."

Source: Anonymous.

living, he generally answers by telling you he works for Sumitomo, Mitsubishi, or Matsushita, rather than that he is a chauffeur, an engineer, or a chemist.

Power and Achievement

Although there is some power-seeking by business managers throughout the world, power seems to be a more important motivating force in South American countries. In these countries, many business leaders are not only profit-oriented but also use their business positions to become social and political leaders. One way to measure achievement is by the amount of money in the bank, and another is social rank. These last aspirations are particularly relevant to the United States.

COMMUNICATION STYLES

Edward T. Hall, professor of anthropology and for decades a consultant to business and government on intercultural relations, tells us that communication involves much more than just words. His article, "The Silent Language of Overseas Business," which appeared in the *Harvard Business Review* in 1960, remains a most worthwhile read. In it he describes symbolic meanings of *time, space, things, friendships,* and *agreements,* and how they vary across cultures. In 1960, Hall could not have anticipated the innovations brought on by the Internet. However, all of his ideas about cross-cultural communication apply to that medium as well.

No language readily translates into another because the meanings of words differ widely among languages. For example, the word "marriage," even when accurately translated, can connote very different things in different languages—in one it may mean love, in another restrictions. Though it is the basic communication tool of negotiators working in foreign lands, Americans often fail to develop even a basic understanding of even one other language, much less master the linguistic nuances that reveal unspoken attitudes and information.

Verbal communication, no matter how imprecise, is at least explicit. But much business communication depends on implicit messages that are not verbalized. Hall goes on to say, "In some cultures, messages are explicit; the words carry most of the information. In other cultures . . . less information is contained in the verbal part of the message since more is in the context."[3]

Based on decades of anthropological fieldwork, Hall places 11 cultures along a high context–low context scale:

High Context (meaning is implicit in communication)
Japanese
Arabian
Latin American
Spanish
Italian
English (UK)
French
North American (United States)
Scandinavian
German
Swiss
Low Context (meaning is explicit in communication)

Communication in a high-context culture depends heavily on the contextual (*who* says it, *when* it is said, *how* it is said) or nonverbal aspects of communication, whereas the low-context culture depends more on explicit, verbally expressed communications.

A brief exemplar of the high/low-context dimension of communication style regards an international negotiator's description of a Los Angeles business entertainment event. "I picked him [a German client] up at his hotel near LAX and asked what kind of food he wanted for dinner. He said, 'Something local.' Now in LA local food is Mexican food. I'd never met anyone that hadn't had a taco before! We went to a great Mexican place in Santa Monica and had it all, guacamole, salsa, enchiladas, burritos, a real Alka-Seltzer kind of night. When we were done I asked how he liked the food. He responded rather blandly, 'It wasn't very good.'"

The American might have been taken aback by his client's honest, and perhaps too-direct, answer. However, the American knew well about German frankness[4] and just rolled with the "blow." Germans, being very low-context oriented, just deliver the information without any social padding. Most Americans would soften the blow some with an answer more like, "It was pretty good, but maybe a bit too spicy." And, a high-context oriented Japanese individual would really pad the response with something like, "It was very good. Thanks." But then he would never order Mexican food again.

While an American or German might view the Japanese response as less than truthful, from the Japanese perspective, he would be just preserving a harmonious relationship. Indeed, the Japanese have two words for truth, *honne* (true mind) and *tatemae* (official stance). The former delivers the information and the latter preserves the relationship. And, in high-context Japan, the latter is often more important.

TIME

North Americans are a more time-bound culture than Middle Eastern and Latin American cultures. Our stereotype of those cultures is that "they are always late," and their view of us is "you are always prompt." Neither statement is completely true, though both contain some truth. What is true, however, is that the United States is a very time-oriented society—time is money to us—whereas in other cultures, time is to be savored, not spent. Insights into a culture's view of time may be found in its sayings and proverbs. For example, compare the following adages:

- "Those who rush arrive first at the grave." *Spain*
- "The clock did not invent man." *Nigeria*
- "If you wait long enough, even an egg will walk." *Ethiopia*
- "Before the time, it is not yet the time; after the time, it's too late." *France*

Hall defines two time systems in the world: monochronic and polychronic time. *M-time,* or *monochronic time,* typifies most North Americans, Swiss, Germans, and Scandinavians. These Western cultures tend to concentrate on one thing at a time. They divide time into small units and are concerned with promptness. M-time is used in a linear way and it is experienced as being almost tangible in that one saves time, wastes time, bides time, spends time, and loses time. Most low-context cultures operate on M-time. *P-time,* or *polychronic time,* is more dominant in high-context cultures, where the completion of a human transaction is emphasized more than holding to schedules. P-time is characterized by the simultaneous occurrence of many things and by a great involvement with people. P-time allows for relationships to build and context to be absorbed as part of high-context cultures.

One study comparing perceptions of punctuality in the United States and Brazil found that Brazilian timepieces were less reliable and public clocks less available than in the United States. Researchers also found that

Brazilians more often described themselves as late arrivers, allowed greater flexibility in defining *early* and *late,* were less concerned about being late, and were more likely to blame external factors for their lateness than were Americans.[5] Please see similar comparisons of 31 countries in exhibit 3.3.

Exhibit 3.3   Speed Is Relative

Rank of 31 countries for overall pace of life [combination of three measures: (1) minutes downtown pedestrians take to walk 60 feet, (2) minutes it takes a postal clerk to complete a stamp-purchase transaction, and (3) accuracy in minutes of public clocks].

Overall Pace	Country	Walking 60 Feet	Postal Service	Public Clocks
1	Switzerland	3	2	1
2	Ireland	1	3	11
3	Germany	5	1	8
4	Japan	7	4	6
5	Italy	10	12	2
6	England	4	9	13
7	Sweden	13	5	7
8	Austria	23	8	9
9	Netherlands	2	14	25
10	Hong Kong	14	6	14
11	France	8	18	10
12	Poland	12	15	8
13	Costa Rica	16	10	15
14	Taiwan	18	7	21
15	Singapore	25	11	4
16	United States	6	23	20
17	Canada	11	21	22
18	South Korea	20	20	16
19	Hungary	19	19	18
20	Czech Republic	21	17	23
21	Greece	14	13	29
22	Kenya	9	30	24
23	China	24	25	12
24	Bulgaria	27	22	17
25	Romania	30	29	5
26	Jordan	28	27	19
27	Syria	29	28	27
28	El Salvador	22	16	31
29	Brazil	31	24	28
30	Indonesia	26	26	30
31	Mexico	17	31	26

Source: From Robert Levine, "The Pace of Life in 31 Countries," *American Demographics,* November 1997.

The American desire to get straight to the point and get down to business is a manifestation of an M-time culture, as are other indications of directness. The P-time system gives rise to looser time schedules, deeper involvement with individuals, and a wait-and-see-what-develops attitude. For example, two Latin Americans conversing would likely opt to be late for their next appointments rather than abruptly terminate the conversation before it came to a natural conclusion. P-time is characterized by a more flexible notion of being on time or late. Interruptions are routine; delays to be expected. It is not so much putting things off until *mañana* as it is the concept that human activity is not expected to proceed like clockwork.

Most cultures offer a mix of P-time and M-time behavior, but have a tendency to be either more P-time or M-time in regard to the role time plays. Some are similar to Japan, where appointments are adhered to with the greatest M-time precision but P-time is followed once a meeting begins. The Japanese see U.S. businesspeople as too time-bound and driven by schedules and deadlines that thwart the easy development of friendships. The differences between M-time and P-time are reflected in a variety of ways throughout a culture.

When businesspeople from M-time and P-time cultures meet, both parties need to be able to make adjustments so that a harmonious relationship develops. Often clarity can be gained by specifying tactfully, for example, whether a meeting is to be on "Mexican time" or "American time." An American who has been negotiating successfully with the Saudis for many years says he has learned to take plenty of paperwork kinds of things to do when he travels there so he can put waiting time to good use. Others schedule appointments in their offices so they can work until their P-time friend arrives. The important thing for the American negotiator to learn is to adjust to P-time in order to avoid the anxiety and frustration that comes from being out of synchronization with local time. As global markets expand, however, more businesspeople from P-time cultures are adapting to M-time.

BUSINESS ETHICS AND BRIBERY

Before the Enron and WorldCom crises, to most Americans, the word corruption meant bribery. Now, in the domestic context, fraud has moved to a more prominent spot in the headlines. However, for U.S. companies engaged in international markets in the 1970s, bribery became a national issue with public disclosure of political payoffs to foreign recipients by U.S. firms. At the time, there were no U.S. laws against paying bribes in foreign countries. But for publicly held corporations, the Securities and Exchange Commission's (SEC) rules required accurate public reporting of all expenditures. Because the payoffs were not properly disclosed, many executives were faced with charges of violating SEC regulations. The issue took on proportions greater than that of nondisclosure because it focused national attention on the basic question of ethics. The business community's defense was that payoffs were a way of life throughout the world: If you didn't pay bribes, you didn't do business.

One of the obstacles to Shell's development of the Peruvian gas fields in the late 1990s was the corrupt Fujimori administration as described in the introduction. The decision to pay a bribe creates a major conflict between what is ethical and proper and what is profitable and sometimes necessary for business. Many global competitors perceive payoffs as a necessary means of accomplishing business goals. A major complaint of U.S. businesses was that other countries did not have legislation as restrictive as the United States' Foreign Corrupt Practices Act (FCPA). The U.S. advocacy of global anti-bribery laws has led to an accord by the member nations of the Organization for Economic Co-operation and Development (OECD) to force their companies to follow rules similar to those that bind U.S. firms. To date, 33 of the world's largest trading nations, including the United States, have signed the OECD Convention on combating the bribery of foreign public officials in international business transactions. In Latin America, the Organization of American States (OAS) has taken a global lead in ratifying an agreement against corruption. Long considered almost a way of business life, bribery and other forms of corruption now have been criminalized.

An international organization called Transparency International (TI) is dedicated to "curbing corruption through international and national coalitions encouraging governments to establish and implement effective laws, policies and anti-corruption programs." Please visit their excellent website www.transparency.org. Among its various activities, TI conducts an international survey of businesspeople, political analysts, and the general public to determine their perceptions of corruption in 179 countries. In the Corruption Perception Index (CPI), shown in part in exhibit 3.4, Denmark, Finland, and New Zealand, all with scores of 9.4 out of a maximum of 10, were perceived to be the least corrupt, and Myanmar and Somalia, with scores of 1.4, as the most corrupt. TI also ranks 21 bribe-

Exhibit 3.4   Transparency International CPI Indices

Country Rank	Country	2007 CPI Score [2006 Bribe Payers' Index]
1	Denmark	9.4
1	Finland	9.4
1	New Zealand	9.4
4	Singapore	9.3 [6.7]
4	Sweden	9.3 [7.6]
6	Iceland	9.2
7	Netherlands	9.0 [7.3]
7	Switzerland	9.0 [7.8]
9	Canada	8.7 [7.5]
9	Norway	8.7
11	Australia	8.6 [7.6]
12	Luxembourg	8.4 [7.5]
12	United Kingdom	8.4 [7.4]
14	Hong Kong	8.3 [6.0]
15	Austria	8.1
16	Germany	7.8 [7.3]
17	Japan	7.5 [7.1]
19	France	7.3 [6.5]
20	USA	7.2 [7.2]
21	Belgium	7.1 [7.2]
22	Chile	7.0
25	Spain	6.7 [6.6]
28	Portugal	6.5 [6.5]
34	Taiwan	5.7 [5.4]
41	Italy	5.2 [5.9]
43	Malaysia	5.1 [5.6]
43	S. Africa	5.1 [5.6]
43	S. Korea	5.1 [2.8]
56	Greece	4.6
61	Cuba	4.2
61	Poland	4.2
64	Turkey	4.1 [5.2]
68	Colombia	3.8
72	Brazil	3.5 [5.7]
72	China	3.5 [4.9]
72	India	3.5 [4.6]
72	Mexico	3.5 [6.5]
72	Peru	3.5
79	Saudi Arabia	3.4 [5.8]
94	Panama	3.2
105	Egypt	2.9
123	Niger	2.6
123	Vietnam	2.6
131	Philippines	2.5
143	Indonesia	2.3
143	Russia	2.3 [5.2]
150	Azerbaijan	2.1
150	Kenya	2.1
162	Bangladesh	2.0
162	Venezuela	2.0
177	Haiti	1.6
179	Somalia	1.4

paying countries, and the ranking is reported in exhibit 3.4 in its entirety. TI is very emphatic that its intent is not to expose villains and cast blame, but to raise public awareness that will lead to constructive action. As one would expect, those countries receiving low scores are not pleased; however, the effect has been to raise public ire and debates in parliaments around the world—exactly the goal of TI.

The reader will note that the CPI could have predicted the cultural clash that was part of the Peruvian gas field project by the relatively good marks on bribery for the Dutch (9.0 and [7.3]), British (8.4 and [7.4]), and Americans (7.2 and [7.2]) vis-à-vis the low score for the Peruvians (3.3), as listed in exhibit 3.4.

CULTURE'S INFLUENCE ON STRATEGIC THINKING

Finally, it is important to recognize that culture influences thinking in companies around the world from the bottom to the very top, including strategic decision making by executive boards. Perhaps MIT economist Lester Thurow provided the most articulate description of how culture influences managers' thinking about business strategy.[6] Others are now examining his ideas in even deeper detail. Thurow distinguished between the British-American "individualistic" kind of capitalism and the "communitarian" form of capitalism in Japan and Germany. The business systems in the latter two countries are typified by cooperation among government, management, and labor, particularly in Japan. Contrarily, adversarial relationships among labor, management, and government are more the norm in the United Kingdom, and particularly in the United States. We see these cultural differences reflected in Hofstede's results—on the IDV scale the United States is 91, the United Kingdom is 89, Germany is 67, and Japan is 46.

We also find evidence in our own studies of these differences in a comparison of the performance of American, German, and Japanese firms.[7] In the less individualistic cultures, labor and management cooperate—in Germany, labor is represented on corporate boards, and in Japan, management takes responsibility for the welfare of the labor force. Because the welfare of the workforce matters more to Japanese and German firms their sales revenues are more stable over time. American-style layoffs are eschewed. The individualistic American approach to labor–management relations is adversarial—each side takes care of itself. So we see damaging strikes and huge layoffs that result in more volatile performance for American firms.

Circa 2000 the American emphasis on competition looked like the best approach, and it appeared that business practices around the world were converging on the American model. But, it is important to recall that key word in Adam Smith's justification for competition—"frequently." It's worth repeating here: "By pursuing his own interest he frequently promotes that of society. . . ." Smith wrote *frequently,* not *always,* or even *most of the time.* A competitive, individualistic approach works well in the context of an economic boom. During the late 1990s, American firms dominated Japanese and European ones. The latter seemed stodgy, conservative, and slow in the then hot global information economy. However, downturns in a competitive culture can be ugly things. A review of the performance and layoffs at Boeing during the commercial aircraft busts of the late 1990s and early 2000s is instructive.

It should also be mentioned that Thurow and the others writing in the area omitted a third kind of capitalism—that common in Chinese cultures.[8] Their distinguishing characteristics are a more entrepreneurial approach and an emphasis on *guanxi* (one's network of personal connections)[9] as the coordinating principle among firms. This third kind of capitalism is also predicted by culture. Chinese cultures are high on PDI and low on IDV and the strong reciprocity implied by the notion of *guanxi* fits the data well.

A SYNTHESIS: RELATIONSHIP-ORIENTED VS. INFORMATION-ORIENTED CULTURES

With increasing frequency, studies note a strong relationship between Hall's high/low context and Hofstede's Individualism/Collectivism and Power Distance indices. For example, low-context American culture scores relatively low on power distance and high on individualism, while high-context Arab cultures score high on power distance and low on individualism. This is not at all surprising given that Hofstede leans heavily on Hall's ideas in developing and labeling the dimensions of culture revealed via his huge IBM database. Indeed, the three dimensions, high/low context, IDV, and PDI are correlated above the $r = 0.6$ level, suggesting all three dimensions are largely measuring the same thing.[10] Likewise, when we compare linguistic distance (to English) to the other three dimensions we see similar levels of correlations among all four dimensions. And while metrics for other dimensions of business culture do not yet exist, a pattern is evident. Please see exhibit 3.5.

Exhibit 3.5 Dimensions of Culture, A Synthesis

Information-Oriented (IO)	Relationship-Oriented (RO)
Low context	High context
Individualism	Collectivism
Low power distance	High power distance (including gender)
Bribery less common	Bribery more common
Low distance from English	High distance from English
Linguistic directness	Linguistic indirectness
Monochronic time	Polychronic time
Internet	Face-to-face
Foreground	Background
Competition	Reduce transaction costs

The pattern displayed is not definitive, only suggestive. Not every culture fits every dimension of culture in a precise way. However, the synthesis is useful in many ways. Primarily, it gives us a simple, yet logical way to think about many of the cultural differences in management style and business systems we have described in this chapter. For example, American culture is low-context, individualistic (IDV), low in power distance (PDI), obviously close to English, monochronic time oriented, linguistically direct, foreground focused,[11] achieves efficiency through competition, and, therefore, it will be categorized hereafter in the book as an *information-oriented culture*. Alternatively, Japanese culture is high-context, collectivistic, high in power distance, far from English, polychronic (in part), linguistically indirect, background-focused, achieves efficiency through reduction of transaction costs, and therefore it can be properly categorized as a *relationship culture*. All this is so even though both the United States and Japan are high-income democracies. Both cultures do achieve efficiency, but through different means. The American business system uses competition, while the Japanese depends more on reducing transaction costs.

The most managerially useful aspect of this synthesis of cultural differences is that it allows us to make predictions about unfamiliar cultures. Reference to the three metrics available gives us some clues about how business systems work in a wide variety of cultures and how consumers and/or business partners will behave and think. Hofstede has provided scores for 78 countries and regions, and we have included them in exhibit 2.3 on page 41. Find a country on his lists and you have some information about business systems and negotiators from there. One can expect Sweden to be an information-oriented culture and Russia to be a relationship-oriented culture and so on. Moreover, measures of linguistic distance (any language can be used as the focal one, not just English) are available for every country, indeed, every person. Thus, we would expect that someone that speaks Vietnamese as his first language to be relationship-oriented. And, that leads us nicely to a discussion of how culture impacts negotiation style in the next chapter.

CHAPTER 4

CULTURAL DIFFERENCES IN NEGOTIATION STYLE[1]

Never offer to teach a fish to swim.

—American proverb

Many high-stakes poker players wear sunglasses. Some high-stakes negotiators are even resorting to Botox treatments before important meetings.[2] Yes, everyone knows that nonverbal behaviors count, but few bother to count them. We do here. We also consider verbal bargaining strategies and cultural values as well. In particular, we compare across cultures in several countries to see how communication behaviors and thinking processes vary at the negotiation table. Based on our counting, we develop pictures of negotiation styles considered appropriate in several countries, how they vary, and how the differences cause problems in international negotiations (see exhibit 4.1).

Exhibit 4.1

The Russian Kiss (Moscow). What an adventure. It was 1989, and it was Thomas Lee's last night in town after a two-week stay. The Mezh (Mezhdunarodnaya Hotel) had been comfortable for the first week. But he still wasn't over his jet lag by the time he got to the Sputnik Hotel for week two. There's an 11-

hour time difference between Newport Beach and Moscow. And nothing got better at the Sputnik. The food, furniture, linens, laundry, electrical power, and plumbing were all . . . well, intermittent is the kindest adjective one might use. In the 1950s, the Sputnik was most likely a nice place. In fact, in the 1950s, Moscow was probably a nice place. In 1989 it wasn't nice, but it was interesting.

Despite Tom's personal problems with the business infrastructure in Moscow, his work had gone well and his host, Leonid, had dragged him out once again for a bit of a going-away party. This time it was the Russian equivalent of the old Ed Sullivan Show, but staged in a huge smoke-filled, booze-guzzling restaurant. There were singers, dancers, jugglers, and fire-eaters. Most were scantily clad, but all were very talented in their specialties.

Between the acts came the food, oceans of it, including wave after wave of greasy sliced salami and sliced cucumbers. Lots of cucumbers—obviously cucumbers shipped well, even over rough Russian roads. And there was absolutely no reason to smoke at dinner. The concentration of Winston and Marlboro smoke floating free in the air was far greater than anyone could possibly suck out the end of any one cigarette. And the alcohol—relentless toasting. Thick red wine, volumes of vodka, and Moscow beer. Whatever you put your hand on first was fine. Tom had asked about the red-label Moscow beer the first time it was served to him in the Cosmos Hotel two weeks earlier. He inquired, "Is this the most popular brand?" His hosts had all gotten a good laugh at his free-enterprise naiveté—one replied, "Yes, it's not only the most popular, in fact, it's the only brand!"

The two weeks had been a test of Tom's physical stamina—a big change from decaf, cappuccinos, and huevos rancheros in seaside patio cafes in California. He had entertained these same comrades in Newport Beach and Disneyland, now they were returning the favor. Good friends and colleagues, all wonderful people. Despite the partying or perhaps because of the partying, Tom was feeling quite at home, quite comfortable with this Russian. Remarkable. And then

Leonid kissed him. In saying good-bye to Tom at his hotel, Leonid wrapped his arms around him, gave him a big hug, and planted his lips right on his cheek!

Now Tom knew that Russian men kiss each other on the cheeks. He'd seen *Doctor Zhivago* in the theaters and newspaper pictures of even Khrushchev or Gorbachev issuing kisses of greeting. The French do the same thing, although you'd assume there's a difference in technique. And before the trip Tom had read about this "cultural difference stuff" in a couple of different books. Manners of greeting vary from country to country.

And now his cross-cultural quandary? Should he kiss Leonid back? And if he were to, how should he do it? After all, how hard you squeeze someone's hand says a lot in the United States. In Japan, the intricacies of bowing properly are learned only after years of practice. Back in the States there are all kinds of kisses—pecks, smooches, wet ones, French ones, passionate, and passionless. This Russian kiss included much more lip than the typical touching of cheeks Tom had experienced in greeting women colleagues in Brazil, France, and Spain. Would a peck be impersonal? But if he were to do it wrong, Tom could just picture Leonid getting into the cab, rubbing his check with his coat sleeve, and cursing those "sloppy Americans." Ringo's refrain, "All ya' gotta do is act naturally," simply didn't help Tom on that Moscow street in front of the Sputnik Hotel.

THE PERVASIVE IMPACT OF CULTURE
ON NEGOTIATION BEHAVIOR

The primary purpose of this chapter is to demonstrate the extent of cultural differences in negotiation styles and how these differences can cause problems in international business negotiation. The material here is based on our systematic study of the topic over the last three decades in which the negotiation styles of more than 1,500 businesspeople in 17 countries (21 cultures) were considered.[3] The work has involved interviews with experienced executives and participant observations in the field, as well as behavioral science laboratory work including surveys and analyses of videotaped negotiations. The countries studied were Japan, Korea, China (Tianjin, Guangzhou, Taiwan, and Hong Kong), Vietnam, the Philippines, Russia, Israel, Norway, the Czech Republic, Germany, France, the United Kingdom, Spain, Brazil, Mexico, Canada (English- and French-speaking), and the United States. The countries were chosen because they constitute America's most important present and future trading partners.

Looking broadly across the several cultures, two important lessons stand out. The first is that regional generalizations very often are not correct. For example, Japanese and Korean negotiation styles are quite similar in some ways, but in other ways they could not be more different. The second lesson learned from our program of research is that Japan is an exceptional place: On almost every dimension of negotiation style considered, the Japanese are on or near the end of the scale. For example, the Japanese use the lowest amount of eye contact of the cultures studied. Sometimes, Americans are on the other end. But actually, most of the time Americans are somewhere in the middle. The reader will see this illustrated by the data presented in this section. The Japanese approach, however, is most distinct, even sui generis.

Cultural differences cause four kinds of problems in international business negotiations at the levels of:

1. Language
2. Nonverbal behaviors
3. Values
4. Thinking and decision-making processes[4]

The order of these differences is important; the problems lower on the list above are more serious because they are more subtle. For example, two negotiators would notice immediately if one were speaking Japanese and the other German. The solution to the problem may be as simple as hiring an interpreter or talking in a common third language, or it may be as difficult as learning a language. Regardless of the solution, the problem is obvious. Cultural differences in nonverbal behaviors, on the other hand, are almost always hidden below our awareness. That is to say, in a face-to-face negotiation participants nonverbally—and more subtly—give out and take in a great deal of information. Some experts argue that this information is more important than verbal information. Almost all this signaling goes on below our levels of consciousness. When the nonverbal signals from foreign partners are different, negotiators are most apt to misinterpret them without even being conscious of the mistake. For example, when a French client consistently interrupts, Americans tend to feel uncomfortable without noticing exactly why. In this manner, interpersonal friction often colors business relationships, goes undetected, and, consequently, goes uncorrected. Differences in values and thinking and decision-making processes are hidden even deeper and therefore are even harder to cure. We discuss these differences here, starting with language and nonverbal behaviors.

DIFFERENCES AT THE LEVEL OF LANGUAGE

Translation problems are often substantial in international negotiations. And, when languages are linguistically distant, greater problems should be anticipated. Particularly daunting can be work in multi-country negotiations. Often the language used is English, but it may be spoken as a second language by most executives at the table. Indeed, native speakers from England, India, and the United States often have trouble understanding one another. As mentioned in chapter 2, exact translations in international interactions are a goal almost never attained.

Moreover, language differences are sometimes exploited in subtle ways. We have witnessed another interesting way to take advantage of speaking more than one language. Many senior executives in foreign countries speak and understand some English, but prefer to speak in their "stronger" native language and use an interpreter. Thus, we've seen a senior Russian negotiator asking questions in Russian. The interpreter then translated the question for his American counterpart. While the interpreter spoke, the American directed his attention (gaze) toward the interpreter. However, the Russian's gaze was directed toward the American. Therefore, the Russain could carefully and unobtrusively observe the American's facial expressions and nonverbal responses. Additionally, when the American spoke, the senior Russian had twice the response time. Because he understood English, he could formulate his responses during the translation process.

What's this extra response time worth in a strategic conversation? What's it worth to be able to carefully observe the nonverbal responses of your top-level counterpart in a high-stakes business negotiation? Later in the book we'll talk more about some of the other strategic and tactical advantages of knowing more than one language. We will also discuss in some detail how to manage interpretors and the interpretion process toward mitigating some of the disadvantages of monolingualism. For example, it may often be useful for the American side to bring their own interpreter as well. But for now, our point is a simple one—bilingualism is not a common characteristic for Americans, and therefore we afford our competitors with greater language skills a natural advantage in international commerce.

Unfortunately, Americans are clearly near the bottom of the languages skills list, although Australians often assert that they are even worse. Moreover, according to the Pew Research Center, young people in America are becoming less interested in learning a second language.[5] The same is true for Canada and generally in Western Europe. Moreover, since 9/11, American undergraduate students are spending less time in study abroad programs than previously. Worse still, foreign-language teaching resources in the United States are inadequate to satisfy even the decreasing demand. Likewise, the Czechs are now throwing away a hard-earned competitive advantage: Young Czechs are not studying Russian anymore. It is easy to understand why, but the result will be a generation of Czechs who cannot leverage their geographic advantage because they will be unable to speak to their neighbors to the east. All this is so despite the manifest importance of language skills in the fast globalizing world of business.

American managers often complain regarding foreign clients and partners breaking into side conversations in their native languages. At best, it is seen as impolite, and quite often American negotiators are likely to attribute something sinister to the content of the foreign talk— "They're plotting or telling secrets."

This is a frequent American mistake. Many times the purpose of such side conversations is to straighten out a translation problem. For instance, one Korean may lean over to another and ask, "What'd he say?" Or, the side conversation can focus on a disagreement among members of the the foreign team. Both circumstances should be seen as positive signs by Americans—that is, getting translations straight enhances the efficiency of the interactions, and concessions often follow internal disagreements. But because most Americans speak only one language, neither circumstance is appreciated. People from other countries are advised to give Americans a brief explanation of the content of their first few side conversations to assuage such sinister attributions.

But, there are problems at the level of language beyond translations and interpreters. Data from simulated negotiations are informative. In our study, the verbal behaviors of negotiators in 15 of the cultures (6 negotiators in each of the 15 groups) were videotaped. The numbers in the body of exhibit 4.2 represent the percentages of statements that were classified into each category listed. That is, we classified 7 percent of the statements made by Japanese negotiators as promises, 4 percent as threats, 7 percent as recommendations, and so on. The verbal bargaining behaviors used by the negotiators during the simulations proved to be surprisingly similar across cultures. Negotiations in the 15 cultures studied were composed primarily of information-exchange tactics—questions and self-disclosures. Note that the Israelis are on the low end of the continuum of self-disclosures. Their 30 percent (near the Japanese, Spaniards, and the English-speaking Canadians at 34 percent) was the lowest across all 15 groups, suggesting that they are the most reticent about giving (that is, communicating) information. Overall, however, the patterns of verbal tactics used were surprisingly similar across the diverse cultures.

ADDING NONVERBAL BEHAVIORS TO THE MIX

Anthropologist Ray L. Birdwhistell demonstrated that less than 35 percent of the messages in conversations are conveyed by the spoken word while the other 65 percent are communicated nonverbally.[6] Albert Mehrabian,[7] a UCLA psychologist, also parsed where meaning comes from in face-to-face interactions. He reports:

7 percent of the meaning is derived from the words spoken;
38 percent from paralinguistic channels, that is, tone of voice, loudness, and other aspects of how things are said; and
55 percent from facial expressions.

Of course, some might quibble with the exact percentages (and many have), but our work also supports the notion that nonverbal behaviors are crucial—how things are said is often more important than what is said.

Some early evidence of the salience of nonverbal behaviors was the global success of Charles Chaplin's pantomine-based movies even after the invention of "talkies." His 1931 *City Lights* proved wildly popular at the

Exhibit 4.2 Verbal Negotiation Tactics (the "what" of communications)

Bargaining Behaviors and Definitions	Cultures*				
	JPN	KOR	TWN	CHN**	RUSS
Promise. A statement in which the source indicated its intention to provide the target with a positive reinforcing consequence.	7+	4	9	6	5
Threat. Same as promise, except that the reinforcing consequences are thought to be noxious or unpleasant.	4	2	2	1	3
Recommendation. A statement in which the source predicts that a pleasant environmental consequence will occur to the target.	7	1	5	2	4
Warning. Same as recommendation, except that the consequences are thought to be unpleasant.	2	0	3	1	0
Reward. A statement by the source that is thought to create pleasant feelings for the target.	1	3	2	1	3
Punishment. Same as reward, except that the feelings are thought to be unpleasant.	1	5	1	0	1
Normative appeals. A statement in which the source indicates that the target's behavior conforms with social norms or is in violation of social norms.	4	3	1	1	1
Commitment. A statement by the source to the effect that its future bids will not go below or above a certain level.	15	13	9	10	1
Self-disclosure. A statement in which the source reveals information about itself.	34	36	42	36	40
Question. A statement in which the source asks the target to reveal information about itself.	20	21	14	34	27
Command. A statement in which the source suggests that the target perform a certain behavior.	8	13	11	7	7

*For each, group n = 6
**Northern China (Tianjin and environs).
+Read "7 percent of the statements made by Japanese negotiators were promised."

Cultures (continued)*									
ISRL	GRM	UK	FRN	SPN	BRZ	MEX	FCAN	ECAN	USA
12	7	11	5	11	3	7	8	6	8
4	3	3	5	2	2	1	3	0	4
8	5	6	3	4	5	8	5	4	4
1	1	1	3	1	1	2	3	0	1
2	4	5	3	3	2	1	1	3	2
3	2	0	3	2	3	0	2	1	3
5	1	1	0	1	1	1	3	1	2
10	9	13	10	9	8	9	8	14	13
30	47	39	42	34	39	38	42	34	36
20	11	15	18	17	22	27	519	26	20
9	12	9	9	17	14	7	5	10	6

time, and as actor, writer, and producer, he insisted on silence. Indeed, on a trip to California, Albert Einstein had asked to be introduced to Chaplin. Chaplin invited him to the Hollywood premier of *City Lights* and commented as they walked down the red carpet, "They cheer me because they all understand me, they cheer you because no one understands you."[8]

Finally, the latest findings from the new brain sciences are confirming the relative importance of nonverbal communications. For example, Donald Hoffman tells us in his path-breaking book, *Visual Intelligence*,[9] that over half the capacity of the brain is dedicated to the single sense of sight and making sense of what we see. And almost all this processing of visual input happens instantly and below our level of consciousness. Literally, actions speak louder than words, particularly when it comes to building interpersonal trust and human relationships.

Exhibit 4.3 provides analyses of some linguistic aspects and nonverbal behaviors for the 15 videotaped groups, that is, *how* things are said. Although these efforts merely scratch the surface of these kinds of behavioral analyses, they still provide indications of substantial cultural differences. Note that, once again, the Japanese are at or next to the end of the continuum on almost every dimension of the behaviors listed. Their facial gazing and touching are the least among the 15 groups. Only the Northern Chinese used the word *no* less frequently, and only the Russians used more silent periods than did the Japanese.

A broader examination of the data in exhibits 4.2 and 4.3 reveals a more meaningful conclusion: The variation across cultures is greater when comparing linguistic aspects of language and nonverbal behaviors than when the verbal content of negotiations is considered. For example, notice the great differences between the Japanese and Brazilians in exhibit 4.2 vis-à-vis exhibit 4.3.

What follows are further descriptions of the distinctive aspects of each of the 15 cultural groups videotaped. Certainly, conclusions of statistically significant differences between individual cultures cannot be drawn without larger sample sizes. But, it's worthwhile to briefly consider the suggested cultural differences.

Japan

Consistent with most descriptions of Japanese negotiation behavior, the results of this analysis suggest that the Japanese style of interaction is among the least aggressive (or most polite). Threats, commands, and

Exhibit 4.3 Linguistic Aspects of Language and Nonverbal Behaviors ("how" things are said)

Bargaining Behaviors (per 30 minutes)	Cultures*														
	JPN	KOR	TWN	CHN**	RUSS	ISRL	GRM	UK	FRN	SPN	BRZ	MEX	FCAN	ECAN	USA
Structural Aspects															
"No's." The number of times the word no was used by each negotiator.	1.9	7.4	5.9	1.5	2.3	8.5	6.7	5.4	11.3	23.2	41.9	4.5	7.0	10.1	4.5
"You's." The number of times the word you was used by each negotiator.	31.5	35.2	36.6	26.8	23.6	64.4	39.7	54.8	70.2	73.3	90.4	56.3	72.4	64.4	55.1
Nonverbal Behavior															
Silent periods. The number of conversational gaps of ten seconds or longer.	2.5	0	0	2.3	3.7	1.9	0	2.5	1.0	0	15.3	1.1	0.2	2.9	1.7
Conversational overlaps. Number of interruptions.	6.2	22.0	12.3	17.1	13.3	30.1	20.8	5.3	20.7	28.0	15.6	10.6	24.0	17.0	5.1
Facial gazing. Number of minutes negotiators spent looking at opponent's face.	3.9	9.9	19.7	11.1	8.7	15.3	10.2	9.0	16.0	13.7	74.6	14.7	18.8	10.4	10.0
Touching. Incidents of bargainers touching one another (not including handshaking).	0	0	0	0	0	0	0	0	0.1	0	4.7	0	0	0	0

*For each group, n = 6
**Northern China (Tianjin and environs).

warnings appear to be de-emphasized in favor of the more positive promises, recommendations, and commitments. Particularly indicative of their polite conversational style was their infrequent use of *no* and *you* and facial gazing, as well as more frequent silent periods. More details are provided in John's new book, *Doing Business in the New Japan.*

Korea

Perhaps one of the more interesting aspects of this analysis is the contrast of the Asian styles of negotiations. Non-Asians often generalize about the Orient; the findings demonstrate, however, that this is a mistake. Korean negotiators used considerably more punishments and commands than did the Japanese. Koreans used the word *no* and interrupted more than three times as frequently as the Japanese. Moreover, no silent periods occurred between Korean negotiators.

China (Northern)

The behaviors of the negotiators from Northern China (i.e., in and around Tianjin) were most remarkable in the emphasis on asking questions (34 percent). Indeed, 70 percent of the statements made by the Chinese negotiators were classified as information-exchange tactics. Other aspects of their behavior were quite similar to the Japanese, particularly the use of *no* and *you* and silent periods. See John's new book, *China Now,* for details.

Taiwan

The behavior of the businesspeople in Taiwan was quite different from that in China and Japan, but similar to that in Korea. The Chinese negotiators in Taiwan were exceptional in the time of facial gazing—on the average, almost 20 of 30 minutes. They asked fewer questions and provided more information (self-disclosures) than did any of the other Asian groups.

Russia

The Russian style was quite different from that of any other European group, and, indeed, was quite similar in many respects to the style of the

Japanese negotiators. They used *no* and *you* infrequently and used the most silent periods of any group. Only the Japanese did less facial gazing, and only the Chinese asked a greater percentage of questions.

Israel

The behaviors of the Israeli negotiators were distinctive in four respects. As mentioned above, they used the lowest percentage of self-disclosures, apparently holding their cards relatively close. Alternatively, they used by far the highest percentages of promises and recommendations, utilizing these persuasive strategies unusually heavily. They were also at the end of the scale regarding the percentage of normative appeals (at 5 percent), with the most frequent reference to competitors' offers. Perhaps most importantly the Israeli negotiators interrupted one another much more frequently than negotiators from any other group. Indeed, this important nonverbal behavior is most likely to blame for the "pushy" stereotype often used by Americans to describe their Israeli negotiation partners.

Germany

The behaviors of German negotiators are difficult to characterize because they fell toward the center of almost all continua. However, the Germans were exceptional in that they had a high percentage of self-disclosures (47 percent) and a low percentage of questions (11 percent).

United Kingdom

The behaviors of British negotiators were remarkably similar to those of Americans in all respects.

Spain

Diga is perhaps a good metaphor for the Spanish approach to negotiations evinced in our data. When you make a phone call in Madrid, the usual greeting on the other end is not *hola* ("hello") but is, instead, the command *diga* ("speak"). It is not surprising, then, that the Spaniards in the videotaped negotiations likewise used the highest percentage of commands (17 percent) of any of the groups and gave comparatively little information (self-disclosures, only 34 percent). Moreover, they interrupted one another more frequently than any other group, except for their Mediterranean neighbors from Israel, and they used the terms *no* and *you* very frequently.

France

The style of the French negotiators was perhaps the most aggressive of all the groups. In particular, they used the highest percentage of threats and warnings (together, 8 percent). They also used interruptions, facial gazing, and *no* and *you* very frequently compared with the other groups, and one of the French negotiators touched his negotiation partner on the arm during the simulation.

Brazil

The Brazilian businesspeople, like the French and Spanish, were quite aggressive. They used the second-highest percentage of commands of all the groups. On average, the Brazilians said the word *no* 42 times, *you* 90 times, and touched one another on the arm about 5 times during 30 minutes of negotiation. Facial gazing was also high.

Mexico

The patterns of Mexican behavior in our negotiations are good reminders of the dangers of regional or language-group generalizations. Both verbal and nonverbal behaviors were quite different than those of their Latin American (Brazilian) or continental (Spanish) cousins. Indeed, Mexicans answer the telephone with the much less-demanding *Bueno* (short for "good day"). In many respects, the Mexican behavior was very similar to that of the negotiators from the United States.

French-Speaking Canada

The French-speaking Canadians behaved quite similarly to their continental cousins. Like the negotiators from France, they too used high percentages of threats and warnings, and even more interruptions and eye contact. Such an aggressive interaction style would not mix well with some of the more low-key styles of some of the Asian groups or with English speakers, including English-speaking Canadians.

English-Speaking Canada

The Canadians who speak English as their first language used the lowest percentage of aggressive persuasive tactics (threats, warnings, and punishments totaled only 1 percent) of all 15 groups. Perhaps, as communications researchers suggest, such stylistic differences are the seeds of the interethnic discord witnessed in Canada over the years. With respect to international negotiations, the English-speaking Canadians used noticeably more interruptions and *nos* than negotiators from either of Canada's major trading partners, the United States and Japan.

United States

Like the German and British negotiators, the Americans fell in the middle of most continua. They did interrupt one another less frequently than all the others, but that was their sole distinction.

These differences across the cultures are quite complex, and this material by itself should not be used to predict the behaviors of foreign counterparts. Instead, great care should be taken with respect to the aforementioned dangers of stereotypes. The key here is to be aware of these kinds of differences so that the Japanese silence, the Brazilian "no, no, no . . . ," or the French threat are not misinterpreted.

DIFFERENCES IN MANAGERIAL VALUES

We mentioned managerial values in the previous chapter. Four of them—objectivity, competitiveness, equality, and punctuality—which are held strongly and deeply by most Americans seem to frequently cause misunderstandings and bad feelings in international business negotiations.

Objectivity

"Americans make decisions based upon the bottom line and on cold, hard facts." "Americans don't play favorites." "Economics and performance count, not people." "Business is business." Such statements well reflect American notions of the importance of objectivity.

We highly recommend *Getting to Yes*, the single most successful book on the topic of negotiation, for both American and foreign readers.[10] The latter will learn not only about negotiations but, perhaps more important, about how Americans think about negotiations. The authors are quite emphatic about "separating the people from the problem," and they state, "Every negotiator has two kinds of interests: in the substance and in the relationship." This advice is probably quite worthwhile in the United States or perhaps in Germany, but in most places in the world such advice is nonsense. In most places in the world, particularly in relationship-oriented cultures, personalities and substance are not separate issues and cannot be made so.

For example, consider how important nepotism is in Chinese or Hispanic cultures. Experts tell us that businesses don't grow beyond the bounds and bonds of tight family control in the burgeoning "Chinese Commonwealth." Things work the same way in Spain, Mexico, and the Philippines. And, naturally, negotiators from such countries not only will take things personally but will be personally affected by negotiation outcomes. What happens to them at the negotiation table will affect the business relationship regardless of the economics involved.

Competitiveness and Equality

Simulated negotiations can be viewed as a kind of experimental economics wherein the values of each participating cultural group are roughly reflected in the economic outcomes. The simple simulation used in this part of our work represents the essence of commercial negotiations—it has both competitive and cooperative aspects. At least 40 businesspeople from each culture played the same buyer–seller game, negotiating over the prices of three products. Depending on the agreement reached, the "negotiation pie" could be made larger through cooperation (as high as $10,400 in joint profits) before it was divided between the buyer and seller. The results are summarized in exhibit 4.4.

The Japanese were the champions at making the pie big. Their joint profits in the simulation were the highest (at $9,590) among the 21 cultural groups involved. The Chinese in Hong Kong and the British businesspeople also behaved cooperatively in our negotiation game. The Czechs and the Germans behaved more competitively. The American pie was more average-sized (at $9,030), but at least it was divided relatively equitably (51.8 percent of the profits went to the buyers). Conversely, the Japanese and particularly the South Korean and Mexican businesspeople split their pies in strange (perhaps even unfair) ways, with buyers making

Exhibit 4.4 Cultural Differences in Competitiveness and Equality

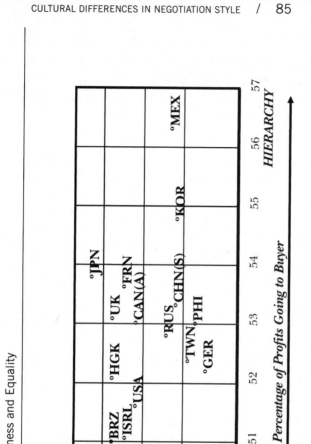

higher percentages of the profits (53.8 percent, 55.0 percent, and 56.7 percent, respectively). The implications of these simulated business negotiations are completely consistent with the comments of other authors and the adage that in Japan (and apparently in South Korea and Mexico as well) the buyer is "kinger." Americans have little understanding of the Japanese practice of granting complete deference to the needs and wishes of buyers. That is not the way things work in the United States. American sellers tend to treat American buyers more as equals, and the egalitarian values of American society support this behavior. The American emphasis on competition and individualism represented in these findings is quite consistent with the work of Geert Hofstede[11] detailed in chapter 2, which indicated that Americans scored the highest among all the cultural groups on the individualism (versus collectivism) scale. Moreover, values of individualism/collectivism have been shown to directly influence negotiation behaviors in several other countries.

Finally, not only do Japanese buyers achieve higher profits than Americans buyers, but compared with American sellers ($4,350), Japanese sellers also get more of the commercial pie ($4,430) as well. Interestingly, when shown these results, Americans in executive seminars still often prefer the American seller's role. In other words, even though the American sellers make lower profits than the Japanese, many American managers apparently prefer lower profits if those profits are yielded from a more equal split of the joint profits.

Time

"Just make them wait." Everyone else in the world knows that no negotiation tactic is more useful with Americans, because no one places more value on time, no one has less patience when things slow down, and no one looks at their wristwatches more than Americans do. The material from the last chapter on P-time versus M-time is quite pertinent here. Edward T. Hall in his seminal writing best explains how the passage of time is viewed differently across cultures and how these differences most often hurt Americans.

Even Americans try to manipulate time to their advantage, however. As a case in point, Solar Turbines Incorporated (a division of Caterpillar) once sold $34 million worth of industrial gas turbines and compressors for a Russian natural gas pipeline project. Both parties agreed that final negotiations would be held in a neutral location, the south of France. In previous negotiations, the Russians had been tough but reasonable. But in Nice, the Russians were not nice. They became tougher and, in fact, completely unreasonable, according to the Solar executives involved.

It took a couple of discouraging days before the Americans diagnosed the problem, but once they did, a crucial call was made back to head-quarters in San Diego. Why had the Russians turned so cold? They were enjoying the warm weather in Nice and weren't interested in making a quick deal and heading back to Moscow. The call to California was the key event in this negotiation. Solar's people at their headquarters in San Diego decided to allow their negotiators to take their time. From that point on, the routine of the negotiations changed to brief, 45-minute meetings in the mornings, with afternoons at the golf course, beach, or hotel, making calls, and doing paperwork. Finally, during the fourth week, the Russians began to make concessions and to ask for longer meet-ings. Why? They could not go back to Moscow after four weeks on the Mediterranean without a signed contract. This strategic reversal of the tactic of time pressure yielded a wonderful contract for Solar.

DIFFERENCES IN THINKING AND DECISION-MAKING PROCESSES

When faced with a complex negotiation task, most Westerners (notice the generalization here) divide the large task up into a series of smaller tasks. Issues such as prices, delivery, warranty, and service contracts may be set-tled one issue at a time, with the final agreement being the sum of the se-quence of smaller agreements. In Asia, however, a different approach is more often taken wherein all the issues are discussed at once, in no ap-parent order, and concessions are made on all issues at the end of the dis-cussion. The Western sequential approach and the Eastern holistic approach do not mix well.

That is, American managers often report great difficulties in measur-ing progress in negotiations, particularly in Asian countries. After all, in America, you are half done when half of the issues are settled. But in China, Japan, or Korea nothing seems to get settled. Then, surprise, you are done. Often, Americans make unnecessary concessions right before agreements are announced by the other side. For example, one American department store executive who traveled to Japan to buy six different con-sumer products for her chain lamented that negotiations for the first product took an entire week. In the United States, such a purchase would be consummated in an afternoon. So, by her calculations, she expected to have to spend six weeks in Japan to complete her purchases. She considered raising her purchase prices to try to speed things along. But before she was able to make such a concession, the Japanese quickly agreed on the other five products in just three days. This particular manager was, by her own admission, lucky in her first encounter with Japanese bargainers.

This American businesswoman's near blunder reflects more than just a difference in decision-making style. To Americans, a business negotiation is a problem-solving activity, the best deal for both parties being the solution. To a Japanese businessperson, on the other hand, a business negotiation is a time to develop a business relationship with the goal of long-term mutual benefit. The economic issues are the context, not the content, of the talks. Thus, settling any one issue really is not that important. Such details will take care of themselves once a viable, harmonious business relationship is established. And, as happened in the case of our retail goods buyer, once the relationship was established—signaled by the first agreement—the other "details" were settled quickly.

American bargainers should anticipate such a holistic approach to be common in Asian cultures and be prepared to discuss all issues simultaneously and in an apparently haphazard order. Progress in the talks should not be measured by how many issues have been settled. Rather, Americans must try to gauge the quality of the business relationship. Important signals of progress can be the following:

- Higher-level executives from the other side being included in the discussions;
- Their questions beginning to focus on specific areas of the deal;
- A softening of their attitudes and position on some of the issues—"Let us take some time to study this issue";
- At the negotiation table, increased talk among themselves in their own language, which often means they're trying to decide something; and
- Increased bargaining and use of lower-level, informal, and other channels of communication.

IMPLICATIONS FOR MANAGERS AND NEGOTIATORS

Considering all the potential problems in cross-cultural negotiations, particularly when you mix managers from relationship-oriented cultures with those from information-oriented ones, it is a wonder that any international business gets done at all. Obviously, the economic imperatives of global trade make much of it happen despite the potential pitfalls. But an appreciation of cultural differences can lead to even better international commercial transactions—it is not just business deals but creative and highly profitable business relationships that are the real goal of international business negotiations. That leads us to Rule #3: Don't just adjust to cultural differences; exploit them as well.

CHAPTER 5

BEYOND NATIONAL CULTURE AND OTHER IMPORTANT MATTERS

"... as humorous as a German."

Some might suggest that the material we have presented so far in this book is classic stereotyping. Does everybody really act the same in Germany, Brazil, or Thailand? Should we prejudge others based on their nationality or ethnic background or the language(s) they speak? The short answer is of course "no." There is as much danger in stereotyping executives as there is in stereotyping anyone else. Indeed, it's worth while to consider two prominent foreign executives who haven't conformed to the stereotypes of their countrymen.

Our favorite is Dieter Zetsche, CEO of DaimlerChrysler before it dissolved. Despite Karl sounding more like Groucho Marx in the chapter 3 epigraph, Germans are still often stereotyped by their fellow Europeans for their lack of humor. Indeed, there's a postcard you can buy in the lobby of the European Union Parliament building that pokes fun at the diversity of the EU members' cultures. "The Perfect European should be . . . humble as a Spaniard, generous as a Dutchman (ah, the penny-stretching joke again), sober as the Irish, and humorous as a German, etc." Now, judging by the comical Dr. Z ad campaign that he approved and starred in, Dieter Zetsche has a pretty good sense of humor. However, we should point out that the ad campaign aired only in the United States and Canada. And one of the criticisms of the campaign is that Dr. Z wasn't really very funny. But, we liked it anyway. Another much larger decision made by Zetsche that better demonstrates his unusual German character was his advocacy of and leadership in the takeover of Chrysler. The Germans don't like instability, yet he talked his colleagues into a major investment in one of the most unstable businesses on the planet, the American automobile market. Ouch.

Or consider Akio Morita, the now-deceased founder of Sony Corporation—an unusual, albeit very successful, Japanese businessman. He was described as outgoing, adventurous, and molded in the American entrepreneurial spirit. His top-down decision-making style was also well known. Such characteristics made him an outcast in Japanese industry initially, and his company concentrated on developing markets in the United States first. In fact, part of his legacy is the acceptance of a Welshman, a *gaijin*, one Sir Howard Stringer, as CEO of the Japanese powerhouse.

Here's the point: So far we've talked about culture as it influences negotiation behavior in international commerce. We have provided you the best tools available for predicting and understanding the behavior of your foreign counterparts. These will help if applied diligently. But, obviously you've got more work to do to really get to know your business partners. You don't negotiate with countries, cultures, or companies. You negotiate with people. And any one person's behavior is determined by a number of factors aside from culture—personality, industry and/or company culture, expatriate experiences, age, gender, regional differences, even brain chemistry. We can't help with the last, or the blood type that might interest a Japanese executive, or the Asian calendar year in which you're born—pig, snake, etc. But herein we comment on what influences some of these other factors.

NEGOTIATION STYLES DIFFER ACROSS INDUSTRIES

We have found important differences in negotiation styles across industries in most countries. One dramatic contrast, for example, is that between the banking and retailing industries. Negotiations with bankers in all countries will almost always proceed in the most conservative and traditional ways—nobody wants a daring banker. Indeed, the flamboyant Mario Conde, ironically known as *"El Tiburon"* (the Shark), owner of the fourth-largest bank in Spain, voted by his countrymen as the most admired businessman in the land in 1990, and frequently featured handsomely on the cover of *El Tiempo* magazine at the time, has spent most of his last few years in jail for his daring "banking" practices. Ordinarily, however, major retailers in most countries will tend to take more aggressive approaches in business strategies and at the negotiation table compared to their banking counterparts.

Quantitative estimates of how behaviors and attitudes differ across industries are few and far between. But we have come across some numbers (based on survey data) on how industries differ on one important dimension of international business—the prevalence of corruption and bribery. Transparency International (www.transparency.org) suggests that corruption will be a problem to the greatest extent with firms involved in public works/construction or arms and defense. Alternatively, they rate light manufacturing and agriculture as the "cleanest" industries. Please see exhibit 5.1 for scores on additional industries.

Generally, the major firms in established industries will negotiate in the traditional ways of their cultures. Smaller firms, particularly if they have been exposed previously to international transactions, and if they are in newer industries, may take a more flexible, less traditional approach to business negotiations. But the key word is "may."

Company Culture

Anyone that's worked for two companies in the same industry and country knows that companies have cultures, that is, ways of doing things, ways

Exhibit 5.1   Bribery in Business Sectors

Business Sector	Score	Business Sector	Score
Public works/ construction	1.3	Heavy manufacturing	4.5
Arms and defense	1.9	Banking and finance	4.7
Oil and gas	2.7	Civilian aerospace	4.9
Real estate/property	3.5	Forestry	5.1
Telecoms	3.7	IT	5.1
Power generation/ transmission	3.7	Fishery	5.9
Mining	4.0	Light manufacturing	5.9
Transportation/storage	4.3	Agriculture	5.9
Pharmaceuticals/medical care	4.3		

Source: Transparency International

of thinking, etc. Indeed, many a merger or acquisition strategy that made great sense on paper has failed in implementation because of what some call differences in "management style." Think Dieter Zetsche's Daimler-Chrysler as a prominent example. Forty years ago, you could read in the *Harvard Business Review*, "When a company seeks to merge, it usually wants a partner whose operations will complement it in some manner, such as product line, marketing, or manufacturing capability. But a successful combination depends at least as much on compatibility of fundamental business "styles."[1] One may recall the recent examples of incompatibility in the United States was the initial friction between AOL and Time Warner executives after their 2001 merger. One industry analyst described it most colorfully in September 2002: "AOLTW has already undergone a slew of personnel shakeups, which has seen top executives falling from the beleaguered company like rotted fruit from a tree. Former Time Warner CEO Gerald Levine in January, while company COO and interim head of AOL Robert Pittman followed in July. Pittman's departure came as part of an overall restructuring of the company that shifted power away from the renegade new media side and into Time Warner's old media court."[2]

Indeed, corporate goals and growth strategies have much to do with corporate culture and everyday decision making *and* negotiation style. The stodgy "old media" versus creative "new media" just described is just one kind of clash. Or take Neiman Marcus versus its sister brand/store Bergdorf Goodman. Both are high-end department stores, jointly owned, and they often even trade executives. But the latter specifically aspires to serve only New York City, while Neiman Marcus is now expanding fast across the Unites States. This affects their management cultures in many ways. Or just imagine how a Microsoft/Apple merger might work?

Our favorite proof of the importance of corporate culture in negotiations comes straight from the cover of the aforementioned most popular trade book, published in Russia, about negotiating with Americans, Peter Shikerev's *Dolphins and Sharks*. The title is chess-champion ingenious as it begs the question, who's who? Are the Americans the sharks, or is it the Russians? Recall his answer: There are sharks and dolphins in the business culture of both countries, and you better be careful that you're working with the dolphins. Indeed, many would argue that Michael Eisner transformed Disney from a dolphin into a shark. And both Microsoft and Wal-Mart are also renowned for their aggressive negotiation styles. Perhaps it has something to do with size? One study at the Wharton Business School found that General Motor's procurement costs in the late 1990s were twice those of Chrysler because GM was viewed as a "much less trustworthy organization" by its own suppliers.[3]

Our own studies demonstrate that company culture influences negotiation styles. For example, we have found negotiators in both Canadian and Filipino companies that are reputed to be more people-oriented (as opposed to finance-oriented) to be more cooperative in their negotiations with Americans. That is, they are more likely to behave like dolphins. As we describe in the next chapter, a key component of your intelligence gathering will be determining the reputations of both the people and the firms with which you are negotiating. The bottom line—look for the blowholes.

Negotiators with Expatriate Experiences

Foreign executives with experience living or working in the United States will usually adjust their bargaining style and appear to understand a Western approach. For example, we have noticed in our negotiation simulations that Japanese executives living only six months in the United States unconsciously begin to reflect the communication style (eye contact, conversational rhythm) of American bargainers. And the Korean choreography of the flying chair described in the introduction depended in part on the thrower's knowledge of Americans based on his U.S. MBA.

But the degree to which foreign executives will understand and respond to the American style of negotiations can differ depending on the length and quality of their stay in America. The answers to simple questions such as, "How long did you spend in the United States?" and, "What were your responsibilities there?" will help gauge their understanding. Generally, higher-level expatriate tours of duty (such as head of a subsidiary or middle manager) are shorter (three to five years) and involve primarily contact with their own headquarters personnel at home. Alternatively, staff or trainee assignments are for five to six years and entail much more contact with American suppliers and clients. Thus, foreigners with earlier and/or lower-level staff experience in the United States can be expected to be more familiar with Western negotiation practices.

You should also be aware that most foreign businesspeople with such a bicultural competence are able to switch their American style on and off. We have seen, for example, Mexican associates that can play either role—languishing in business entertainment and non-task talk, or in other circumstances getting down to business uncomfortably fast.

And, as we mentioned before, you are more likely to focus your attention on executives with long expatriate experiences because they speak English better, they appear to understand you better, and they appear to be smarter. This is a mistake. Often, the foreign executive with long expatriate experience is the least influential in the group.

Age

The ancient Greeks complained about the younger generation. Socrates circa 500 BC opined: "Youth today love luxury. They have bad manners, contempt for authority, no respect for older people and talk nonsense when they should work. Young people do not stand up any longer when adults enter the room. They contradict their parents, talk too much in company, guzzle their food, lay their legs on the table, and tyrannize their elders." Sound familiar? Indeed, the generational divide is widening as younger people are better able than their elders to keep up with the almost daily changes in communication systems and other technologies.

So we should expect age-based differences in communication, interaction, and of course, negotiation styles in other countries as well as at home. Around the world, most generation gaps are marked by formative events, and astute negotiators should be alert for mention and/or signs of them. Consider how the baby boom generation has affected American culture. Then there's Generation X, Nexters, the Internet Generation, etc. Our favorite is the new generation of kids with wheels on their shoes. We wonder if the latter will be less patient in their negotiations in the 2030s.

In Britain, the demise of industrial supremacy has had an interesting effect on the generations. A recent survey[4] there asked about words associated with the term "industry." Britons under age 25 most often answered: money, busyness, booming, computers, success, and technology. Their over-45 countrymen who directly witnessed Britain's industrial demise answered: factory, decline, dirt, strike, China, and masculinity/maleness. This signals quite a difference in outlook across the age groups there.

In China, the Cultural Revolution of the late 1960s, when universities were closed and faculties were sent to be reeducated on western farms, has left a "Lost Generation" of very smart people who do not participate in executive roles there. Or think of how different the views will be of the young Russian businesspeople now learning about commerce and the wisdom of the market compared to their elders who were immersed in Marxist teachings. Indeed, a Moscow colleague born in the 1950s gloomily told us that the benefits of the demise of communism will only be felt by his children.

We get some measure of the extent of the generation gap around the world with reference to exhibit 5.2. The good news in the Pew Research Center report[5] is that support for globalization and international interdependence is growing in most places around the world. However, the notable exception is Latin America. Also, 30- and 40-year-olds in Europe seem to be, on average, less interested in global cooperation than the age cohorts above and below them.

CULTURE AND COUNTRY DO NOT ALWAYS COINCIDE

Can we generalize about national styles of negotiation? We think so and indeed have done so. But almost all natives of any country can quickly describe the nuances of culture across regions in their homeland. Mexicans say there are really five Mexicos. Vietnamese argue there are three very different cultures in their country—north, south, and middle. The toughest negotiators in Japan are from Yokohama, in Spain from Valencia, and in China from Shanghai. Languages mark significant regional differences.

Exhibit 5.2   Mixed Support for Globalization

	Age			
	18-29 %	30-49 %	50-64 %	65+ %
North America	43	35	35	27
Western Europe	41	37	40	36
Eastern Europe	39	30	30	7
Latin America	36	36	44	45
West Africa	75	66	58	61
East/South Africa	59	51	48	31
Conflict Area*	50	50	45	39

Persons responding "Very good" to the question "How do you feel about the world becoming more connected through greater economic trade and faster communication?"
*Countries included in the Middle East/Conflict area are Egypt, Jordan, Lebanon, Pakistan, Turkey, and Uzbekistan
Source: Pew Research Center

Freeway signs near Barcelona mark exits in both Catalán and Castilian Spanish, *sortida* and *salida*, respectively. But, not very respectfully, Catalán taggers often paint over the word *salida* in protest. Indeed, review Hofstede's data in exhibit 2.3 on page 41. He distinguished between French- and Flemish-speaking Belgians, English- and French-speaking Canadians, and so on. Indeed, if he were to replicate his study in the United States now, he'd need to consider measuring the work values of Spanish-speaking Americans separately. And, of course, even then there would be an argument about lumping together immigrants from Mexico and Cuba living in the United States.

Particularly in the larger nations, regional differences can heavily impact negotiation behavior. Joel Garreau, a long-time demographer at the *Washington Post*, eloquently described the cultural variation across the North American continent in his still excellent read, *The Nine Nations of North America*.[6] In exhibit 5.3 we've listed the nine, along with their "capitol cities." He based his demarcations on differences in public opinion polls he'd noticed over the years. For example, during the 1970s, the federal government imposed a national 55 mph speed limit. At the time, folks in Boston thought it made sense—fuel was expensive after all, and distances were short and streets narrow. But their fellow countrymen in Boise thought the idea was insane. They were much closer to cheaper sources of fuel, but much further from their families and friends. Or, think for a moment about the comparative rate of words produced in a conversation in New York vs. New Orleans. In chapter 13 we even go as far as to say that negotiation styles in California will be, *by nature*, more creative than those in New York.

Perhaps the most obvious place to look for large cultural differences within countries is within the most populous ones. While tiny Switzerland includes four different official languages on its currency—French, German, Italian, and Romansch, a 20-rupee note in India lists its 13 official languages in addition to Hindi and English. Indeed, there is more cultural diversity in terms of religions and languages on the subcontinent of India than there is in all of Europe. And let's consider China. Below we present summaries of regional nuances in negotiation styles detailed in *China Now*[7]:

Northeastern Negotiators. Forthright—this is the stereotype of Northeastern businesspeople held by their southern neighbors. Negotiators from the three northeastern provinces above the Yangtze are certainly industrious, competent businesspeople. They are generally

Exhibit 5.3   The Nine Nations of North America

- The Industrial Foundry (Philadelphia)
- New England and the Maritime Provinces of Canada (Boston)
- Dixie, The Southern States (Atlanta)
- The Intermountain West or Empty Quarter (Denver)
- Hispanic Southwest and Mexico or Mexamerica (Los Angeles)
- Pacific Northwest or Ecotopia (San Francisco)
- Great Plains or Breadbasket (Kansas City)
- Latin American Rim or Islands (Miami)
- Quebec

---

honest and plain-spoken to the point of being considered uncouth. They are also not known for their risk-taking propensity or creativity. *Beijing Area.* Negotiators from the Beijing area are known for their unusual (within China) bureaucratic sloth and imperialist perspective, both yielding a relatively uncommon lack of creativity, that is, thinking outside the box. Indeed, since they have often defined the box in the first place, they are not used to thinking of ways to escape it. The one note of caution about these generalizations is the growing cosmopolitanism of managers working in and around the capitol city.

Shanghai Area. The negotiators from the Shanghai area are renowned in China for shrewdness. They are outgoing, big talkers, and big spenders. They will try to impress you in ways and to extents you won't see anywhere else in China. For them, anything is possible—they are very creative thinkers. Folks that grow up speaking the Shanghai dialect are quite clannish and cunningly political. Some in China describe them as calculating, even devious. But, more than anything else, they are successful, really the dominant business group on the Mainland.

The South. Chinese in the south have always been the closest to foreign influences. This has yielded a special entrepreneurship and spontaneity. Negotiators are reputed to be relatively honest and forthright. They are less calculating than folks in Shanghai. But, they are excellent traders and particularly interested in making a quick buck.

Hong Kong. The business culture in Hong Kong is distinct from the general descriptions in important ways. Almost all the Chinese negotiators you deal with in Hong Kong will be bilingual, at least speaking English fluently. Indeed, their English is probably better than yours. As Hong Kong executives have learned English, they've also absorbed British culture in a deep way. However, for most, their first language is Cantonese. Among Chinese speakers around the world, Cantonese is considered the roughest dialect. It almost always sounds like an argument is going on, and the swearing possible and practiced in Cantonese is legendary—it can sound incredibly vulgar at times. But if you get mad at them, face is lost on both sides of the table, and usually the deal is dead. Finally, humility and indirection are more emphasized in southern than in northern China as well.

Taiwan. The behavior in general, and language in particular, of the people on Taiwan are considered by other Chinese to be the most conservative. That is, neither Confucius's influence nor the Mandarin spoken was mitigated by Communist philosophies and rule. Consequently, in Taiwan, age, rank, and family play the most powerful roles among all Chinese. Companies tend to be managed directly from the top and the decision-making style is autocratic. Managers are at the same time down-to-earth and practical, but on occasion daring.

Singapore. The salient difference between the Chinese managers in Singapore and on the Chinese mainland is the historical influence of the British. Their English-language skills are of course most apparent. But there are underlying values for following rules and generally straightforward (not devious) business dealings. Also, Singapore Chinese tend more toward individualism that most other Chinese. Things may move fast, even very fast, and decision making tends toward the autocratic.

Overseas Chinese. Overseas Chinese managers, often born and raised in countries such as Indonesia, Thailand, the Philippines, Canada, and the United States are at least bicultural, and therefore are capable of thinking and conversing as "natives" in their native countries. But they can also turn on the entrepreneurial spirit and skillful bargaining of their south coast Chinese ancestors quite quickly. They will continue to be tough customers and even tougher competitors, particularly on their home turf.

The commercial values and behaviors of overseas Chinese will be best indicated by their fluency in Chinese dialects, how recently they immigrated, and where they were educated at university. So as you get to know the Chinese folks across the negotiation table, whether they be in Bangkok or Boston, it makes sense to take an interest in their personal history. It would also be just plain interesting.

Including the Chinese Diaspora in the discussion just above makes a nice segue for the brief, but essential discussion of Joel Kotkin's *Tribes*[8] and his argument that cultures not only vary within countries, but some cultures also span countries. Indeed, the notion of nation is losing steam in the twenty-first century. Kotkin explains that tribes that cross national boundaries have been leading the global economy for centuries, and, indeed, are still today. He describes in interesting detail the dominance of the Jews, the British, the Japanese, the Indians, and, of course, the diasporic Chinese. All of these groups have in common the following: (1) a strong ethnic identity, with a sense of mutual dependence and emphasis on family structure; (2) a global network based on tribal trust that allows the group to function collectively; and (3) a passion for technology and a belief in education and scientific progress.[9] Kotkin also predicts the rising influence of new tribes—the Mormons and Armenians.

RACIAL AND ETHNIC PREJUDICES

Very few countries in the world share America's ideals of racial and ethnic equality. We say "ideals" because sometimes Americans aren't very good at ignoring color and race. The fear of foreigners that often drives prejudices is a natural thing; and the more foreign, the greater the fear. Indeed, our best pals these days are the British. Same language, same religion, a shared Anglo culture, we love their brands and call their TV "educational," and they own more of America than any other foreign nation. British accents make people sound smarter. This is so even though we've fought two wars against them and they very certainly have their own separate national interests.

As Americans go east from England, the fear of foreignness begins to grow. Just pass through the Chunnel and they're already speaking unintelligibly, rejecting American TV, and eating horses and frogs and snails. Go all the way to East Asia and they're using characters instead of an alphabet, beliefs are based on Confucius and Buddha, and the diet includes raw fish in Japan or dogs, cats, rats, lizards, snakes, grubs, bugs, and quite literally anything with digestible protein in China. So because the language, religion, values, and culture of East Asians are more different (than Europeans to Americans) we tend to understand them less and fear them more.

Recall the shrill outcry of the 1980s when Japan bought so much American real estate and so many American companies. One of

Newsweek's 1987 cover stories was, "Your Next Boss May Be Japanese." Even then, the British owned more of America. And now why don't we hear the same alarm about European investments in America? Japan's 1980s appetite for American assets pales in comparison to Germany's 1990s gorging on the likes of Bankers Trust, Random House, and Chrysler. Indeed, history tells us we should fear Germany more than Japan. But instead we fear the more unfamiliar. Our xenophobia dominates our memories.

Americans who demonstrate this kind of ethnic prejudice will not be successful in foreign countries. Your clients will easily read such feelings, and business discussions simply will not proceed.

Unfortunately, racism is prevalent in all countries, but with different targets and different expressions. For example, we thought it was strange that an American multinational company we worked with had no German sales representatives working in its German office despite the size of their revenues from that large market. When we asked the Dutch sales manager why, he said, "We couldn't find anyone qualified." When we asked again over a few beers, we got the real answer. This particular sales manager just didn't like Germans. Perhaps it was their humor?

Particularly among the hierarchical relationship cultures in Asia, old historical feuds still fuel problems. Consider the current political dustups among China, Japan, and South Korea for just a glimpse of the millennia-old bad feelings. Racial prejudices in Japan can be quite a problem. In fact, some argue that racial prejudice is a particular problem in Japan because of the nation's history of isolationism and the resulting ethnic homogeneity. And this ethnic homogeneity will certainly persist, given Japan's virtual ban on alien naturalization. But our concern here is not social reform. Rather, we must consider how racial and ethnic prejudice influences the efficiency of international business negotiations.

Let us begin by saying that your foreign clients and partners expect to deal with American executives who are Caucasian and male. This is their stereotype of "the American business executive." And although many foreigners have trouble handling Americans in general, they at least know more about Caucasian males. After all, take a look at a list of American presidents.

These expectations and stereotypes often have caused difficulties in international negotiations. Take Japan for example. Americans of African, Asian, or even Japanese heritage are often assumed by the Japanese to be second-class citizens. For example, we know of one second-generation

Japanese American municipal official who was traveling on business to Japan. He and his younger Caucasian male assistant were greeted at the airport by their Japanese hosts. The Japanese assumed the Japanese American was second in command and treated him accordingly. When they learned otherwise, the Japanese hosts were mortified by their mistake. They had lost face, and much time had to be spent patching things up, including bringing in a new set of hosts. Such a circumstance may seem a bit comical, but the relationship suffered. And in a land where personal relationships are so important, this was a serious problem.

It is interesting to contrast the relative successes of Chinese Americans in promoting commercial relationships in China. Indeed, most of the huge foreign investments into the Middle Kingdom have been and are still being managed by the worldwide Chinese diaspora. They know the language, culture, and often have relatives in China. Trade often follows immigration. Alternatively, fewer Japanese have immigrated to the United States in recent years and thus have lost some of the associated advantages. In Japan, if you're not a citizen, you're not quite Japanese anymore.

Americans who don't fit the foreign executives' stereotype may make them uncomfortable at first. African or Asian American executives traveling to other countries should realize this and anticipate having to work harder at establishing credibility initially. When minority executives are sent to negotiate with foreign clients, the foreigners should be notified ahead of time who is coming and who is in charge.

We do note that things are changing almost everywhere in this respect. Younger executives can be expected to have a broader, less prejudiced view of the world and international business. And generally, minority Americans are treated as foreigners first and minorities second. Once the initial surprise is overcome, most foreign executives will get down to the business of personal relationships and the economics of the deal. It also helps immensely to have two U.S. Secretaries of State in a row that happen to be African Americans.

GENDER BIAS IN INTERNATIONAL BUSINESS

There are two obstacles women must confront in international negotiations: (1) the perception, at least in the United States, that women aren't effective negotiators; and (2) the fact that the progress American women have made toward equality in management professions isn't shared by their foreign counterparts, yielding the perception here in the United States that female business executives will not be accepted as equals by their foreign counterparts. Both of these perceptions are false.

Women as Business Negotiators

We know from our own studies of gender differences in negotiation among MBA students, and a raft of other similar studies, that women do not achieve the same levels of profits as do men in simulated negotiations in a laboratory setting. We also know that real-life American women make less money than men, and one of the key reasons is that they do not ask for as much money as their male counterparts. Thus, we see the commonly misconstrued conclusion that women do not negotiate as well as men, at least in the United States. The reader will notice however, that neither of these negotiation settings (laboratory or salary negotiations) reflect the reality of the potential for creative commercial relationships that drive international commerce.

In a recent study of the pricing decisions made by American men and women veterinarians we again see the expected lower prices set by women. However, unlike their male counterparts, the women vets took into consideration customer traits and the number of associates in their practices. That is, the women vets charged higher prices when they had more associates, but the men did not. Moreover, linguistics expert Deborah Tannen reports:

> In general, women are more comfortable talking one-on-one. The situation of speaking up in a meeting is a lot closer to boys' experience of using language to establish their position in a large group than it is the girls' experience using language to maintain intimacy. That's something that can be exploited. Don't wait for the meeting; try to make your point in advance, one-to-one. This is what the Japanese do, and in many ways American women's style is a lot closer to the Japanese style than to American men's.[10]

The fundamental point here is that American women are better at managing personal relationships than American men. They literally pay more attention to those folks with whom they work. They are more relationship-oriented than their male counterparts. And that trait will tend to serve them well (perhaps even better) in international negotiations.

Acceptance of American Businesswomen in Other Countries

The misperception that American businesswomen will not be accepted in other cultures is a bit more complicated. While it is true that women in other countries do not share the same level of equality that American women do, in some cases, they're actually better off. Exhibit 5.4 shows that the United States trails only Norway and Sweden when it comes to gender parity in corporate board membership. A broader measure of gender equality has been compiled by the World Economic Forum (www.weforum.org), and it finds that America ranks #22 of the 115 nations reviewed. Saudi Arabia and Yemen, ranked 114 and 115 respectively, are at the bottom of the list, whereas Sweden and Norway, at #1 and #2, top the gender equity survey. However, things are improving for women in interesting ways around the world. For example, in the United States, where

Exhibit 5.4   Female Directors on Corporate Boards as % of total, March 2004

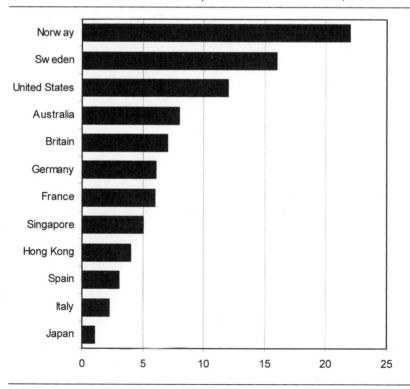

Source: Ethical Investment Research Service, March 2004.

women have seen substantial improvements in business opportunities, 57 percent of undergraduate students are women. This trend has taken hold in other countries as well, mostly in Europe, but even in such places as Iran (ranked #108 in the survey) and Saudi Arabia, which are known for their systematic repression of women. The consequence of this sea change in undergraduate enrollments is a changing landscape in professional programs in the United States. About half of law and medical students in America are women. Women now comprise about 30 percent (down from 40 percent in the 1990s) of MBA classes around the country and about 20 percent in U.S. engineering programs.

But, the gender bias against women managers that exists in some countries, coupled with myths harbored by male managers, does create reluctance among U.S. multinational companies to offer women international assignments. Although women constitute nearly half of the U.S. workforce, they represent relatively small percentages of the employees who are chosen for international assignments—only 18 percent.

Despite the substantial prejudices against women in many foreign countries, evidence suggests that prejudices foreign women executives face may be overestimated and that the treatment local women receive in their own cultures is not necessarily an indicator of how foreign businesswomen are treated. It would be inaccurate to suggest that there is no difference in how male and female managers are perceived in different cultures, but this does not mean that women are not successful in international negotiations.

The key to success for both men and women often hinges on the strength of a firm's backing. When a woman manager receives proper training and the strong backing of her firm, she usually receives the respect commensurate with the position she holds and the firm she represents. To be successful, a woman needs a title that gives her immediate credibility in the culture in which she is working, and a support structure and reporting relationship that will help her get the job done. In short, with the power of the corporate organization behind her, resistance to her gender either does not materialize or is less troublesome than anticipated. Once business negotiations begin, a business host's willingness to engage in business transactions and show respect to a foreign businessperson grows or diminishes depending on the business skills he or she demonstrates, regardless of gender. As one executive stated, "The most difficult aspect of an international assignment is getting sent, not succeeding once sent."

Exhibit 5.5 A Ford Executive's Comments

We interviewed Julie Willoughby, an American female executive assigned international negotiation responsibilities by Ford Motor Company. While her initial experiences with her clients in Japan (ranked #80 on the aforementioned World Economic Forum gender equality survey, and at the bottom of exhibit 5.4) were not much fun, she subsequently became quite effective with her foreign counterparts. She attributes her ultimate effectiveness to the strong support of her Ford team members and her own recognition of the importance of building personal relationships with the Japanese. She explains:

> My husband, also a Ford manager working with Japanese clients, and I decided to have a few of our Mazda associates over for an "All-American" dinner during their next trip to Detroit. So, we started out inviting three people to our home. We thought this would be a nice intimate way to get to know one another and provide the Japanese with an honest-to-goodness homemade American meal. By the eve of the dinner word had gotten out and we had thirteen for dinner. They sort of invited themselves, they changed their meetings around, and some even flew in from the Chicago Auto Show. We had a wonderful time and for the first time they saw me as a person. A mom and a wife as well as a business associate. We talked about families, some business, not particulars, but world economics and the auto industry in general. The dinner party was a key turning point in my relationships with Mazda.[11]

We talked with Muneo Kishimoto (then president of Mazda North America Inc.), and formerly one of Willoughby's counterparts at Mazda, to get the Japanese perspective on dealing with American women. He told us Julie was always professional in demeanor and dress. Interestingly, he emphasized the importance of the latter. He considered her very capable and noted her patience with his discomfort in speaking English. He didn't think of her as a woman but as an "American business executive."

But perhaps most important, Kishimoto independently confirmed the value of the dinner party at Willoughby's home.

That's when he and his colleagues perceived her as a "person." And as we have emphasized throughout the book, personal relationships are crucial to successful dealings with Japanese businesspeople. American men can establish personal relationships in bath houses, golf club locker rooms, Ginza bars, and the like, if their livers can stand the strain. But American women have to be more creative. Many of the more traditional recreational activities are not appropriate for mixed company. But the personal touch is still necessary.

The aspects of the Ford/Mazda relationship managed by Willoughby and Kishimoto proved worthwhile for both companies. Indeed, both executives were subsequently promoted to positions of greater responsibility. And they remain good friends even though their jobs have changed.

Another female executive we talked with at Ford also attributed her success with Japanese clients to taking them out fishing on the Huron River near her home; again establishing a personal relationship in a different way from the traditional all-male drinking fests common at the time in Japan. Of course, we love this second story!

Nancy Adler, a professor of management at McGill University in Montreal, found that North American women executives are successfully managing relationships with Japanese clients.[12] She echoes the idea that American women are foreigners first and women second, and they interact with Japanese managers as such. It is true that they don't fit into the traditional routine of golf, Ginza nightclubs, and bath houses, but with time, they are accepted because of their professional expertise. Nancy makes several key recommendations:

Give a woman every opportunity to succeed. Send her in full status—not as a temporary or experimental expatriate—with the appropriate title to communicate the home company's commitment to her. Do not be surprised if foreign colleagues and clients direct their comments to the male managers rather than the new female expatriate in initial meetings, but do not accept such behavior. Redirect discussion, where appropriate, to the woman. Such behavior should not be interpreted as prejudice, but rather as the reaction to an ambiguous, a traditional situation.

The female expatriates Nancy interviewed had a number of suggestions for other women following in their footsteps. First, as they suggest, presume naiveté, not malice. Realize that sending women to Asia is new, perceived as risky, and still fairly poorly understood. In most cases, companies and foreigners are operating on untested assumptions, many of which are faulty, and not out of a basis of prejudice.

Several other women managers we've talked with add that the attitudes and behaviors of their American colleagues are crucial to setting the right tone. An early reference or, better yet, deference to the expertise of the woman team members will help a great deal. The managerial implication here is the same as in the previous section on racial and ethnic prejudice. When women travel to foreign countries, they must anticipate the attitudes of their clients. With patience and an understanding of the cultural differences, women can be effective. Indeed, it is most interesting to note that three of the last six U.S. Trade Representatives and two of the last three U.S. Secretaries of State have been women.

Business negotiations across cultures are difficult undertakings, particularly in such a fast-changing world. Much can go wrong besides the economics of the deal. In this chapter, we have tried to address some delicate but very real problems beyond those of national culture. We don't have all the answers. But we hope to have made you aware of these important, often hidden, pitfalls of business negotiations with colleagues in foreign countries.

Finally, it will be your job to get to know your negotiation counterparts with respect to all these background characteristics, through both your research ahead of the negotiations and once they commence. This knowledge will help you better predict and assess their behaviors. This knowledge will help you discern whether you're working with sharks or dolphins. This knowledge will help you see more options in your evolving business relationship and these are the crucial keys to creativity.

PART II

THE GLOBAL NEGOTIATION— A CREATIVE PROCESS

N ow we turn our focus to the heart of *The New Rules*. We start with the tail of the fish, the *knowledge* that powers the entire process.

4. Gather intelligence and reconnoiter the terrain.

Next we turn to the body, the center of the fish—*communication*.

5. Design the information flow.
6. Invest in personal relationships.
7. Persuade with questions.
8. Make no concession until the end.

Finally, we consider the head of the fish—the *creativity* that yields the best possible long-term, mutually beneficial commercial relationships among people, companies, even countries.

9. Use techniques of creativity.
10. Continue creativity after negotiations.

Chapters 4 through 6 encompass a new way to negotiate, the best practices from our long observation of and participation in a variety of negotiations around the world.

CHAPTER 6

INTELLIGENCE GATHERING

It has always been my private conviction that any man who pits
his intelligence against a fish and loses has it coming.

—John Steinbeck

The Battle of Tarawa was a disaster. It was the second American amphibious assault in World War II, but it was the first time U.S. Marines faced an organized opposition to a beach landing. Thirty-five thousand American troops attacked 4,713 entrenched Japanese soldiers on that small Pacific island on November 20–23, 1943. The Marines prevailed, killing all but 17 Japanese. American casualties were 1,001 killed and 2,296 wounded. Most of the Americans died during the initial assault. The waves of landing craft carrying troops heading for the beach at Tarawa went aground on a submerged coral reef. Neither naval charts nor aerial reconnaissance revealed the dangerous obstacle that lurked just below the surface hundreds of yards off the beach. The Marines were forced to wade the long stretch in hip-deep water under tremendous Japanese fire. Many drowned under the weight of their own equipment. It was painfully apparent to staff planners of all armed services that the success of future amphibious invasions of Japanese-held territory would be in jeopardy if there was no way of knowing what obstacles, both natural and man-made, lay seaward of the beach, and if there was no way of clearing such obstacles. The U.S. Navy's Underwater Demolition (and later SEAL) Teams were created to fulfill this new mission.

We reiterate—we do not see international business negotiations as anything like battles—they are instead opportunities for creativity and innovation. But, the main point of our Tarawa tale is the importance of being there. Intelligence gathering is usually conducted from a distance. Reconnaissance means going there, visiting the offices of your potential clients and/or partners, or, as Peter Drucker put it so eloquently in an article for the *Wall Street Journal,* "Management by Walking Around, Outside."[1]

Sticking with the military metaphor a bit longer, we'll use the term "HUMINT" as it is euphemistically called within the espionage world. NATO defines HUMINT as "A category of intelligence derived from information collected and provided by human sources."[2] To negotiate, you need to acquire as much HUMINT about your counterpart as possible. Ultimately, the more HUMINT you acquire the more successful your negotiations will be. At some point, you will be meeting with your negotiations counterparts and asking them a long series of questions to mostly confirm what you have learned previously from other sources. We call this a "double echo."

As a first step, most of us find ourselves obtaining intelligence from open sources: "OSINT" or open source intelligence.[3] That is, overt, as opposed to covert, public information readily accessible through the media, public records, and professional and academic sources. Within this context, the way in which we acquire this information is critical and is the topic of this chapter. The process by which lead negotiators gather, coordinate, and analyze intelligence has typically been unstructured and strategically uncoordinated. If information is a valued commodity, a more disciplined approach is necessary. We propose a *strategic intelligence gathering mechanism* to help us navigate, the fish tail begins both to steer and propel our negotiations. As you recall in exhibit I.1 on page 10, the "tail" of the fish consists of two components, *Environmental Scanning* and the *"Three Priorities": planning, preparation, and procedures.* In this chapter, we consider the first component, and in the next chapter, we address the second component.

First, by way of a general explanation, we recognize that not all negotiations will require the same level of strategic intelligence gathering effort. The smaller the stakes, the less effort negotiators should give to this early process. On the other hand, smaller, less significant negotiations can be useful as technique-development exercises to be subsequently expanded upon and used in the more important, higher-stakes negotiations.

OSINT SOURCING

We are very fortunate to live at a time when OSINT is literally at our fingertips. The Internet makes the task of aggregating this information much easier. There are a series of websites that provide assistance, public and private. The U.S. federal government provides a wealth of potentially pertinent information about companies and countries through the Commerce Department. Both the World Bank and the International Monetary Fund are also sources of important financial and economic data and reports. Here we will highlight sources that we have found quite useful in preparing for our own international negotiations.

CIA World Factbook

The *CIA World Factbook* (www.cia.gov/cia/publications/factbook/index. html) is a quick reference guide to a specific country or region, providing information on geography, people, government, economy, communications, transportation, military and transnational issues and reference maps. It presents the information that may serve as the foundation for subsequent research. Simply put, it is a great starting point. Of course, the reader will note that information from the CIA necessarily carries with it the political biases of the United States. However, given this caveat we still recommend its use for recent general information that can be compared across the more than 100 countries and regions included in their database. Please see the excerpt regarding the Czech Republic. Or better yet, go directly to the website and pick a country with which you are familiar and you be the judge of the accuracy and usefulness of this easy-access, free resource.

> The Czech Republic is one of the most stable and prosperous of the post-Communist states of Central and Eastern Europe. Growth in 2000–05 was supported by exports to the EU, primarily to Germany, and a strong recovery of foreign and domestic investment. Domestic demand is playing an ever more important role in underpinning growth as interest rates drop and the availability of credit cards and mortgages increases. The current account deficit has declined to around 3% of GDP as demand for Czech products in the European Union has increased. Inflation is under control. Recent accession to the EU gives further impetus and direction to structural reform. In early 2004, the government passed increases in the Value Added Tax (VAT) and tightened eligibility for social

benefits with the intention to bring the public finance gap down to 4% of GDP by 2006. However, due to significant increases in social spending in the run-up to June 2006 elections, the government is not likely to meet this goal. Negotiations on pension and healthcare reforms are continuing without clear prospects for agreement and implementation. Privatization of the state-owned telecommunications firm Cesky Telecom took place in 2005. Intensified restructuring among large enterprises, improvements in the financial sector, and effective use of available EU funds should strengthen output growth.

Economist Intelligence Unit

The Economist Intelligence Unit (EIU; www.eiu.com) describes itself as providing "a constant flow of analysis and forecasts on more than 200 countries and eight key industries." EIU "help[s] executives make informed business decisions through dependable intelligence delivered online, in print, in customized research as well as through conferences and peer interchange."[4] EIU represents the next level of analysis. Its products are for sale (an annual subscription runs in four figures), it facilitates the initial aggregation of information, and it undertakes preliminary analyses. At an intermediate level, within the industries they target, we have found EIU to be very helpful. Below we provide a taste of their services, and you can compare with what the *CIA Factbook* says about the Czech Republic. You will notice that the data listed are more up-to-date and even include forecasts.

A three-party coalition, comprising the Civic Democratic Party (ODS), the Christian Democratic Union-Czechoslovak People's Party (KDU-CSL) and the Green Party won a confidence vote in parliament in January 2007, after two rogue deputies from the Czech Social Democratic Party (CSSD) agreed to abstain from the vote. The effectiveness of the new government will depend on the ability of the prime minister, Mirek Topolanek, to balance the demands of his diverse governing coalition with those of the CSSD; given that the government does not have an absolute majority in parliament, support from the CSSD is crucial. Domestic demand will drive economic expansion, as net trade will provide less of a stimulus to growth than in 2004–05, owing to the slower increase in import demand in the euro zone. Real GDP growth is therefore forecast to slow to 4.9% in 2007 and to 3.9% in 2008. Inflation will rise in 2007, owing to increases in regulated prices, but will decelerate in 2008. The

Economist Intelligence Unit forecasts that the current-account deficit will remain above 4% of GDP, owing to solid domestic demand.

Oxford Analytica

Oxford Analytica (www.oxan.com) describes itself as "an international, independent consulting firm drawing on a network of over 1,000 senior faculty members at Oxford and other major universities and research institutions around the world."[5] If the *CIA Factbook* is a Chevy and EIU a Cadillac, then Oxan is a Lamborghini. Fees run at five figures depending on what you order. So, among the publicly accessible sources, Oxford Analytica is one of the very best. They describe their reputation as resting "on their ability to harness the expertise of pre-eminent scholar experts to provide business and government leaders with timely and authoritative analysis of world events. It is a unique bridge between the world of ideas and the world of enterprise." A review of their clients clearly reflects the level of professionalism they strive for and apparently attain. Below is the briefest excerpt from their website on the topic of "Energy Security in Russian-Western Relations:"

Outlook. Chronic volatility in the Middle East, Africa and Latin America creates an opportunity for Russia and the West to build energy partnerships based on strong political engagement and mutual investment. Yet until now, such partnerships have not materialised due to the lack of consensus on the fundamentals of energy security. Frictions over conflicting policies that Russia and the West pursue in what Moscow considers to be its legitimate 'sphere of influence' will exacerbate tensions over energy policy even in the long run.

The EU will persist in its attempts to diversify sources of energy imports, placing a special emphasis on the Caspian. At the same time, Brussels will be cautious not to spoil relations with Russia over diverging approaches to the CIS. By contrast, the United States will continue with its harsh criticism of Russia's energy policies and step up efforts to enhance energy security of the friendly regimes in Eastern Europe and the Caucasus.

Conclusion: Rising energy prices and Moscow's growing international clout have turned Russian-Western energy trade into a traditional security issue. Unless Russia, the United States and the EU learn to insulate the energy dialogue from their differences on geopolitical and domestic policy issues, they will remain locked in a vicious circle of mutual distrust, trading accusations across both sides of the 'energy counter.'

Datamonitor MarketLine Business Information Center

We have found this resource particularly helpful. Available online at dbic.datamonitor.com, it provides profiles of 10,000 U.S. and international companies including strategic (SWOT) analyses, top competitors, and location and subsidiary information. It also includes 2,000 U.S. and international industry profiles with competitors, market shares, market size, and volume/value forecasts. Also included are 50 Country Profiles with economic, market, and industry analyses of the countries' business environments.

Factiva

Factiva (www.factiva.com) is an excellent source for global business and non-business news from newspapers, magazines, newswires, and trade and industry journals. It is available in many language formats. The service charges a nominal fee per each article viewed.

ENVIRONMENTAL SCANNING

The term "environmental scanning" is not indigenous to negotiations but rather, it derives from international marketing. In an attempt to understand the "market" international marketers sought to understand the "environment" into which products or services were to be introduced. From a negotiations perspective we find this initial methodology to be particularly helpful in understanding the "external conditions" that may lead to a particular posture or position within a negotiation. Environmental *scanning* as opposed to *analysis* implies a continuous monitoring of the key environmental factors—that is, before, during, and after negotiations. So, we first focus on these extrinsic factors and the role that they can actually play within the negotiation process.

As you will note, we identify initially ten aspects of the environment that can affect negotiations: Political, Legal/Regulatory, Physical/Geographic, Demographic, Economic, Financial, Technological, Social/Cultural, Extent and Nature of Competition, and Other (see exhibit I.1, page 10). Initially, information on the first eight factors is relatively easily obtainable through the electronic sources outlined among others, but the role that each plays within the overall negotiation process is more difficult to glean. We suspect that much of the responsibilities for obtaining this information will be delegated to the corresponding team members. For example, the legal/regulatory will most probably be addressed by domestic counsel working with his or her corresponding counsel in a particular country, financial analysis will correspond to the finance people, etc. What is important, however, is that each aspect be analyzed and integrated toward serving the overall negotiation process and strategy. The management of this process of environmental scanning clearly falls on the shoulders of the lead negotiator. Finally, our list of these ten factors can also serve as a checklist for international negotiation teams, helping to ensure a comprehensive analysis of potentially important external factors.

The Political Environment

Besides the immediate importance that one might give to political risk, namely the possibility of asset expropriation, confiscation, or domestication, the political environment is more subtle from the perspective of overarching strategic goals that may not be immediately obvious. As we saw with the Korean semiconductor example in the first chapter, it was Korea, and specifically the Korean government, that was under a heightened sense of pressure to maintain national competitiveness in the face of globalization and the interdependence of the U.S. and Korean markets for new cellular phone features. Although not completely determinative, this heightened sense of pressure from a society where nationalism is important may well have played a role in the chair being thrown and the deal being cut in favor of the Koreans.

Similarly, from another perspective, the political environment may also proscribe what strategy or tactic may be used. If negotiating in a socialist country for example, sensitivity to social issues and specifically labor issues may be more important. Certainly we can see evidence of this issue in China as both Wal-Mart and McDonald's have recently capitulated to unionization in their operations in the Middle Kingdom. Besides the legal/regulatory differences, such a political environment may be similarly hostile to overt capitalist profit maximization and more receptive to a collaborative "labor force" friendly arrangement. Whether specifically addressed during negotiations, such political considerations may prove crucial.

Lastly, we can see clear examples of political considerations transforming into legal/regulatory ones in many countries. One example is Venezuela and the United States. The Hugo Chavez regime, toward building his personal political power, has moved strongly in the direction of more controls, even nationalization, of foreign oil companies. Of course, the huge profits reaped by the multinational oil companies in 2006 pushed his political agenda along quite smartly. A Chinese purchase of American oil producer UNOCAL was thwarted by public and political outcry, as was DP World's (a Dubai company) purchase of several U.S. port operations. In the latter case, the transaction was approved by the Bush administration, but the Dubai firm sold off the assets in the midst of the political firestorm over having a Middle Eastern firm controlling U.S. port facilities. Both these prominent issues have now yielded new legislation on Capitol Hill to tighten regulations and scrutiny of foreign purchases of security-related assets in the United States.

Legal/Regulatory Environment

First a few words on the limitations of a formal legal and business education. While it may seem to some obvious to put the burden of this aspect on internal legal staff, it has been our experience that legal counsel, in the United States, has been trained to focus primarily on two critical factors: risk and control. By focusing on these two factors most corporate attorneys seek to mitigate risk (preferably to zero) and maximize control. From a domestic negotiations perspective, most do that well. But few American attorneys have been formally trained in the science and art of global negotiations, let alone creative processes. We therefore address this environmental aspect from the perspectives of both the attorney and the businessperson.

If you are an attorney, we ask you to honestly assess your formal training. In all likelihood, you have focused three years of law school and a significant amount of time on acquiring very specific state law. Little or no time has been spent understanding the laws of other countries, and even less on the idiosyncrasies of the societies that formed those laws. In this regard, you are no different than any other professional such as an accountant, engineer, or physician. Yes, you have had perhaps a course in international business transactions, or perhaps you have been involved in a foreign transaction where you managed to "cut the deal." But, we suspect that it was done with some uncomfortable self-doubt about your own professional preparation and your capabilities to foresee future problems and assess lessons learned. We therefore suggest you seek out the help you need to feel comfortable on the international stage.

For businesspeople, many of the points we highlighted about the attorney also apply, but with a modification: At business school, you've learned to focus on cutting the deal toward maximizing shareholder value, and risk and control become secondary considerations. The problem you face is that legal/regulatory frameworks in other countries are not often based on the same emphases and perspectives. This is your challenge.

Legal/regulatory environments differ across national and cultural boundaries and they represent distinct legal philosophies. Important negotiations will most likely require the retaining of local counsel. The importance of choice of local counsel and his/her ability to work with the negotiation team can not be overstated. Perhaps more so than any other party, the role of local counsel as a facilitator, liaison, and intermediary with the host country and its laws is of utmost importance. But, this individual or firm must be capable of interacting with the negotiation team. Too often this key relationship is ignored or at least undervalued.

Physical/Geographic Environment

Anyone who's been to Beijing or Hong Kong during August or September can appreciate the importance of the physical environment for not only the content, but also the process of negotiations. It will certainly be interesting to see how the marathoners manage the air pollution in the capitol city at the 2008 Olympics. A windy day might blow away the industrial air pollution, but it also might blow in a dust storm from the east. Certainly environmental concerns will be prominent issues in many negotiation settings—from natural gas production sites in the Amazon jungle to high-rise construction in the Netherlands. And, as we learned in the introduction, local geographical conditions can affect negotiators and negotiations in adverse ways, whether it be ten-hour jet lag, germs in rivers or tap water, or the lung-searing air pollution on a hot summer day in Mexico City. And, we can add the impact that the physical environment has on the population, or how a region's climate can affect the character of its people, or the ability to construct, build, ship, transport, or conduct business when the climate will not permit you to do so.

Such a lesson was learned on the banks of the Urubamba River in the headlands of the Amazon in Peru by a group of American executives negotiating the logistics of bringing in heavy equipment along the river. Not understanding that the Urubamba is sufficiently deep to allow barges to navigate up to the construction site only during certain parts of the year, they began to develop a work schedule that did not anticipate the ebb and flow of the rainy season. As it turned out, during three months, no work was going to be accomplished no matter how persuasive the arguments in the associated negotiations.

This principle also applies to the windy conditions along the southern tip of Spain: staying in the "Levante" makes for a good discount on hotels on the beach. When the Levante blows, it kicks up sand such that catching rays on the beach becomes very uncomfortable. Locals and well-traveled tourists use this knowledge to negotiate better hotel rates, especially if done up front. Similarly, in other countries where sun is a premium, hotels have been known to discount if not grant free night stays when the sun has not shown; this as a concession to attract sun worshipers.

Demographic Trends

At first you may assume that demographic trends fall clearly within the scope of marketing analysis and few would doubt that. We, however, propose this environmental analysis from a negotiation-specific perspective. To understand the demography of a country is to understand the dynamic nature of the population—its births, deaths, migration, aging—and in so doing begin to understand the thought patterns of that population.

Here again, we remind you of the Korean semiconductor case, and the composition of the Korean negotiation team. Three different generations were represented: the mature, institutionalized executive; the middle-aged senior staffer, who bridged the gap between the older and the younger staff members; and the young MBA who was more international and Westernized. Each generation had its corresponding mindset; each had his own corresponding knowledge pool; each had to be persuaded with consideration to his "Korean-ness" and his particular generation.

Globalization has made demographic trends much more important. The mobility of labor and the forces of immigration are systematically turning the stereotypical characteristics of homogeneous cultures into the melting pots we are seeing around the world. Japanese companies are now run by Welshmen (Sony), Frenchmen of Lebanese descent (Nissan), and Korean immigrants (Softbank). To negotiate in France, it is no longer necessary to talk with a Gaul. A cursory review of the French demographics will quickly confirm that you may be sitting across the table from an Algerian or a Polynesian or a Caribbean when you're negotiating with a

French company. We need only look to the U.S. high-tech industry to realize that it has a tremendous amount of Indian and East Asian influence, and that diversity often offers a vibrant creativity, providing key opportunities for cognizant negotiators.

Economic Conditions

Economic conditions are of course related to political ones. Moreover, demographics and geography also intersect in interesting ways. Aging baby boomers and a lack of land in the United States makes real estate development in NAFTA neighbor Mexico, particularly along the beaches, particularly attractive circa 2008. But the economic environment as a distinct analysis point may assist negotiators in understanding some of the macro tendencies or perspectives that may play into the negotiations.

Here again, we focus on the concept of risk and control. As with the law, the economic conditions of a particular nation state may very well influence some of the concessions and negotiating points of a particular transaction. Needless to say, the government's attitudes toward the open market, liberalization of trade, and business in general are of critical importance. Add to that the currency risk, including potential convertibility risk, the risk of repatriation of funds, and the tax implications of all this and you have quite a basket of concerns that must be considered in any negotiations.

Of course, the prominent example at the time of this writing is energy prices. Business relationships in a wide variety of industrial sectors that made sense when oil was at $40/barrel in 2004 make little sense or perhaps better sense when oil sits at $95/barrel. With higher oil prices, a plethora of global pipeline projects are favored, while highway construction projects and car-dependent suburban development both lose way to mass transit and telecommunications projects.

Financial Environment

Also obviously related to economic conditions, financial conditions refer to the means by which finances are managed and obtained, and the use of banks and financial institutions as a means of "dealing" in the particular country. As with the legal expertise often required, the person in charge of finance, whether the CFO or the VP of Finance or even someone lower down the management ladder, must be able to understand the particular financial issues that a particular international transaction entails. But the lead negotiator must also have a fundamental understanding of these as well.

A variety of financial considerations can be critically important to negotiations. Whether the account can be held in dollars or only in a specific national currency may well lead to a different posture as to the underlying transaction. Certainly, depending on the structure of business projects and proposals, a wide variety of government incentives and support may be available to help finance international commerce. For example, some countries seeking to attract foreign investment may make the financial environment more attractive to offshore firms than local ones. Others may provide incentives for local firms only. In either case, international partnerships involving both local and offshore enterprise may make the most sense.

Technological Environment

The important role played by technology within negotiations cannot be overestimated. As we have described, and as we will emphasize in subsequent chapters, international business negotiations are a creative activity. Creativity thrives in an environment of information. And, all the new communications technologies deliver information in increasingly efficient ways.

We can initially analyze the technological environment from an inbound perspective. That is, in the early stages of negotiations initial exchanges may be done either by telephone, fax, or e-mail. However, it should be understood that all countries and cultures don't utilize communications technologies and practices equally. Some of the differences are reflected in the usage numbers listed in exhibit 6.1. Computer and Internet usage per capita in the United States outpaces those in the other countries listed. The differences in cell phone usage are more interesting. The United States does not dominate and India is woefully behind its developing nation peers, China, Brazil, and Russia. But most remarkable is the fact that there are more cell phones than people in both the U.K. and Hong Kong! The numbers do tell you about the hardware in usage, but the usage culture varies as well. For example, Korean and Japanese companies are not getting the most out of their technology investments. A recent report[6] listed three reasons: (1) fun factor—smart phones are viewed more as a toy than a tool; (2) face time—if you're not in the office, no one thinks you're working; and (3) info-fear—companies worry that laptop-

Exhibit 6.1   Technology Usage across Countries (Per 1,000 persons)

Country	Personal Computers	Internet	Cell Phones
USA	749	630	617
UK	599	628	1021
Japan	542	587	716
Hong Kong	608	506	1184
Germany	561	500	864
Brazil	105	120	357
Russia	132	111	517
China	41	73	258
India	12	32	44

Source: World Bank (World Development Indicators, 2004).

toting commuters could misplace sensitive data. But as the world becomes more globalized, more and more countries and companies will have video conference capabilities that will most certainly assist in the negotiation process. Knowledge of whether a country or a company has sufficient bandwidth and a culture conducive to accommodating video conferences will certainly bear on the decision to get on an airplane or just "dial up" your international counterparts.

Knowledge of the technological environment is also important from a knowledge management/economics perspective. We think it can be safely said that the higher the technological level, the more educated and skilled the labor force tends to be. Furthermore, the higher the techno-logical level, the more likely it is that competition will have taken root. The higher the technical capabilities of the negotiators, the lower the transaction costs and it is more likely that multiple individuals can be vir-tual, the flow of information will be facilitated, and the negotiation process is likely to be more sophisticated and efficient. But, it must be re-membered that managers from relationship-oriented cultures such as Japan or Hong Kong, even with their copious technology assets, will still tend to favor face-to-face meetings more than someone from an informa-tion-oriented culture like the United States or Germany.

Social/Cultural Environment

As detailed in the other chapters in this book, this aspect of the environment arguably encompasses all the others. Its complexity must be understood in order to be as successful in global negotiations as one would hope to be.

Nature and Extent of Competition

The nature and extent of competition represent an interesting twist to the Environmental Scanning methodology. Although much may be obtained through open sources, every international businessperson immediately recognizes that in this regard much of the truly critical information is not public. In fact, the most sensitive information on the nature and extent of competition would probably be obtained through alternative sources. How that information is obtained may be critical.

Before we dive into those waters however, further attention should be given to the way in which we conceptualize competition. When we say "competition" we mean both foreign and domestic. We not only include the large multinational corporation with extensive capabilities but also the smaller firm that is well connected locally, that has an excellent grasp of the market, and, more importantly, the necessary personal relationships to bring about "David and Goliath" kinds of consequences.

By conceptualizing competition in this manner, we begin to delve into less OSINT gathering techniques. Word-of-mouth information, HUMINT, will be important. Here the waters are very deep, dark, and menacing. Moral, ethical, legal, and business judgment come into play. Indeed, some national governments have often been accused of using their espionage resources to gain commercially important intelligence. One accusation included electronic eavesdropping of commercial conversations aboard Air France airliners crossing the Atlantic.[7] We cannot give you specific advice here other than to be honest and forthright in your business dealings. But it seems that despite all the corporate policies about ethical behavior, some at the top ignore the documents they sign. We offer a story about a CEO of one of America's largest companies as instruction (see exhibit 6.2).

Other Environments

Although our checklist for environmental scanning is comprehensive, we have included an "other" category as well. That is, once you have gone through this checklist with your negotiation team, carefully developing the scenarios and briefings to support the actual negotiation processes, you will still have to sit back at your final meeting and ask the question, "OK, what are we not thinking of? There must be something."

Exhibit 6.2   Shades of Gray

After a particularly grueling series of interviews lasting more than six hours, a young international law student found himself sitting across from the CEO of one of the largest multinational corporations in the world. The CEO looked at the now exhausted but confident student and said: "Young man, you have passed all the tests we could possibly have given you. You have the grades, the qualifications. You have successfully proven yourself to all those with whom you have met. All we need to determine now is whether you and I get along."

The student thought to himself, "Well this should be relatively easy."

"I only have one question for you," stated the CEO: "Are you ethical?"

Here again the student seemed somewhat relieved. "Of course I'm ethical," and he then listed all his "ethical" accomplishments: he had been an altar boy, an Eagle Scout, he worked for various organizations as a volunteer; all clearly portraying a man with a very well-defined moral compass.

"Excellent!" said the CEO, "but you won't be working for us."

Shocked and not believing what he had just heard, the student composed himself and responded, "Good enough, but rarely does a young person like me have the opportunity to sit before one of the captains of industry, I hope to learn something from the experience. What did I do or say wrong?"

"Good enough," responded the CEO, "It's pretty simple. If you are completely black, meaning unethical, I'm in jail. If you are completely white, I'm non-competitive. I strongly suggest to you that from now on you will be in a gray world. Oh, and by the way, there are shades of gray."

To step into international waters is to step into a gray world. Often light doesn't penetrate the depths. The laws and customs of one nation may not necessarily coincide with those of your own. What is right for one is not right for the other, and yet you may find yourself precisely there.

RECONNAISSANCE, GOING THERE

We have always marveled at how political campaign advance teams go into an unknown city and within 24 hours understand the lay of the land, the key players, the best restaurants, who is who, and who does what to whom and still have time to get that beer before the candidate arrives. In so doing, they have their fingers on the pulse of the city. It is an uncanny skill they have; to recognize what it is that is important and utilize that information to the benefit of their client.

To some extent, a lead negotiator, responsible for the negotiations, must accomplish the same task except in a foreign city with conditions that are many times unknown and indiscernible from afar. Going there to get a look at the negotiation partners' facilities and neighborhoods and to get a sense of how they fit into their own communities is invaluable. No matter how complete the preliminary research and the environmental scanning, going there gives the negotiator an opportunity to see, smell, hear, taste, and feel the places where she and her team will be working. The trip will also provide an important triangulation of the data and analyses conducted at home. There's a reason why the Japanese are renowned for this type of preparation—recall LePoole's comments from before, " . . . they spend days getting to know their opponents." It works! The investment in travel expenses and executive time pays off handsomely for them. For you, new considerations and new avenues for creativity will present themselves, as well as those dangerous hidden coral reefs. It will be the responsibility of the lead negotiator to look out into the distance and be able to navigate those waters.

CHAPTER 7

DESIGNING RICH KNOWLEDGE FLOWS: THE CONFLUENCE OF TIMING, TECHNOLOGY, AND PLACE

Listen to the river and you will get a trout.
—Irish Proverb

THE CONCERT OF "THE THREE PRIORITIES"

George Frideric Handel composed a series of orchestral move-ments, often considered as three suites, called *Water Music.* It pre-miered in the summer of 1717 when King George I requested a concert on the River Thames. That original concert was performed by 50 musicians who joined the king on his barge. The king was so pleased with the music that he ordered Handel to play the suites three times during the trip. As a composer, Handel learned how to "negotiate" his music. He coaxed out of every instrument, every musician, a melody or harmony that moves the listener still. In a similar manner, the negotiator must coax, cajole, and persuade not only his or her team to produce the best, he or she must move the other side as well.

In Handel's *Water Music,* the order of the three movements or suites was undetermined, and the order didn't matter. Similarly, the order in which we present the three priorities—preparation, planning, and process design—is somewhat arbitrary, because in practice negotiators often must undertake all three tasks simultaneously. Indeed, the decisions about people, strategic goals, and procedures must be made with respect to one another, that is, in concert. These preliminary steps then provide a scheme to manage the flow of information toward maximizing the creative output of international business negotiations.

PREPARATIONS

The initial step in preparing for international business negotiations is often the selection of company representatives. Negotiators come from all ranks of firms, depending on the size of the firms involved and the size and importance of the transaction. Selection of the best representatives can make or break a business relationship. More than one American company has found that sending the wrong people to handle negotiations overseas has led to costly failures.

We all have our own ideas about what makes a good negotiator. About one hundred years before Handel entertained King George on the Thames, Sir Francis Bacon told us to use "bold men for expostulation, fair-spoken men for persuasion, crafty men for inquiry and observation." Today, characteristics such as persistence, extroversion, a nimble tongue, a quick wit, or an affable demeanor come to mind. Such characteristics sound good, but do they really make a difference in business negotiations? Are they effective in other countries? Based on our discussion in the previous chapters, one would conclude that what makes a good bargainer in the United States may not lead to the best bargaining outcomes with foreign clients. So whom do we send overseas? What skills and personality traits should we look for in prospective representatives of our companies?

Key Bargainer Characteristics

Our reading of the literature on international negotiations, our continuing research on the topic, our interviews with experienced bargainers, and our own experiences as negotiators in international business transactions all suggest the following list of bargainer characteristics to be particularly important in international negotiations. They are:

1. Listening ability
2. Social intelligence
3. Willingness to use team assistance
4. Self-confidence
5. High aspirations
6. Influence at headquarters
7. Language skills

Representatives with these qualities should be sought to fill temporary or more permanent positions in negotiating with foreign clients and partners. The seven key bargainer characteristics are obviously interrelated and the reasons for their importance are further described below.

Listening Ability

The ability to listen is crucial in any bargaining context. Negotiation is by definition joint decision-making. And decisions should be made with as much information as possible, including information about the client's or partner's needs and preferences. In order to achieve the most favorable bargaining solution for both sides, bargainers must be vigilant for all the subtle indications of clients' real interests. Also, good listening is the initial step in persuasion. Before trying to change the minds of those across the bargaining table, it is best to determine, through good questions and attentive listening, what the other side needs to know. There is little point in extolling the virtues of one's product when one's potential customer already believes it is the best available or when quick delivery is foremost in his or her mind. Finally, in international transactions, one's listening abilities are put to the most difficult test—ascertaining meaning in the context of less-than-fluent English and different nonverbal vocabularies. The bottom line—good listeners serve to maximize the flow of information.

Social Intelligence

We mentioned the importance of personal relationships in business negotiations, and such transactions are very much a social activity, particularly in relationship-oriented cultures. Social intelligence, the ability to get along with other people, not only smoothes the social contact points but also tends to encourage the flow of information from the other side of the table. Thus better, more informed, and creative decisions can be made regarding the business relationship.

Daniel Goleman has written the definitive book on this topic, *Social Intelligence: The New Science of Human Relationships*.[1] You will note that his definition of social intelligence encompasses other aspects of our list:

> *Social Awareness:* Social awareness refers to a spectrum that runs from instantaneously sensing another's inner state, to understanding her [or his] feelings and thoughts, to "getting" complicated social situations. It includes:
>
> - Primal empathy: Feeling with others; sensing nonverbal emotional signals.
> - Attunement: Listening with full receptivity; attuning to a person.
> - Emphatic accuracy: Understanding another person's thoughts, feelings, and intentions.
> - Social cognition: Knowing how the social world works.
>
> *Social Facility:* Simply sensing how another feels, or knowing what they think or intend, does not guarantee fruitful interactions. Social facility builds on social awareness to allow smooth, effective interactions. The spectrum of social facility includes:
>
> - Synchrony: Interacting smoothly at the nonverbal level.
> - Self-presentation: Presenting ourselves effectively.
> - Influence: Shaping the outcome of social interactions.
> - Concern: Caring about others' needs and acting accordingly.

The reader will of course recognize that (1) Goleman is generally describing a relationship-orientation; and (2) exercising social intelligence across cultures will take extra effort and careful reflection about differences particularly in nonverbal behaviors.

Willingness to Use Team Assistance

This trait can make a crucial difference in international business negotiations. Expertise in technical details, financial matters, cultural considerations, and the all-important maintenance of business relationships is simply too much to expect of one person—even an American executive. Application engineers, financial analysts, interpreters, and foreign agents should be included and used when appropriate. The additional expense may be an important investment. Also, observation of negotiations can be a valuable training experience for younger members of an organization. Even if they add little to the discussion, their presence may make a difference. Additional team members will provide at least another set of ears and different perspectives that can enhance creativity as well.

Self-Confidence

The job of the representative is one of the most difficult of all. Bridging the gap between companies and cultures can be exhausting work. Negotiations are being conducted not only with clients but also with the home office. Clients question your company's policies. Sales managers question the time and money you invest in building personal relationships, and so on. Self-confidence, or belief in one's own ideas, will be an important personal asset for those working in such situations of role ambiguity. Self-confidence will also be important in putting new ideas on the table.

High Aspirations

High aspirations regarding the business deal are key. One of the basic lessons of the hundreds of bargaining studies mentioned earlier is that bargainers who ask for more in the beginning end up getting more. Thus, given two otherwise equal executives, the one with higher aspirations is the better one to send. Negotiators with higher aspirations will not be satisfied with just getting to yes; they will be more interested in truly creative outcomes.

Influence at Headquarters

This characteristic will be particularly important in international negotiations. We mentioned above the difficulty of the international representative's job—bridging both organizational and cultural barriers. Many representatives we have interviewed suggest that the toughest part of business negotiations is selling the agreement to headquarters. Moreover, there is danger in presenting the other side's point of view too well—your own management might trust you less. In choosing a representative for negotiations in a foreign country, influence at headquarters is a criterion worth much consideration.

Language Skills

No bargainer characteristic is more important in international negotiations, yet more ignored, than the possession of the pertinent foreign language skills. Whenever we talk to groups of executives, we ask them what they're looking for in graduating business students. Almost always, the first things they mention are good communication skills. Letter and report writing and presentations to clients and internal groups are crucial parts of "making things happen" in the United States. In our business schools, we emphasize the development of such skills. We give our students extensive instructions, practice, and feedback in the cultivation of such skills.

Now comes the paradox: As the markets of American companies become more global, why aren't managers asking for graduates with foreign-language skills? In American industry, at the present time, there is still little payoff for fluency in Chinese or Spanish. In fact, the lockstep curricula in almost all U.S. business schools preclude mastery of the language necessary to make things happen in a foreign country.

We used to be better at this. For example, in a course list bulletin from the University of Southern California Business School dated 1921—when American companies were taking over dominance of world markets from the British—of the 46 classes offered, nine were international business-oriented. Listed were courses in commercial Spanish, French, German, and Chinese. In business school in 1921 we were teaching our students how to write a letter to a client in Spain *in Spanish!* It must have been important then. And it is clearly important today.

Some of our undergraduates are recognizing that the world has changed from American economic dominance to broad economic interdependence. In particular, there have been dramatic increases in enrollment in Chinese language and education abroad courses in China over the last few years. However, language training in the United States still reflects history rather than reality. In our high schools, more students are taking Latin than Chinese. Even though France is our ninth most important market behind number eight South Korea, more than ten times as many students take French as take Korean.

Many American executives who lack fluency in foreign languages argue that English is the international business language. And when American firms dominated world markets in the 1960s and 1970s, this was true. But now the global customers can choose between American, Chinese, Japanese, German, and even Korean suppliers. Indeed, during the 1990s the Koreans spent millions of dollars on Chinese language lessons in preparation for their growing trade with the People's Republic of China. Their investment has paid off handsomely in China, particularly in the northern parts.

Perhaps the most important reason why foreign language skills aren't yet valued in American companies is a more personal one. By nature, we all like to hire and promote younger executives with skills and backgrounds similar to our own. "If foreign languages were not a part of my education, then the people I hire don't need those skills either. After all,

I'm quite successful enough, even though my Spanish vocabulary is limited to *hasta la vista,*" goes the conventional wisdom.

Management Implications

Hiring young executives with language skills and living experiences abroad is crucial. Business schools are burgeoning in many countries around the world and perhaps the best managers to represent your firm overseas will be graduates of their new business and law schools. Also, folks who have immigrated from countries where other languages dominate will prove particularly valuable for both their language and cultural skills. But it's also never too late to gain something from language training. As soon as you begin to study German or Portuguese, you begin to have a greater appreciation for the deeper nuances of the cultures. As soon as you learn that there is more than one way to say "you" in Spanish or Chinese, you begin to understand how social rank influences not just conversational style but also all behaviors and thinking in Mexico and Spain or China and Singapore.

Other Factors

Patience will be critical around the world, particularly in the relationship-based cultures. Negotiations and decisions take longer—particularly the early stages of non-task sounding and information exchanges. Also, quiet men and women should be sent to most Asian countries such as Thailand, Japan, and the Philippines. By "quiet," we mean individuals who are good listeners, are comfortable with silence, and genuinely respectful of other people.

Another concern is ethnocentrism. We all suffer from this to a degree. But even those with the broadest views will be put to the test in many developing countries. Individuals harboring chauvinistic cultural attitudes will almost always do poorly in Indonesia or Malaysia, where mutual respect and deference anchor all interpersonal contact. A curious mind, a genuine tolerance, and interest in how folks do things in different places will all be helpful. Finally, while most countries around the world have five-star hotels, most fast-developing countries themselves are not five-star hotels. Glamour and sophistication will often be found elsewhere. So, a personal ruggedness will also make a difference.

Selecting the Team

Now that we know what we're looking for in a negotiator who can be sent overseas, how do we measure these important personality traits? We have four options. First, the most frequently used personnel selection device is the interview. Prospective representatives might be asked to assess their own characteristics, and some factors may actually be assessed during the interview—listening ability, for example. Second, paper-and-pencil psychological tests are often used in employment and assignment decisions. However, we feel this approach is the least useful. Third, observation of the various characteristics during actual business negotiations is perhaps the best measure. Fourth, when field observations are not possible, as with new employees, role playing and observation are the next best methods of measuring personality traits and predicting future performance.

The selection, training, and deployment of a negotiation team should be carefully considered at the very earliest stages. Ideally, the team will have worked together previously. Within a perfect world, the team will have already undergone various stages of progressively more complex negotiating events. The ranks of the team will reflect the various roles and responsibilities implicit in the transaction. There would most likely be a lead negotiator who would be responsible for the entire negotiation, the development of the strategy, the tactics and maneuvers, with the corresponding personality traits that would permit global negotiations to proceed. Others might be selected more for their special sets of knowledge—legal, financial, technical, and so on.

The next considerations are how many negotiators to send and what levels of management are appropriate? Decisions regarding negotiation team composition must be made with consideration of who will be on the other side of the table.

An important rule of negotiation team composition is to remember that in relationship-oriented cultures social status is more important and talk tends to flow horizontally across levels, not vertically between levels. Also, what is talked about varies from level to level. That is, when top executives are present, they talk to corresponding top executives about primarily non-task-related matters. Executives at other levels may be asked questions (with short answers expected), but the focus of such meetings is the development of personal relations at the top level. When only middle managers and operational staff are present, middle managers confirm decisions and commitments to corresponding middle managers.

Or, middle managers listen while operational staff members exchange information and try to persuade one another. Given these circumstances, it is our recommendation that an American negotiation team should reflect the composition and behaviors of negotiation teams from other countries.

Our final comment regarding negotiation team selection concerns interpreters. As we mentioned earlier, very few Americans speak foreign languages. Thus, despite the disadvantages of using an interpreter, they are often a necessity. Particularly when substantive discussions begin, having your own interpreter will be important for two reasons. First, you will need to brief the interpreter before discussions begin. Second, you will need to sit with the interpreter after the negotiations end each day to assess results and the interests of the other side. Without your own interpreter, neither option is open to you.

The best interpreters will be a help in the negotiations not only by translating, but by communicating the meanings intended. Interpreters can hurt or help you, and generally you get what you pay for. Their fees vary depending on the level of technical knowledge and competence you require. But you can never spend too much money on interpretation services. Interpreters should be briefed on the background and terminology of the deal but not necessarily on your strategies. It must be remembered that interpreters are third parties. Even though they are paid by you they have different, personal motives and agendas.

NEGOTIATOR TRAINING

Many companies in the United States provide employees with negotiations training.[2] For example, through his training programs, Chester Karrass[3] has taught more people ("close to a million") to negotiate than any other purveyor of the service[4]—see his ads in almost all in-flight magazines of domestic American air carriers. Karrass's basic course is offered in more than a dozen foreign countries in English and Spanish where appropriate. However, very few companies offer training for negotiations with managers from other countries.

Perhaps more surprising is the lack of cultural content in the training of our government's diplomats. Instead, in most schools of diplomacy the curricula cover language skills, social and diplomatic skills, and knowledge specific to the diplomatic profession, including diplomatic history and international relations, law, economics, politics, international organizations, and foreign policies. Cultural differences in negotiation and communication styles are seldom considered.

We have worked with companies such as Allergan, Conexant, Honeywell, Intel, and AT&T in developing and delivering programs on international negotiations. In particular, with our consultation, Ford Motor Company has offered its executives over the years the widest array of international negotiation programs, including courses on Japan, South Korea, and China.

Unfortunately, Ford is one of the only major American companies making such a commitment to training its executives. Even Ford's innovative efforts are really just a first step toward increasing effectiveness in their Asian partnerships and operations. We have advised many of the best American firms to consider how their hiring practices, which, for example, place almost no emphasis on foreign-language skills over the years, have not kept up with their increasingly global strategies. Training will help in the short run, but who will be running the global operations of American firms in 2015? In 2025?

We are currently developing a new international negotiations training program for another Fortune 100 firm that includes their European, American, and Asian employees. The pedagogy of the week-long course will include *The New Rules*, of course, and the videotaping of simulated negotiations with systematic feedback among the participants. That is, the foreign managers will give the Americans advice for improvement, and the Americans will do likewise for them. We see this interactive approach to international negotiations training as the wave of the future.

PLANNING

Unless trained specifically in negotiations, rarely do executives, lawyers, or businesspeople create a negotiation plan. We recognize that at first the concept of a negotiation plan seems as abstract as a Pollock painting, yet it is precisely within that realm that we find ourselves many times. That is, trying to cope with that which cannot be precisely expressed. We attempt therefore to give structure to that which is fluid.

By planning, we mean strategic planning. We mean logically thinking out the goals and objectives, and sequentially, methodically, rhythmically, working toward the attainment of those goals. We do this by means of tactics. Tactics represent the manner in which we begin to take the general steps toward the attainment of those goals and objectives. Tactics are filled with minor maneuvers that represent the individual action items that in turn implement the strategy.

For example, the strategic goal of one of our clients was the creation of a joint venture with a Saudi firm to build a series of desalinization plants. To realize this strategic goal, a number of potential partners had to be identified. Thus, the opening tactic was for our client to attend several desalinization conferences that included potential Saudi partners. Once at the conferences, the targeting of and talking with executives of individual companies was the next step. Each conversation within that scenario represented another step toward the strategic goals and objectives. Indeed, all preliminary activities—telephone calls, other contact points, and human intelligence gathering were considered part of a structured negotiation strategy.

Once viable clients and or partners have been identified, and once meetings have been scheduled, then more specific plans are drawn in earnest. Any experienced business negotiator will tell you that there's never enough time to get ready. Given the typical time constraints of international negotiations, planning must be accomplished efficiently. The homework must be done before bargaining begins. We provide the following checklist to foreign clients help them reach their goal of efficiency in planning for bargaining:

1. Assessment of the situation and the people;
2. Facts to confirm during the negotiation;
3. Agenda;
4. The best alternative to a negotiation agreement (BATNA);
5. Concession strategies; and
6. Team assignments.

Assessment of the Situation and the People

It is only common sense to learn as much as possible about a potential client or partner before negotiations begin. As we've delineated in previous chapters, all kinds of information might be pertinent depending on the nature of the contemplated business relationship. We assume that the various sorts of financial data and competitive information that may be relevant have been collected and organized as part of the environmental scanning described in the previous chapter. Now, the focus will be more narrow and information will be garnered from people within your company, associated companies, or perhaps intermediary firms. The last will often be the key source of information as they will often know the people with whom you will be bargaining.

It should be clearly understood that knowing who you will be bargaining with, particularly in relationship-oriented cultures, is far more important than most Americans would assume. If you and your business associates step off the plane with no personal or professional perspectives on individuals you will be meeting, you can expect little success once the meetings begin.

In addition to the public sources of information about foreign companies and executives, informal sources should be consulted. Other American companies that have dealt with the courted foreign firm might be valuable sources of information.

Once the file on the foreign company is complete, it is time to evaluate carefully your own company's situation. The kind of economic analysis you have undertaken regarding the courted company should be replicated in your own company. Most often the other side will do the same, and you need to anticipate what they know about you. Finally, your own instructions from top management and your authority limits should be clearly understood. This latter aspect of preparations is often taken for granted, and lack of attention to this detail can cause serious problems during and after the negotiations. Frequently, American managers in the heat of a long negotiation will overstep their authority and make commitments that later must be retracted. "I'll take full responsibility," runs the cliché.

Facts to Confirm during the Negotiation

No matter how careful the analysis and how complete the information available, all critical information and assumptions should be reconfirmed at the negotiation table. As part of the preparations, a list of such facts should be discussed among the members of the negotiation team, and specific questions should be written down. We have found again and again that surprises (both pleasant and unpleasant) often surface as part of this confirmation of facts.

Agenda

Most business negotiators come to the negotiation table with an agenda for the meeting in mind. We feel it is important to do two things with that agenda. First, write out the agenda for all members of your negotiating team. Second, don't try to settle each issue one at a time. The latter recommendation goes against the grain of the typical American sequential approach. However, in any bargaining situation it is better to get all the issues and interests out on the table before trying to settle any one of them. This will be particularly true when the other side consists of representatives from an Asian company. Such an approach will also tend to maximize the creativity of the process.

Negotiators from other countries will often seem less organized (even disorganized) with respect to an agenda. For example, Asian agendas often permit skipping around among selected topics. Perhaps most frustrating for Americans, Asians will often reopen issues that were seemingly closed. Indeed, consistent with the holistic approach described previously, for Asians nothing is settled until everything is settled. Patience will be key.

The Best Alternative to a Negotiated Agreement

Fisher and Ury, in their popular book, *Getting To Yes,* point out that an often skipped crucial aspect of negotiation preparations is a clear definition of the best alternative to a negotiated agreement, or BATNA. They suggest, and we agree, that negotiators and managers must spend time considering what happens if this particular business relationship doesn't work out. "Is there another foreign firm to court or should we just concentrate on our domestic business for now and try again later?" The BATNA sets the cutoff point where negotiations no longer make sense. But it is more than a simple bottom line; it is a kind of contingency plan. Moreover, your list of viable alternatives defines your power in the negotiation. And be assured that you will hear about your competitors from your counterparts in other countries, particularly in China.

One of the best descriptions of the importance of BATNA and the way to enhance one's strategic alternatives is reporter Daniel Michaels[5] 2003 *Wall Street Journal* article, "Boeing and Airbus in Dogfight to Meet Stringent Terms of Iberia's Executives." We include it here as exhibit 7.1. It's an interesting read.

Exhibit 7.1   Iberia Airlines Enhances Its BATNA

MADRID—One day last April, two model airplanes landed in the offices of Iberia Airlines.

They weren't toys. The Spanish carrier was shopping for new jetliners, and the models were calling cards from Boeing Co. and Airbus, the world's only two producers of big commercial aircraft.

It was the first encounter in what would become a months-long dogfight between the two aviation titans—and Iberia was planning to clean up.

Airbus and Boeing may own the jetliner market, with its projected sales of more than $1 trillion in the next 20 years, but right now they don't control it. The crisis in the air-travel industry makes the two manufacturers desperate to nail down orders. So they have grown increasingly dependent on airlines, engine suppliers and aircraft financiers for convoluted deals.

Once the underdog, Airbus has closed the gap from just four years ago—when Boeing built 620 planes to Airbus's 294—and this year the European plane maker expects to overtake its U.S. rival. For Boeing, Iberia was a chance to stem the tide. For Airbus, Iberia was crucial turf to defend.

Iberia and a few other airlines are financially healthy enough to be able to order new planes these days, and they are all driving hard bargains. Enrique Dupuy de Lome, Iberia's chief financial officer and the man who led its search for wide-body jets, meant from the start to run a real horse race. "Everything has been structured to maintain tension up to the last 15 minutes," he said.

Throughout the competition, the participants at Iberia, Boeing and Airbus gave *The Wall Street Journal* detailed briefings on the pitches, meetings and deliberations. The result is a rarity for the secretive world of aircraft orders: an inside look at an all-out sales derby with globetrotting executives, huge price tags and tortuous negotiations over everything from seats to maintenance and cabin-noise levels. The rivals' offers were so close that on the final day of haggling, Iberia stood ready with multiple press releases and extracted last-minute concessions in a phone call between the airline's chairman and the winning bidder.

By that point, both suitors felt like they'd been through the wringer. "With 200 airlines and only two plane makers, you think we'd get a little more respect," said John Leahy, Airbus's top salesman.

Airbus, a division of European Aeronautic Defense & Space Co., reckoned it had a big edge. It had sold Iberia more than 100 planes since 1997. Mr. Leahy thought last summer that he might even bag the contract with minimal competition. In June he had clinched a separate deal with Iberia for three new Airbus A340 widebodies.

But Mr. Dupuy made Mr. Leahy fight for the order—and so enticed Boeing to compete more aggressively. Then, "just to make things interesting," Mr. Dupuy said, he upped the pressure by going shopping for secondhand airplanes. These are spilling onto the market at cut-rate prices as the airline industry's problems force carriers to ground older jets with their higher operating costs.

Iberia is one of the industry's few highly profitable carriers, thanks to a thorough restructuring before the national carrier was privatized in early 2001. The world's No. 18 in passenger traffic, with a fleet of 145 planes, it has benefited by flying few routes to North America, where air travel is in tatters, and by dominating the large Latin American market.

The Spanish carrier was looking to replace six Boeing 747-200 jumbo jets more than 20 years old. It wanted as many as 12 new planes to complete a 10-year modernization program for Iberia's long-haul fleet. Based on list prices, the 12-plane order was valued at more than $2 billion.

Iberia's Mr. Dupuy, 45 years old, a soft-spoken career finance man, first needed to woo Boeing to the table. The U.S. producer had last sold Iberia planes in 1995, and since then the carrier had bought so many Airbus jets that Boeing considered not even competing. But in late July, Mr. Dupuy met Toby Bright, Boeing's top salesman for jets. Over dinner in London, according to both men, Mr. Dupuy told Mr. Bright that Iberia truly wanted two suppliers, not just Airbus.

The Boeing sales chief was skeptical, and he recalled thinking at the time, "You're running out of ways to show us." Having worked as Boeing's chief salesman in Europe, Airbus's home turf, he had heard similar lines from customers who eventually bought Airbus planes. So he wondered: "Are we being brought in as a stalking horse?"

Last Chance

Yet replacing Iberia's old 747s with new 777s would be Boeing's last chance for years to win back Iberia. The argument against Boeing was that an all-Airbus fleet would make Iberia's operations simpler and cheaper. Still, going all-Airbus might weaken Iberia's hand in future deals. Airbus would know that the carrier's cost of switching to Boeing would require big investments in parts and pilot training.

Picking Planes   Iberia's airplane choices from Airbus and Boeing

	Airbus	*Boeing*
Model	A340-600	777-300ER
Catalog Price	$190 million	$215 million
Seats (Iberia configuration)	350	374
Engines	4	2
Engine maker	Rolls-Royce	General Electric
Introduced	2002	2003
Earlier model	A340-300 (introduced 1993)	777-300 (introduced 1998)

Source: The Companies

In early November, Airbus and Boeing presented initial bids on their latest planes. The four-engine Airbus A340-600 is the longest plane ever built. Boeing's 777-300ER is the biggest twin-engine plane.

The new A340 can fly a bit farther and has more lifting power than the 777. The new Boeing plane is lighter, holds more seats and burns less fuel. The Boeing plane, with a catalog price around $215 million, lists for some $25 million more than the A340.

Mr. Dupuy, whose conference room is decorated with framed awards for innovative aircraft-financing deals, set his own tough terms on price and performance issues including fuel consumption, reliability and resale value. He won't divulge prices, but people in the aviation market familiar with the deal say he demanded discounts exceeding 40%.

As negotiations began, Mr. Dupuy told both companies his rule: Whoever hits its target, wins the order. The race was on.

Mr. Bright, who had been appointed Boeing's top airplane salesman in January of 2002, pitched the Boeing 777 as a "revenue machine." He insisted that his plane could earn Iberia about $8,000 more per flight than the A340-600 because it can hold more seats and is cheaper to operate. A burly 50-year-old West Virginian, Mr. Bright joined Boeing out of college as an aerospace designer. He knew the new Airbus would slot easily into Iberia's fleet. But he also felt that Mr. Dupuy's target price undervalued his plane.

At Airbus, Mr. Leahy also fumed at Iberia's pricing demands. A New York City native and the company's highest-ranking American, he pursues one goal: global domination over Boeing. Last year he spent 220 days on sales trips.

To Iberia, he argued that his plane offered a better investment return because the A340 is less expensive to buy and is similar to Iberia's other Airbus planes. From a hodge-podge of 11 models in 1997, Iberia now flies five types, and replacing the old 747s with A340s would trim that to four—offering savings on parts, maintenance and pilot training.

Even before presenting Airbus's offer, Mr. Leahy had flown to Madrid in October to make his case. On Nov. 18, he once again took a chartered plane for the one-hour flight from Airbus headquarters in Toulouse, France, to Madrid. For two hours that evening, he and his team sat with Mr. Dupuy and other Iberia managers around a table in Mr. Dupuy's office, debating how many seats can fit on a 777. Those numbers were crucial to the deal because each seat represents millions of dollars in revenue over the life of a plane but also adds weight and cost.

Boeing had told Iberia that its 777 could hold 30 more seats than the 350 Iberia planned to put on the Airbus plane. Mr. Leahy argued that the Boeing carries at most five more seats. "Get guarantees from Boeing" on the seat count, Mr. Leahy prodded the Iberia managers.

At Boeing, Mr. Bright was eager to soften Iberia's pricing demand. His account manager, Steve Aliment, had already made several visits to pitch the plane, and in late November, Mr. Bright sent him once again to protest that Iberia didn't appreciate the 777's revenue potential. Boeing desperately wanted to avoid competing just on price, so Mr. Bright pushed operating cost and comfort.

On the Airbus side, Mr. Leahy also was feeling pressured because a past sales tactic was coming back to haunt him. In 1995, when Iberia was buying 18 smaller A340s and Mr. Dupuy expressed concern about their future value, Mr. Leahy helped seal the deal by guaranteeing him a minimum resale price, which kicks in after 2005. If Iberia wants to sell them, Airbus must cover any difference between the market price of the used planes and the guaranteed floor price.

The guarantee is one of the tools that Mr. Leahy has used to boost Airbus's share of world sales to about 50% today from 20% in 1995. Boeing rarely guarantees resale values.

Mr. Dupuy had wanted guarantees because they lower his risk of buying, and thus cut his cost of borrowing. What mattered now was that the guarantees also freed him to sell the planes at a good price. Early in the competition, he suggested to both Airbus and Boeing that he might eventually replace all of Iberia's A340s with Boeings—and potentially stick Airbus with most of the tab.

"If we didn't have the guarantees, the position of Airbus would be very strong," Mr. Dupuy said in an interview. Instead, "we have a powerful bargaining tool on future prices."

On Dec. 4, Mr. Leahy flew again to Madrid to try to persuade Iberia to close a deal by year's end. Running through a presentation in Mr. Dupuy's office, Mr. Leahy and five colleagues ticked off fuel and maintenance costs for their plane. They asserted that passengers prefer the plane because it is quieter than the 777 and has no middle seats in business class.

Mr. Dupuy then rattled Mr. Leahy's cage with a new scenario: Iberia managers would be flying off next week to look at used Boeing 747-400 jumbo jets. Singapore Airlines had stopped flying the planes and was offering to lease them at bargain prices.

Mr. Leahy chided Mr. Dupuy, saying that was "like buying a used car," where a bargain can easily backfire. Mr. Dupuy replied that sometimes buying used makes sense because it offers the flexibility of other options. The message: Iberia could dump its Airbus fleet.

Within Iberia, another debate was ending. Mr. Dupuy heard from his managers the results of a yearlong analysis of the rival planes. The Airbus was cheaper than the Boeing, and the A340's four engines help it operate better in some high-altitude Latin American airports. But Iberia managers had decided they could fit 24 more seats on the Boeing, boosting revenue. And Iberia engineers calculated that the 777 would cost 8% less to maintain than the A340. Maintenance on big planes costs at least $3 million a year, so the savings would be huge over the life of a fleet.

Unaware of Iberia's analysis, the Boeing team arrived in Mr. Dupuy's office on the morning of Dec. 11 with three bound selling documents. One contained Boeing's revised offer, titled "Imagine the Possibilities . . . Iberia's 777 Fleet." Knowing Mr. Dupuy as a numbers guy, the Boeing team peppered him with data showing passengers would choose Iberia because they prefer the 777.

Mr. Dupuy told the salesmen their price was still too high.

By mid-December, Iberia Chairman Xabier de Irala was getting impatient and wanted a decision by the end of the year. On Dec. 18, Boeing's Mr. Bright flew to Madrid. Over a long lunch, Mr. Dupuy reiterated his price target.

"If that's your number, let's give this up," Mr. Bright said. Talks continued cordially, but the men left doubtful they could close the gap. That Friday, Dec. 20, Mr. Dupuy told Iberia's board that prices from Airbus and Boeing were still too high and he would push the used-plane option harder.

Matching easyJet

By the start of the year, Airbus's Mr. Leahy, growing frustrated, arranged a Saturday meeting with Mr. Dupuy. On Jan. 4, the Iberia executive interrupted a family skiing holiday in the Pyrenees and drove two hours along winding French roads to meet Mr. Leahy for lunch.

Mr. Leahy spent four hours trying to convince Mr. Dupuy and a colleague that Airbus couldn't offer a better deal. Mr. Dupuy argued that Airbus had just given steep discounts to British airline easyJet, so it should do the same for Iberia. Annoyed, Mr. Leahy said media reports of a 50% price cut for easyJet were nonsense.

"You get Boeing to give you a 50% discount and I'll send you a bottle of champagne," he told the Iberia executives.

Mr. Bright was frustrated too. In the first week of January, Mr. Dupuy proposed visiting Seattle, where Boeing builds passenger planes. Mr. Bright's reply: If Iberia was unwilling to budge, there was little reason to come. So, when Mr. Dupuy said he would make the 14-hour journey, Mr. Bright was encouraged.

On Jan. 14, Mr. Dupuy and two colleagues arrived in Seattle. In the private dining room of Cascadia, a high-end downtown restaurant, they met for dinner with the Boeing salesmen and Alan Mulally, the chief executive of Boeing's commercial-plane division. Mr. Dupuy was impressed by Mr. Mulally's eagerness and was pleased when he urged Mr. Bright's team to find a way to close the gap.

The next day, the Boeing salesmen offered a new proposal–including a slightly lower price, improved financing and better terms on spare parts, crew training and maintenance support from General Electric Co., maker of the plane's engines.

When Mr. Dupuy left Seattle on Jan. 16, Mr. Bright felt Iberia was relenting a bit on price and that Mr. Dupuy wanted to "find a way to do the deal." Mr. Dupuy was also optimistic about striking a deal with Boeing.

Back in Madrid the next day, he raced off to join Iberia's chairman, Mr. Irala, for a meeting with Mr. Leahy and Airbus President Noel Forgeard. Mr. Irala, a bear of a man who is credited with saving Iberia from bankruptcy eight years ago, told the Airbus executives that Mr. Dupuy's price target remained firm. When the Airbus men relented on a few points, Mr. Irala yielded a bit, too, and spelled out Iberia's remaining targets for Airbus. Mr. Forgeard said a deal looked possible.

As the meeting broke up, Mr. Dupuy was pleased. He felt that Boeing and Airbus were digging deep. And no wonder. The world air-travel market was sinking deeper, and fears of war in Iraq and terrorism had slashed global bookings.

In the next few days, the sales teams from Boeing and Airbus each huddled to refine their offers. Both remained about 10% above Mr. Dupuy's price targets. Each called him several times daily, pushing for concessions. Mr. Dupuy didn't budge. On Jan. 23, he told Iberia's board that both companies could do better. The board scheduled a special meeting for the following Thursday, Jan. 30.

Energized by the Seattle meetings, Mr. Bright pushed his team "to go all out to win this bid," and they worked around the clock. Mr. Bright phoned Mr. Dupuy daily from Seattle and occasionally fielded his calls at 3 a.m., Pacific time. By late January, Boeing had cut its price by more than 10% after haggling over engine price with GE and financing with leasing firms. The 777 was now less than 3% above Mr. Dupuy's target–so close that Mr. Bright asked for a gesture of compromise from Iberia.

Mr. Dupuy was impressed by Boeing's new aggressiveness. But Airbus was also closing the gap so quickly, he said, that he could offer no concessions. To Mr. Leahy, he talked up Boeing's willingness to deal. "I was just talking to Toby ..." Mr. Dupuy told Mr. Leahy during several conversations, referring to Mr. Bright. Airbus improved its offer further.

On Wednesday, the day before the deadline, Boeing and Airbus were running about even. In Seattle, Mr. Bright threw some clothes in his briefcase and proposed to Mr. Dupuy that he hop on a plane to Madrid. Mr. Dupuy said the choice was his, but what really mattered was the price target. That day, Mr. Dupuy told Messrs. Bright and Leahy that their bosses should call Mr. Irala with any final improvements before the board meeting.

On Thursday morning, Mr. Bright offered to trim Boeing's price further if Mr. Dupuy could guarantee that Boeing would win the deal. "I can't control Forgeard," Mr. Dupuy replied, referring to the Airbus president, who was due to talk soon with Mr. Irala. Mr. Bright made the price cut without the concession.

"You're very close," Mr. Dupuy told him.

Later, Mr. Forgeard got on the phone with Iberia's Mr. Irala, who said he still needed two concessions on the financial terms and economics of the deal. Airbus had already agreed to most of Mr. Dupuy's terms on asset guarantees and, with engine maker Rolls-Royce PLC, agreed to limit Iberia's cost of maintaining the jets. Mr. Forgeard asked if relenting would guarantee Airbus the deal. Mr. Irala replied yes, pending board approval–and looked over with a grin at Mr. Dupuy, who sat nearby with his laptop open. Mr. Forgeard acquiesced. Mr. Dupuy plugged the new numbers in his spreadsheet. Airbus had hit its target.

That evening, Boeing got a call from Iberia saying the airline would soon announce it had agreed to buy nine A340-600s and taken options to buy three more. Hours later, Boeing posted on its Web site a statement criticizing Iberia's choice as "the easiest decision." Mr. Bright said later that he simply couldn't hit Mr. Dupuy's numbers and "do good business."

In the end, Airbus nosed ahead thanks to its planes' lower price and common design with the rest of Iberia's fleet. By offering guarantees on the planes' future value and maintenance costs, plus attractive financing terms, Airbus edged out Boeing's aggressive package. The deal's final financial terms remain secret.

At Airbus, Mr. Leahy was relieved, but he faced one last slap. Iberia's news release crowed about Airbus's price guarantees on the planes–a detail Mr. Leahy considered confidential. Iberia's Mr. Dupuy said he wasn't rubbing it in. But he had, he boasted, won "extraordinary conditions."

Concession Strategies

Concession strategies should be decided upon and written down before negotiations begin. Such a process—discussion and recording—goes a long way toward ensuring that negotiators stick to the strategies. In the midst of a long negotiation, there is a tendency to make what we call "streaks" of concessions. The only way we have found to avoid this is careful planning and commitment before negotiation.

Of particular concern is the American propensity to "split the difference." Never split the difference! Have specific reasons for the size of each concession you make.

Finally, you will notice very quickly that Chinese or Japanese bargainers, for example, seldom make a concession without first taking a break. Issues and arguments are reconsidered away from the social pressure of the negotiation table. This is a good practice for Americans to emulate.

Team Assignments

The final step in negotiation planning is role assignments. Each American bargainer should understand his or her corresponding role. Other kinds of team assignments might include listening responsibilities, or monitoring the agenda or concession strategies. And perhaps roles should be adjusted to circumstances or over time. For example, as topics shift from commercial to technical, executives with the appropriate expertise might lead exchange speaking versus listening roles. Coordinated teamwork is key.

DESIGNING THE NEGOTIATION PROCESS
TOWARD MAXIMIZING KNOWLEDGE FLOWS

The key to creative negotiations is learning as much about the other side as possible by maximizing the knowledge flowing from their side to yours. Particular people, certain personal relationships, meeting places, times, and communication channels stimulate truthful and copious communications. Others prevent open communication and rich knowledge flows. A key challenge for negotiators is to determine the best means for maximizing these flows.

David Lax and James Sebenius, in their excellent *Harvard Business Review* article (and their subsequent book), make the argument that preparations for negotiations are often more important than the actual talks. We heartily agree and we particularly appreciate a planning tool they recommend, "backward mapping."[6] Taking the concept from a project management perspective, the goal is worked backwards, identifying each step in reverse chronological order to eventually find yourself in the present.

Indeed, in one of our corporate seminars at Boeing, we discovered that the engineers in the group had already begun to "diagram" the negotiation process in a manner familiar to most technical professions. Within a Gant diagram, they had begun to deconstruct the various steps that would be necessary to bring about a good result in a forthcoming negotiation with a parts vendor for an aircraft tail structure. Within this domestic context, the diagram considered each step and did so with a remarkable level of detail and sophistication. We encouraged this type of thought, but asked them to include factors and variables that were not easily quantifiable and then the procedures began to fall apart. We explained that by "procedures" certain steps were going to have to be considered that do not fit well within a perfectly reverse engineered project management goal-setting exercise. It was at this point that the *science* of negotiations met up with the *art* of negotiations for the first time. The engineers came to realize that the vendor wanted a good price but they wanted "other things," such as a long-term relationship with Boeing, the ability to provide other products, the securing of referrals for other Boeing departments. These factors did not fit well within the particular cost/benefit analysis the initial buyer/seller relationship diagram entailed.

We point this out because regardless of the amount of structure we put into the environmental scan and into negotiation planning, preparation, and process design we must always be capable of integrating those unknown and immeasurable factors and considerations that manifest themselves. The fluidity of the process and the improvisational nature of the art are what permit our fish to swim in these deep waters.

So the next aspect of negotiation preliminaries is manipulation of the negotiation situation to maximize knowledge flows. Some of the issues we raise in this section may appear trivial, but the most skilled negotiators and often your foreign clients will consider them. Particularly in a tough negotiation, everything should be working in your favor. If situational factors are working against you, it will be important before the negotiations begin to manipulate them. Also, management of situational factors may be important once the discussions have commenced. In the pages to follow we will consider seven aspects of process design that we feel are particularly important. They are:

1. Location;
2. Physical arrangements;
3. Number of parties;
4. Number of individual participants;
5. Audiences (news media, etc.);
6. Communications channels; and
7. Time limits.

All seven factors are ordinarily set before negotiations begin. All can and should be manipulated to your advantage and to maximize knowledge flows. Anyone can make the difference between success and failure in business negotiations with executives from any country.

Location

The location of the negotiations is perhaps the most important process design element for several reasons, both practical and psychological. The location of the negotiations may have a substantial impact on the legal jurisdiction if litigation is considered. But just having the "home court" is an advantage because the home team has all of its information resources readily available and all the necessary team members close by. Alternatively, the traveling team brings the minimum necessary resources, information, and players, and it stays in hotels. But perhaps a greater advantage the home team enjoys is psychological—a perception of power. If the other side is coming to you, that means you have something they want. You are in control of the scarce resource, whether it be a product or service (you're the seller) or access to a key market (you're the buyer). Smart negotiators will always try to hold negotiations in their own offices. Short of this, a neutral location is best.

The location factor will be even more important when dealing with clients or partners from relationship-oriented cultures, for it communicates power much louder in those places. Thus, in international business dealings we see a strong emphasis on getting to a neutral location, such as a restaurant, karaoke bar, spa, golf course, or some other sort of off-site location.

The U.S. government's current restrictions on visas granted to some foreign executives deliver a big disadvantage to American firms. It will often be impractical to invite your Chinese or Middle Eastern counterparts to visit you given the frequent delays and denials of the American immigration officials. However, you may want to invite them to one of your offices in another country. For example, General Motors negotiators arranged a visit to their Brazilian plant for their Shanghai Auto counterparts during those crucial negotiations.

In the event that you do travel to your partner's home turf, there are some things that can be done to reduce your disadvantages. One is to make arrangements for meeting facilities at your hotel (or your bank, or a subsidiary's office) and invite the other team to call on you. You might argue, "I've already made the arrangements and everything is all set," or "You can get away from the telephone," or perhaps you actually do need to wait for an important FedEx yourself. This may not help much, but it may help some.

Our single favorite example of locations conducive to positive knowledge flows is a variation on the offsite. When John worked as a market analyst for Solar Turbines International, now a San Diego division of Caterpillar, the company owned and operated a corporate boat. This was before the days of cell phones and wireless communications. Clients would be invited for a day of dolphin chasing and deep sea fishing off the tranquil coast of Coronado Island. Time to talk, debate, laugh, drink, and even catch a few fish. And the clients couldn't get away!

Physical Arrangements

Once the negotiation site has been agreed upon, then comes the question of specific physical arrangements. American bargainers should understand that the physical arrangements of the bargaining room will be much more important and will communicate perhaps more, and certainly differently, to foreign executives. We refer you to anthropologist Edward Hall's classic description of the language of space, which we've excerpted in exhibit 7.2. Americans value and feel comfortable with informality. Executives from most other countries value and feel comfortable with formality. If you travel to Thailand for example, Thai businesspcople will manage the physical arrangements of the negotiations such as time, place, refreshments, breaks, etc. (that is, unless you make the arrangements). The only advice we have for Americans in such situations is to ask the Thais where to sit. They will have a specific arrangement in mind, and if you ignore their arrangements, they will feel uncomfortable.

If your foreign partners are calling at your offices, then we recommend setting the physical arrangements to make them feel comfortable and more cooperative. If you wish to communicate that you are interested in the prospective business deal, then the most appropriate atmosphere will be a comfortable living room setting without desks or conference tables. Many chief executives have such furnishings in their offices, and for more reasons than one, a brief non-task encounter with the American CEO may be the appropriate first step. For companies that have frequent visits by foreign clients, a specific room should be set aside and furnished as described. Such a comfortable setting will serve to maximize knowledge flows.

Some firms take steps to create an auction atmosphere in their negotiations by arranging competing bidders to sit in adjacent rooms. Petro-Bras, the Brazilian national oil company, is famous for using this tactic with their suppliers. The involved purchasing agent can easily go from room to room to grind down both suppliers. Wal-Mart is also famous for simply having its vendors sit down in the same room, and the purchasing agent simply runs an auction—the lowest price gets the business. All this is at the opposite end of the high-pressure scale from the aforementioned tipping back of a few Coronas off the Coronado coast. Such pressure tactics will

Exhibit 7.2 The Language of Space

Like time, the language of space is different wherever one goes. The American businessman, familiar with the pattern of American corporate life, has no difficulty appraising the relative importance of someone else, simply by noting the size of his office in relation to other offices around him:

One pattern calls for the president of the chairman of the board to have the biggest office. The executive vice president will have the next largest, and so on down the line until you end up in the "bull pen." More important offices are usually located at the corners of and on the upper floors. Executive suites will be on the top floor. The relative rank of vice presidents will be reflected in where they are placed along "executive row." The French, on the other hand, are much more likely to lay out space as a network of connecting points of influence, activity, or interest. The French supervisor will ordinarily be found in the middle of his subordinates where he can control them.

Americans who are crowded will often feel that their status in the organization is suffering. As one would expect in the Arab world, the location of an office and its size constitute a poor index of the importance of the man who occupies it. What we would experience as crowded, the Arab will often regard as spacious. The same is true in Spanish cultures. A Latin American official illustrated the Spanish view of this point while showing me around a plant. Opening the door to an 18-by-20-foot office in which 17 clerks and their desks were placed, he said, "See, we have nice, spacious offices. Lots of space for everyone."

In the Middle East and Latin America, the [American] businessman is likely to feel left out in time and overcrowded in space. People get too close to him, lay their hands on him, and generally crowd his physical being. In Scandinavia and Germany, he feels more at home, but at the same time the people are a little cold and distant. It is space itself that conveys this feeling.

Source: Edward T. Hall, "The Silent Language in Overseas Business," *Harvard Business Review*, May-June, 1960, pp. 87-96.

make money in the short run, the process has little to do with creativity and ultimately destroys any notions of business relationships.

Number of Parties

In many international negotiations, more than two companies are involved. Often, in addition to a buyer and a seller there are other involved suppliers, engineering consulting firms, banks, trading companies, and government officials. Generally, the more parties involved, the greater the opportunities for creative outcomes, but also the more complex and more difficult the negotiations. Unfortunately, our American impatience often leads us to try to get everyone together and quickly "hammer out" an agreement. Such attempts almost always end in frustration. It is our recommendation that initially negotiations include as few parties as possible—hopefully just representatives of the two primary companies. If more than one other party is involved, we recommend a lobbying approach, which includes meeting with the separate parties individually before calling everyone together. We also note that Peter Shikerev, the Russian author of *Dolphins and Sharks,* tells us that a different approach to lobbying is practiced in his country. Rather than meeting with everyone separately, coalitions are "accumulated" in Russia. You meet with one other party, when you agree you call on a third party, when the three of you agree, then the three of you call on a fourth party, and so on.

After you've reached an agreement with your partners, after you have "gotten to yes," we recommend one additional step wherein all involved parties are included. We will describe such a meeting in more detail in the next chapter, but the idea is to maximize the creativity of the business agreement by going beyond "getting to yes." At this final meeting, the focal questions should be, "Is there some way to make this relationship better for everyone? In particular, is there something we haven't considered?" Having more parties involved will tend to enhance new ideas at this stage.

Number of Individual Participants

In negotiations, Americans are almost always outnumbered. We consider this to be a serious disadvantage. Earlier we mentioned the importance of finding out whom the other side is sending and then putting your team together in response. Moreover, you shouldn't hesitate to include additional members on your team, such as financial or technical experts. The extra expense may be a wise investment.

You should also know that others will try, in sometimes unethical ways, to control numbers of negotiators. We have heard of negotiators who, when faced with large numbers of visiting negotiators, purposefully delayed progress. As a result, some of the other side's team returns home, and the difference in numbers is reduced. We don't suggest you use such tactics, but you should be aware that they may be used against you.

Audiences

In any particular business deal there might be a number of audiences and stakeholders that may exercise influence on the negotiation outcomes. The aforementioned Dubai-owned DP World's bid to acquire several U.S. port operations is a case in point. Consider how many audiences existed:

1. Other suitors and competitors, even foreign ones, including Chinese firms;
2. Governmental agencies–FTC (antitrust), Congress (trade barrier saber rattling), State Department, Commerce Department, the U.S. Trade Representative, and a variety of security agencies;
3. George Bush's donors;
4. The American public;
5. Dock workers' unions;
6. The local and international presses and other media; and
7. Other Middle Eastern firms considering other American acquisitions.

Now consider how the involved companies might have manipulated these various audiences to their advantage. All of the audiences had an interest and a stake in how the DP World talks continued, and certainly some were manipulated through selective leaking of information.

We know such manipulations do occur in deals between foreign companies. Most recently Telenor, a Norwegian cell phone company, has accused its Russian business partner, Altimo, also a telecommunications company, of buying Ukrainian press coverage of their current disputes over assets. We are familiar with other cases in which information was deliberately leaked to the news media to pressure the other negotiating party to agree to the terms of the proposal. It is difficult for the other party to say no to an already publicized agreement. However, extreme caution is advised in this area. Often, the action by one party may result in mistrust and a breakdown in the negotiations. In particular, trying to influence negotiations through leaking information to a foreign press (that is, Americans in a foreign country or vice versa) is quite risky.

You should anticipate that international clients or partners may manipulate audiences for their advantage, particularly their local audiences with which they are more familiar, such as local governments. You should also be aware of audience reactions that may help you, and you should know how to elicit such reactions when appropriate.

Communications Channels

Contemplate for a moment the channels available: face-to-face, through an intermediary, through the press, telephone, conference call, fax, e-mail, instant messaging, text messaging, teleconferencing, videoconferencing, Skype that can combine these, etc. We've tried to be comprehensive in this list, but the "etc." is really the important part of it. It's hard to imagine how communication technologies and their culturally determined uses will evolve as the bandwidth widens. Now you can buy $400,000 HDTV "telepresence" systems. Perhaps this is the technology breakthrough that will deliver on the promise of the videoconferencing concept—but only time will tell. Those of us studying the advantages and disadvantages of different media struggle to keep up with the technological developments. One might conclude that it is always best to meet face-to-face. There all channels are open, verbal and nonverbal. People can touch, smell, even taste one another—recall the Russian kiss. You can also measure attention and comprehension by facial expressions postures, and so on.

However, we are also learning that in international negotiations there are advantages to electronic means. Information flows more smoothly and conveniently over the Internet. That is, when we compare transcripts of face-to-face negotiations with those of e-mail negotiations, in the former we see much miscommunication, missed messages, correcting of errors, and repetition. Indeed, it is hard to listen carefully when you are thinking about what you are going to say next. E-mail allows negotiators to carefully read, even have others consult on specific messages. E-mail also allows time for careful responses. In fact, e-mail works somewhat like talking on the golf course—there you talk on the tee, then while you're chasing your errant shots in separate directions, you have time to carefully consider the information given and your response.

That said, particularly initially, face-to-face negotiations with clients from relationship-oriented cultures are always recommended. Other channels of communication that might be used for negotiations in the United States simply are not effective or acceptable. For example, the Japanese social system is built around almost continuous face-to-face contact. Too much of the important, subtly transmitted information can't be communicated in a letter, memo, fax, e-mail, telephone call, or even by teleconferencing. Written communications also leave a record of interactions that may be eschewed in some circumstances. Also, it is much harder for Japanese bargainers to say no in the face-to-face situation. The social pressure and interpersonal harmony preclude negative responses, and these pressures are not so strong over the phone or e-mail.

The principle management implications are two-fold: (1) ask them about their preferences regarding communication channels; and (2) design communication systems that maximize knowledge flows toward building creativity.

Time Limits

If location is not the single most important aspect of the negotiation situation, then time limits are. Generally, the side that has more time *and knows it* is in a stronger bargaining position. The side with less time is forced to make concessions in order to move the other toward agreement. The use of time can be a powerful bargaining tool.

Ordinarily, time constraints are established by factors beyond the control of negotiators. On the selling side, orders must be secured to keep the factory busy, the expenses of foreign travel are substantial, other customers must be called on, quotas must be filled, and the home office management is in a hurry. Likewise, purchasers must bargain with other suppliers of complementary goods. Purchases must be made before other buyers come on the scene. Purchases must be made according to complex time schedules and before profits can be made from associated operations. Circumstances and company goals set time limits for practically every kind of negotiation and for buyers and sellers alike. Negotiators should try to determine beforehand what the other side's time constraints are. Hopefully, theirs will be shorter than yours. But in any case negotiators can manipulate time limits, or at least the perception of time limits, to their advantage.

Most foreign bargainers have a big advantage when it comes to manipulation of time limits—an American's internal clock apparently ticks much faster and much, much louder. Impatience is perhaps our greatest weakness in international negotiations. We're interested in quick action and immediate results. In contrast, the foreign executive often takes a more careful approach to business transactions. For example, it is much more difficult to rush a Russian decision by imposing a time limit because (1) they will not abandon their more collective approach to decision making, which generally takes longer, particularly if the government is involved, and (2) many Russians would rather make no decision than a bad one. Alternatively, many Americans would rather risk a bad decision than let a potential opportunity slip by.

Americans overseas can also manipulate the other side's perception of their time limits by making hotel reservations for longer or shorter periods than expected. Most foreign clients will check the length of your hotel reservations as part of their pre-negotiation preparation. Your reservations will influence their behavior. Upon your arrival, you will also be asked how long you expect to stay in their country. Negotiators should be aware that something simple like a hotel reservation communicates much, and this channel of communication should be used to your advantage, not theirs.

Another factor related to the timing of negotiations is national holidays and the like. PetroBras once invited a team of American negotiators to bid on a $5 million contract for equipment for an offshore oil platform *right before the Christmas holidays*. Summers are nice in Rio, but the Americans were put at an awful disadvantage in their negotiations there by the unsaid demands of their own families waiting for Santa back home.

In some circumstances it may be possible to impose time limits on foreign negotiators by setting deadlines. The imposition of time limits should only be used in extreme circumstances and should be accompanied with an explanation. Even a comment such as, "When can we expect to hear from you?" can translate into Spanish or Arabic inappropriate impatience. It is probably best to say nothing at all. American bargainers should understand the foreigners' decision processes, anticipate that things will move more slowly, and plan accordingly.

Finally, we need to make one last point about time limits. While creative processes and brainstorming can enhance time pressure, the best international commercial relationships will depend on taking time to develop viable personal relationships and innovative business structures and processes. And, the latter are best not rushed. Indeed, even though Handel was responding to a request by his king, you can tell by his mellow music that he wasn't rushed. And, we know he actually further improved his composition even after it was delivered on the Thames on that lazy summer day.

CHAPTER 8

VIS-À-VIS COMMUNICATIONS

Even a fish wouldn't get into trouble if he kept his mouth shut.

The most difficult aspect of an international business negotiation is the actual conduct of the face-to-face meeting. Assuming that the appropriate people have been chosen to represent your firm, and that those representatives are well prepared, and that the process has been designed to maximize knowledge flows, things can still go wrong at the negotiation table. Obviously, if these other preliminaries haven't been managed properly, then things will go wrong during the meetings.

NON-TASK SOUNDING

Trust and connections can make a big difference in the United States. They're often great to have, but not essential. In all relationship-oriented cultures around the world, they are essential. Getting started in the United States means: (1) sending a letter explaining your business purpose and in it dropping a name or two if possible; (2) a follow-up call for an appointment; (3) five minutes of small talk across her desk (this is the non-task sounding); and (4) you're talking business. There are quite a few more steps to the dance in Asia, Latin America, Southern Europe, India, and Africa.

As we will see in the next chapter most folks on the planet are loathe to use their legal system (attorneys and courts) to clean things up if the business goes sour. They depend on strong and trusting relationships between the people on both sides to mitigate conflicts down the road. And time and money are *invested* in building those relationships *before* getting down to business. Five minutes of non-task sounding in the United States can translate into five days, weeks, or even months of non-task sounding in Shanghai, Lagos, or Rio de Janeiro. There is no other way.

In the United States we tend to trust until given reason not to. In relationship-oriented cultures, suspicion and distrust characterize all meetings with strangers. In such places, it is difficult to earn trust because business will not even begin without it. Instead, trust must be transmitted via personal connections or intermediaries. That is, a trusted business associate of yours must pass you along to one of his trusted business associates and so on. So the key first step in non-task sounding in many countries is finding the personal links to your target organization and/or executive.

Those links can be hometown, family, school, or previous business ties. In some places, they can be institutional—as in Japan where your banker can do the introductions. In China or India, the links must be based on personal experience. For example, you call your former classmate and ask him to set up a dinner meeting with his friend. Expensive meals at nice places are key to demonstrating that you understand the value of strategic personal relationships. If things go well, his friend accepts the role of your intermediary and in turn sets up a meeting with your potential client or business partner whom he knows quite well.

Often, your intermediary will then arrange a lunch or dinner the night before a visit to the client's offices. The intermediary will attend both. Your intermediary will insist that you spend big bucks on the meal. This is important. Your sincerity will be gauged by the size of the check for this ritual sharing of food. Now for someone who grabs a sandwich at their desk for lunch this will seem inefficient. However, a $500 meal may in fact be a great investment in many places around the world.

The talk at these initial meetings may range widely, even inanely from the American perspective. Even though your intermediary has "blessed" the relationship, your foreign partner will still endeavor to sound you out in the broadest senses—trustworthiness, sincerity, integrity, competence, and so on. S/he will be looking for feelings of interpersonal harmony and connection. And there is no rushing this process. While this "empty questioning" may test your own patience, even your endurance, you should take it as a sign of progress—they're interested.

At some point when you have passed the "total-you test," the client or the intermediary will bring up business. This signals the end to non-task sounding in relationship-cultures. Only the client or intermediary can give this signal. We repeat, only the client or intermediary can give this signal. Not you! And even then, after a brief discussion of business, your foreign client may lapse back into more non-task sounding.

Most Americans make it through the dinner, but at the client's offices the next day they can't keep from making proposals. This is often interpreted as incredibly rude from the foreign perspective. Even when they've been told by their own experienced staff to continue the small talk until the client broaches business, most high-powered Americans can't stand the "delays."

We talked with a group of American executives developing a business relationship with Spanish counterparts. Their complaint was that every time they came to Madrid the trip was exhausting because the Spaniards insisted on continuous late-night eating and drinking. That, combined with jet lag, made the discussions during the days literally physically demanding. We recommended they invite the Spaniards to Houston to continue the work. The Texans countered, "We've tried that, but it's still party late into the night there as well, and there we have to contend with our families!"

The management implications are clear. In foreign countries, actually even in the United States, always, ALWAYS, let the client or intermediary bring up business.

Other minor considerations: Business cards will be required and small gifts (exchanged before leaving the offices) will be appropriate in many countries. For meetings in the United States, setting and formality will be marginally less important for operational level executives, but not much less. Particularly when the foreign firm is the one courted, long periods of non-task sounding, including dinner at a very good restaurant or at your home, are advised.

By the way, we've used the form of the opening of this chapter to let you experience the absence of non-task sounding. Perhaps you wondered why there was no talk of bloody Pacific beaches or concerts on the Thames. Instead, we got right down to business. If you missed the intended relaxing diversions they'll be back in the coming chapters.

Non-task Sounding for Top Executives

The role of top executives in negotiations internationally is often ceremonial. By ceremonial, however, we do not mean unimportant. Ordinarily they are brought into negotiations only to sign the agreement after all issues have been settled by lower-level executives. On occasion, top executives are included earlier in the talks to communicate commitment and importance. In either case, their main activity is nontask sounding. Only vague statements should be made about the potential for a strong, long-lasting business relationship. Specifics must be left up to managers and staff.

Getting top American executives to understand the importance of non-task sounding and to make these adjustments in their behavior may be difficult. One successful way has been to supply them with a list of appropriate questions to ask during the initial meetings with their high-level counterparts. Soccer's a good topic almost everywhere, but a little knowledge about cricket will go a long way in Sydney. Ask your local representatives or intermediaries what topics are appropriate and do a little studying ahead of time.

American executives should be prepared with business cards in the local language and should exchange them if the other side offers. However, when presidents of companies meet, business cards often are not required. Of course, American company presidents should be well briefed about their foreign counterparts in advance.

Finally, when high-level meetings are held in the United States, we recommend a similar approach. Top-level foreign executives, particularly from East Asian cultures, will not be prepared to bargain and will not be persuaded, even when in the United States. It's simply not their role. When American hosts wish to demonstrate the importance of the visit and the deal, we advise sending a limousine to pick up the foreign party at their hotel. The initial meeting between top executives should not be held across a boardroom table, and certainly not across the American executive's desk. Rather, a more comfortable atmosphere, such as a living room or a private room in a high-class restaurant, is preferable. Remember, the extra expense is an investment!

TASK-RELATED EXCHANGE OF INFORMATION

A task-related exchange of information implies a two-way communication process. However, when Americans meet foreigners across the negotiation table, the information flow is very often unidirectional—from the American side to the other. In the paragraphs that follow we will recommend actions for American bargainers that will help them to manage efficiently the give-*and*-take of information.

Giving Information

The most obvious problem associated with providing information to international clients will be the language. It is true that many more foreign executives can speak and understand English than Americans can any second language. English is, after all, the international language of business and technology. However, Americans should be careful of misunderstandings that can arise from the other side's limited knowledge of English. Confusion can result when foreign executives, because of politeness, indicate they understand when in fact they do not. When any doubt exists, Americans should use visual media (slides and brochures) and provide copious written support materials and an interpreter if the other side hasn't. Even when your international partner does provide an interpreter, there may be critical stages of the negotiations when your own interpreter should be included on your negotiation team. Also, be sure to talk to and listen to the executive on the other side of the table even when she or he speaks in their local language. The interpreter should not be the sole focus of your attention.

Regarding written materials, imagine for a moment that you are a Vietnamese executive trying to choose between two competitive offerings. One is written in your native language, and the other is written in a foreign language. Which proposal will you "like" better? Which company will you choose as a vendor? Perhaps you can get by with technical or engineering details in English, but the sections of the proposal that will be reviewed and evaluated by upper Vietnamese management, particularly Party officials, must be written in their native language. We've heard more than once that translation of documents is expensive and takes time. But would you rather have your client spending his time reading your proposal in his second language? And how expensive is losing your next deal?

Once you are comfortable with the language situation, you can turn your attention to more subtle aspects of giving information to your foreign counterparts. The first of these has to do with the order of presentation. In the United States, we tend to say what we want and explain the reasons behind our request only if necessary. That's why the task-related exchange of information goes so quickly. This isn't the ritual in many countries. For example, in Japan they are used to long descriptions of background and context before specific proposals are made. Given this mode of operation, it is not surprising to hear the American executive's complaint about the thousands of questions the Japanese executive asks.

Clearly then, communicating your bargaining interests, your company's needs and preferences, will take longer in almost all foreign countries. Language problems and lengthy explanations will require more meetings, involving more of your people (technical experts) and more of theirs. We strongly recommend patience with this process and anticipation of increased time and money spent at this stage. But at some point, American bargainers will have to terminate such questioning. While answering a thousand questions may be tedious but necessary, answering two thousand questions may not be productive. Instead of answering a repetitious question about delivery again, a variety of responses may work better, including:

1. Apparently delivery is key issue for you. Can you remind me again why?
2. Summarize your previous answer after something like: "I already gave that information to Mr. Park yesterday, but to reiterate . . ."
3. Offer to write down the requested information so that it may be shared with all concerned foreign executives.
4. Generally, a repeated question should be answered the second time in about three minutes. The third time it's asked the answer should be a one-minute summary. If the same question is asked a fourth time, it's probably a persuasive tactic and not information gathering. The appropriate response is then silence or a change of subject.

You should recognize one other thing about foreign questions. The other side often understands, and even expects, that some questions cannot be answered. But they will go ahead and ask them anyway. This is in sharp contrast to the American practice of only asking questions that will be answered. That is, if an American manager asks a question and doesn't get an answer, he often gets upset. This is not necessarily the case with the executives in many other countries.

Finally, we recommend that American bargainers guard against the tendency of making concessions during this exchange of information. We have found that often American negotiators, impatient with the process, will actually make concessions during this second stage of negotiations, before they have even determined the foreign negotiator's position, needs, and interests. It will take great patience indeed to avoid the natural urge to get to the third stage, persuasion, by making concessions in the hopes that they will reciprocate.

Getting Information

Of course, getting information *before* negotiations begin is hugely important. James Sebenius advocated "mapping the players and the process" in international negotiations in another recent *Harvard Business Review* article.[1] We agree, and your intermediary or local advisors will be essential in this activity. Key information will be issues related to the larger context of your business—government or party involvement and the larger economic plans of local, provincial, and/or even national authorities—things not considered or uncovered during your own environmental scanning. Also crucial will be knowledge of the key decision makers: In family businesses, it's almost always the patriarch; in state-owned enterprises it's the top Party official.

Hopefully, your foreign clients will be courting your business. In such a situation, they will be the ones making proposals and supplying you with more information than you probably want. But should your firm be initiating the contact or trying to make the sale, expect great difficulties in getting feedback to your proposals. If you ask a group of Thai executives what they think of your price quote and proposal, they will invariably say something like, "Let us take a look or let us study (or do some research on) it." They may even respond in such a manner even if they think it stinks.

Let's review the reasons behind this behavior. First, executives in many relationship-oriented cultures want to maintain your face-to-face and interpersonal harmony. From the Thai point of view a negative, albeit honest, answer at the negotiation would disrupt the harmony established. American executives are often unable to read the subtle, nonverbal, negative cues that accompany the "Let us study it." Another local executive would read the nonverbal message that "it stinks," but even the most experienced Americans are sometimes unable to process this implied message.

In the United States, another key source of information regarding your client's reaction to your proposals is his or her facial expression. Most of us process such information unconsciously, but we all do pay attention to this channel. Indeed, many American executives report great frustration because of the Chinese negotiator's "poker face." Indeed, some Chinese managers report increasing their eye contact when dealing with Americans to demonstrate interest, but controlling their facial expressions to hide negative reactions.

Indeed, the most efficient way to get feedback from a foreign client may be through the indispensable intermediary. Having talked about all the difficulties in getting honest feedback from many of your foreign partners, you should also understand that some cultures are on the other end of the scale. Remember our Korean chair chucker. Or, for example, both German and Israeli negotiators are famous for their frankness and sometimes brutal honesty. If a German executive thinks your proposal stinks she'll very directly tell you so. An Israeli might take it a step further and tell you it's insulting. Israelis highly value what they call *doogri*, that is, expressing their feelings directly and accurately. Israelis complain they can't get a straight answer from Americans. The problem then for Americans is to not take offense at their pushy use of English and their apparently aggressive manner. It's their culture talking.

PERSUASION

From the American perspective persuasion is the heart of a negotiation. In America, we have a wide range of persuasive tactics that can be and often are employed to change our clients' minds. Among them are promises, recommendations, appeals to industry norms, providing more information, asking questions, and the more aggressive threats and warnings. We have observed Americans using all such persuasive tactics. However, the appropriateness and effectiveness of these approaches varies in other countries. Things are a bit more complicated in many places.

For example, Honeywell Bull had won negotiation rights for an order of 100 ATMs from the Bank of China. Toward the end of the negotiations, the Bank of China buyer asked for deeper price cuts. But to him it wasn't just a matter of thrift. He appealed, "If the price isn't reduced further I will lose face." In other words, "the deal will be off and we'll talk to your competitor." The Honeywell Bull executive responded that he had some room to move in the bid, but the lower price would not allow for training in the United States for the Chinese managers. The Chinese side then asked for a break and came back smiling in ten minutes, agreeing to all the terms. Some might conclude that for Chinese executives, seeing Harvard, UCLA, Hollywood, and Las Vegas is more important than a face-saving price reduction. However, the clever negotiator will understand that his staff's travel to the United States brought much more esteem to the Chinese executive than any mere price break.

As we mentioned in the previous chapter, when the persuasion mode starts in your negotiations in many countries you can expect to hear about your competitors and threats to do business elsewhere. Of course, Americans do the same thing, but with more finesse perhaps. Koreans seem to use this tactic with little compunction. Because American negotiators tend to be in a hurry and tend to focus on "one thing at a time," the development of a symmetrical set of alternatives begins only when troubles crop up with the focal business deal. So most Americans feel like they're being "two-timed" when the "there's-more-than-one-game-in-town" threat is delivered. Americans get mad when the Koreans are just blandly pointing out what they believe should be obvious to everyone.

Another important factor in relationship-oriented cultures is the context in which specific tactics are used. Aggressive influence tactics such as threats, which can only be used by negotiators in higher power positions (usually buyers), should be communicated through intermediaries and informally. And even then, only subtle and indirect threats, commands, and so on, are appropriate. Getting mad ruins relationships. Loud voices and angry tones destroy even longstanding interpersonal harmony. So the intermediary or local representative can be doubly important from the American perspective. First, s/he provides a method of more accurately reading foreign clients, and, second, it makes available to American bargainers persuasive tactics that would be completely inappropriate during the formal talks.

To sum up, if an impasse is reached with foreign clients, rather than trying to persuade in the usual American manner, we recommend use of the following eight persuasive tactics, in the following order and in the following circumstances:

1. Ask more questions. We feel that the single most important advice we can give is to use questions as a persuasive tactic, our Rule #7. This is true in not only relationship-oriented cultures, but anywhere in the world, including the United States. In his book, *The Negotiating Game*, Chester Karrass suggests that sometimes it's "smart to be a little bit dumb" in business negotiations. Ask the same questions more than once: "I didn't completely understand what you meant. Can you please explain that again?" If your clients or potential business partners have good answers, then it's perhaps best if you compromise on the issue. But often, under close scrutiny, their answers aren't very good. And

with such a weak position exposed they will be obligated to concede. Also, questions often put more information on the table, providing leads toward more creative solutions. For all these reasons, questions can elicit key information and can be powerful persuasive devices.

2. Educate. Condescension will kill this approach, so be careful. But re-explain your company's situation, needs, and preferences. You might also make oblique reference to the "internationally recognized business practices" about which most managers in fast-developing countries are becoming more interested. Some executives supply foreign customers with information about their own competitors, again with the intent of education about the overall marketplace.

3. Silence. If you are still not satisfied with their response, try silence. Let them think about it and give them an opportunity to change their position. However, you should recognize that often foreign executives are much better at the use of this tactic than you. If silence is a tactic you find difficult to use, you should at least be aware that some of your foreign partners will use it frequently and naturally.

4. If tactics 1 through 3 produce no concessions, it will be time to change the subject or call a recess and put the intermediary to work. But rather than going directly to the more aggressive tactics (warnings and threats), we recommend repeating the first three tactics using that important communication channel—the intermediary or local representative. The questions and explanations may expose new information or objections that couldn't be broached at the negotiation table.

5. Aggressive influence tactics (warnings and threats, particularly those emphasized with expressions of emotions) may be used in negotiations with most East Asians, for example, only at great risk and in special circumstances. First, they should only be used via the intermediary or your local representative, and even then they should be used in the most indirect manner possible. Second, they should be used only when the American company is clearly in the stronger position. Even in these two circumstances, use of such aggressive persuasive tactics will damage the interpersonal harmony, which may in the long run be to your company's disadvantage. If power relations ever shift (and they always do), the other side will be quick to exploit the change in events. However, if the American side exercises restraint and maintains the interpersonal harmony, then if and when power relations shift, often the other side will consider the American company's interests.

This latter point is difficult for most Americans to believe. But we have witnessed Chinese executives behave in this way several times. For example, a corporate vice president at Honeywell Bull threatened a senior executive at China Post with a lawsuit demanding final acceptance of a signed contract. The China Post executive responded, "Go ahead. You may win the case. But you will be finished in the China market." At a subsequent meeting the Honeywell Bull country manager, schooled in the Chinese style of business negotiations and possessing a good relationship with the China Post executive, was able to smooth things over by appealing to the interests of the long term. The customer responded, "This is the right attitude, I will see what I can do to expedite the final acceptance."

6. If tactics 1 through 5 have not produced concessions on the part of the other firm's negotiators, we suggest the use of time to enable them to consider new information and to reach a decision satisfying almost everyone involved on their side, from technical experts to government officials. As a matter of culture, bargainers in many countries don't make concessions immediately following persuasive appeals without broader consultation. Indeed, the combination of collective decision making and social hierarchy can make things quite complicated with clients from relationship-cultures. Unfortunately, time is perhaps the most difficult tactic for American bargainers to use. We're in a hurry to solve the problem and settle the deal. "Letting things hang" goes against our nature. But it may be necessary. And hopefully they will run into their time limits before you run into yours. Additionally, use of this tactic will require the cooperation and understanding of your home office.

    It should be remembered that executives from most other cultures are skilled in the use of time as a persuasive tactic. Often, group decision making and the long-term approach to business deals seem to enhance the effectiveness of tactical delays for foreign bargaining with Americans. Richard Solomon, President of the U.S. Institute for Peace, explains in his excellent book on the Chinese negotiation style: "Do not expect quick or easy agreement. A Chinese negotiator will have trouble convincing his superiors that he has fully tested the limits of his counterpart's position if he has not protracted the discussions."[2]

7. The next persuasive tactic to use is asking the intermediary to arbitrate your differences. Let them call your clients and meet with them separately as a go-between. We have seen intermediaries often successfully settle otherwise irreconcilable differences.

8. Finally, if all else fails, it may be necessary to bring together the top executives of the two companies in the hope of stimulating more cooperation. A refusal at this stage means the business is finished.

To conclude our discussion of persuasive tactics, we want to emphasize the importance of our recommendations. A mistake at this stage, even a minor one, can have major consequences for your international business relationships. American managers will have to be doubly conscientious to avoid blunders here because often the foreigners' style of persuasion is so different and apparently ambiguous. Remember that the managers from relationship-oriented cultures in particular are looking to establish a long-term business relationship of mutual benefit. Threats and the like don't fit into their understanding of how such a relationship should work. You should also recognize that we are recommending adoption of a Japanese approach to persuasion when bargaining with almost all foreign clients and business partners. We realize our approach takes longer, but in the end you and your company will benefit by such an approach. Finally, smart American negotiators will anticipate the foreigner's use of the persuasive tactics just described.

CONCESSIONS AND AGREEMENT

The final stage of business negotiations involves concessions, building toward agreement. Negotiation requires compromise, or as the Chinese say, "Finding *the way*." Usually both sides give up something to get even more. But the approach used for compromise can vary substantially around the world, particularly East to West.

American and European managers often report great difficulties in measuring progress in their negotiations in Asia. Consequently, Americans often make unnecessary concessions right before agreements are announced by the other side. American bargainers in Asia should expect this holistic approach and be prepared to discuss all issues simultaneously and in an apparently haphazard order. Progress in the talks should not be measured by how many issues have been settled. Rather, Americans must try to gauge the quality of the business relationship. Important signals of progress will be:

1. Higher-level foreign executives being included in the discussions;
2. Their questions beginning to focus on specific areas of the deal;
3. A softening of their attitudes and position on some of the issues;
4. At the negotiation table, increased talk among themselves in their native tongue, which may often mean they're trying to decide something; and
5. Calls for additional meetings, increased bargaining, and use of the intermediary;

6. They ask about new things, potential benefits such as overseas training or even future business.

As part of your team's preparations, it will be important to document concession strategies. When they're agreed to and written down before negotiations begin it's easier for everyone on your side to stick to the "concession schedule," so to speak. Americans need to follow such schedules with care. Trading concessions with foreign bargainers will not work because they view nothing to be settled until everything is settled. We advise making no concession until all issues and interests have been exposed and fully discussed. Indeed, this is our Rule #8: Make no concessions until the end. Even then, concessions should be made, on minor issues first, to help establish the relationship.

Finally, concessions should not be decided upon at the negotiation table. Rather, Americans are advised to reconsider each concession away from the social pressure of the formal negotiations. This again is a Japanese practice that Americans will do well to emulate. Having strategically limited authority can be an important check on runaway concession making.

Minor Distractions

Before closing our discussion of the process of business negotiations, it is important to mention briefly three foreign behaviors that will seem rude to American bargainers but are nothing more than common habits for executives in many other countries. First, for example, your Iranian clients will often break into side conversations—in Farsi. Ordinarily, the purpose of these side conversations is to clarify something Americans have said, that is, getting the translation straightened out. Second, often Chinese executives will enter or leave negotiations in the middle of your comments. This reflects their busy schedule and a different view of "meeting etiquette." Finally, it can be particularly disturbing to be talking to a group of Saudi or Japanese executives and discover that one, perhaps even the senior executive, is "listening while doing other things" or "listening with his eyes shut." Usually this shouldn't be taken personally; it simply reflects a different view of appropriate behavior at meetings. Further, busy foreign executives may also be signaling that they are comfortable with how things are going—if they are not comfortable, they will remain quite attentive.

THE NEW CREATIVITY

Getting to "yes" isn't good enough.

Perhaps the most famous negotiation parable involves an argument over an orange. The most obvious approach was to simply cut it in half, each person getting a fair share. But, when the two negotiators began talking to each other, exchanging information about their interests, a better solution to the problem became obvious. The person wanting the orange for juice for breakfast took that part and the person wanting the rind for making marmalade took that part. Both sides ended up with more. Neither agreement is particularly creative. The parable of the orange becomes a story about creativity when both parties decide to cooperate in planting more orange trees. In a similar way, Boeing buys composite plastic wings for its new 787 Dreamliner designed and manufactured by Japanese suppliers, and then sells the completed 787s back to Japanese airlines, all with a nice subsidy from the Japanese government. This is what we mean by creativity in negotiations.

At business schools these days, we are beginning to learn a lot about creative processes. Courses are being offered and dissertations being proffered with "innovation" being the key buzz word at academic conferences and in corporate boardrooms. And the more we hear about innovation and creative processes the more we are beginning to appreciate that the Japanese approach to international business negotiations, by nature, uses many of the techniques commonly emphasized in any discussion of creative processes. Indeed, there appears to be a fundamental explanation as to why the Japanese have been able to build such a successful society despite their lack of natural resources and relative isolation. While Japanese society does have its own obstacles to creativity—hierarchy and collectivism are two—they have developed a negotiation style that in many ways obviates such disadvantages. Indeed, the ten new rules we've advocated herein nicely coincide with an approach to international negotiations that comes natural to Japanese.

We also must give credit to the luminaries in the field who have long advocated creativity in negotiations. Negotiations expert Howard Raiffa and his colleagues recommend:

> . . . the teams should think and plan together informally and do some joint brainstorming, which can be thought of as "dialoguing" or "prene-

gotiating." The two sides make no tradeoffs, commitments, or arguments about how to divide the pie at this early stage.[3]

In *Getting to Yes,* Roger Fisher and William Ury title their chapter 3 "Invent[ing] Options for Mutual Gain."[4] David Lax and James Sebenius, in their important new book, *3D-Negotiations,*[5] go past getting to yes, and talk about "creative agreements" and "great agreements." Lawrence Susskind and his associates advocate the use of "parallel informal negotiations" toward building creative negotiation outcomes.[6] Our goal here is to push these ideas to the forefront in thinking about business negotiations. The field generally is still stuck in the past, talking about "making deals" and "solving problems." Even the use of terms like "win-win" expose the vestiges of the old competitive thinking. Our point is that a business negotiation is not something that can be won or lost, and the competitive metaphor limits creativity. The problem-solving metaphor does as well. Thus, we offer our new rule #1. Accept only creative outcomes!

One of the smartest people we know working in the area of creative processes is Lynda Lawrence at IdeaWorks, a Newport Beach consulting firm (www.ideaworksconsulting.com). Lynda's expertise combines practice and research—the rich experiences of founding and managing her own advertising agency with a comprehensive study of the topic. She also co-teaches a course in Innovation Processes (Creativity and Diffusion of Innovations) at the Merage School of Business at UC Irvine. She has developed a list of "10 Ways to Generate More Ideas" that we have included here as exhibit 8.1. Read her list and consider how these techniques might be used to stimulate creative thinking in your negotiations.

For the Japanese reader, some things will be quite familiar. It's easy to get Japanese in close physical proximity (#3); they've been living that way for millennia. Japanese companies tend not to specialize in just marketing, engineering, or finance. Each executive may have worked in several functional areas, limiting the "silo effect" often associated disparagingly with American firms (#4). Physical movement (#6), picture the start of the day at your typical Japanese factory. The Japanese also seem to work best in small groups (#6). Silence is definitely ok (part of #6). The Japanese invented *karaoke* (#6 and singing). The Japanese have difficulty criticizing others, especially foreigners (#7). The use of visuals and holistic thinking are natural for Japanese (#7). Breaks are also a common procedure for Japanese (#8). Japanese will work better with familiar folks (#9).

Exhibit 8.1   Ten Ways to Generate More Ideas

---

1. Establish *common goals* of what this "collaboration" would create. A more workable deal? Some common long-term goals? A closer partnership?
2. Establish the *rules of engagement*. The purpose of the exercise is to resolve differences in creative ways that work better for both parties. All ideas are possibilities, and research shows that combining ideas from different cultures can result in better outcomes than those from a single culture.
3. *Trust is key*, and difficult to establish in many cultures. Certain techniques might speed that process a little. Being offsite, for example. Establishing physical proximity that unconsciously signals intimacy.
4. *Add diversity* (gender, culture, extroverts, different work specialties, experts, outsiders) to the group.
5. *Use storytelling*. This both helps establish who you are and what point of view you are bringing to this collaboration.
6. Work in *small groups*. Add *physical movement*. Tell the participants to relax, play, sing, have fun, and silence is ok.
7. Work holistically and using visuals. If, for example, there are three sticking points where neither side is happy, agree to work on those points by spending a short time–ten minutes–on each point where both sides offer "crazy" suggestions. Use techniques of *improvisation*. Neither side should be offended by the *crazy ideas*. No one should criticize. Explain that by exploring crazy ideas that better ideas are often generated.
8. *Sleep on it*.* This enables the unconscious to work on the problems, and gives them time to collect opinions before meeting again the next day. Other kinds of breaks, coffee, etc. are also helpful.
9. Doing this process *over several sessions* allows both sides to feel that progress is being made, and actually generates better and more polished ideas that both sides can invest in.
10. It is the process of creating something together, rather than the specific proposals, which creates *bonding* around a shared task and establishes new ways of working together. Each side feels honored and Americans can feel that something is being accomplished.

Source: Lynda Lawrence, Chief Idea Officer, IdeaWorks Consulting (www.ideaworksconsulting.com)

* The overnight part of #8 is particularly important. Anthropologist and consumer expert Clotaire Rapaille[1] suggests that the transitions between wakefulness and sleep can act as a kind of "whack on the side of the head" that allows new kinds of thinking ". . . calming their brainwaves, getting them to that tranquil point just before sleep" (page 8). By the way, we heartily recommend his book, *The Culture Code*, as a key to understanding cultural differences in behavior.

Perhaps we're stretching to make a few of these connections, and as we've already implied, some of these techniques will seem foreign to Japanese negotiators. For example, diversity is not a strong suit for Japanese—purposefully adding women and other elements of diversity (#4) to their groups would seem odd. Moreover, the Japanese are working on some of their own creativity disadvantages. For example, in Japanese elementary schools you can find rows and columns of third graders bowing and chanting in unison their school motto that ironically might include " . . . we will be independent thinkers."

Indeed, we notice similar changes in the Chinese school systems (imitating the Japanese) as they try to bridge what they also see as a creativity gap vis-à-vis the United States. Reporter Ann Hulbert in the *New York Times Magazine* recently asked the uncomfortable questions: Can China create schools that foster openness, flexibility, and innovations? And what happens to China if it does? She adds, "Even as Americans seek to emulate China's test-centered and math-focused pedagogy, Chinese educators are trying to promote a Western emphasis on critical thinking at home. . . . Throughout China, middle school exams have been abolished and vacation review classes are widely discouraged. . . . The Chinese government worries that too many students have become the sort of stressed-out, test-acing drone who lacks the skills necessary in the global marketplace."[7]

However, the key things the Japanese do in international negotiation that Americans can and should learn are the following: (1) The Japanese are the absolute champion information vacuums on the planet. They listen and let everyone else do the talking. Thus, they use the diversity of their international colleagues (customers, suppliers, competitors, scientists, etc.) to a greater extent than any other society. We often disparage it as copying and borrowing, but in fact being open to everyone's ideas has always been the key to creativity and human progress. The Japanese, like everyone else around the world, are ethnocentric. But, at the same time they very much respect foreign ideas; and (2) the Japanese will only work with dolphins, that is, when they have a choice. Trust and creativity go hand-in-hand. And, they will work to train you to behave more like a dolphin for your own good. Witness the 25-year joint venture between Toyota and General Motors as a prominent example. We provide details about this most successful international joint venture in chapter 13.

We challenge you to employ Lynda's list in your own negotiations—planning, execution, and follow-up; that is, in the tail, body, and head of the fish. This thinking should permeate your thinking and interactions.

Application of principles of creativity will be practically and overtly appropriate in at least three points in your negotiations. Earlier we noted that Howard Raiffa's suggestion that principles of creativity be used in pre-negotiation meetings. Second, we advocate their use when impasses are reached. For example, in the negotiations regarding the Rio Urubamba natural gas project described in the introduction, the involved firms and environmentalist groups reached what at the time seemed to be an irreconcilable difference: roads and a huge pipeline through the pristine forest would be an ecological disaster. The creative solution? Think of the remote gas field as an offshore platform, run the pipeline underground, and fly in personnel and equipment as needed.

Second, once you've gotten to "yes," a scheduled review of the agreement may actually get your business relationship past "yes" to truly creative outcomes. Perhaps you schedule such a review six months after implementation of the agreement has begun. But, the point is that time must be set aside for a *creative* discussion of how can we improve on our business relationship. The emphasis of such a session should always be putting new ideas on the table—the answers to the question "what haven't we thought of?"

CONCLUSIONS

Implementing corporate strategies through business negotiations in other countries, particularly the unfamiliar, but fast-growing ones, will remain one of the most daunting and interesting challenges facing American executives during the next few decades. Actually, executives from around the world are quickly learning to work with one another with increasing globalization; particularly as new, large market countries join the World Trade Organization and begin to harmonize commercial practices. Indeed, this book is all about both marking and stimulating what we see as a world standard for business negotiations. Young people are flooding into MBA programs around the world and learning about concepts like corporate image, brand equity, and the ins and outs of intellectual property. The Internet is also making a huge difference, making efficient communication more available. While currently engineers or government officials usually lead companies, the future bodes well for the new business class. Herein we aspire to inspire a new approach in international commerce—one that defines the old ways of competitive and problem-solving negotiation styles as interesting relics, and advocates a new process of negotiations that elevates creativity as the first goal.

In relationship-oriented cultures such as in Indonesia, Nigeria, and China, there are huge advantages to moving first. Old friendships work their magic only when they are *old*. We recommend investing now in such places, if only in a small venture. This activity will allow your executives and your organization to learn the game. You will be able to develop the essential connections and the cross-cultural competence of your own staff toward understanding and growing the business there in these new places. Foreign language skills and cultural knowledge will continue to be crucial. This means that selecting and promoting native speakers of relevant languages on your own staff—and trusting their advice—is necessary.

Other than arrogance, condescension, and ethnocentrism, *time* has always been the American bargainer's biggest handicap in international business. Impatience will be your enemy in almost all foreign countries. But, impatience is your friend when it comes to making the decision about whether to go or not. We advise studied entry, but there is no better time than now to begin your work.

CHAPTER 9

CONTINUING INNOVATION AFTER NEGOTIATIONS

It is not a fish until it is on the bank.
—Irish proverb

O nce verbal agreements have been reached, it is time to consider what follows the negotiations. In the United States, executives usually talk of "concluding business deals." In many countries executives speak of "establishing business relationships," and we hope this latter approach fast becomes more prevalent in the United States. We've already discussed how such differing views influence negotiation processes. Now we will turn to the subject of how they influence post-negotiation procedures.

CONTRACTS

Contracts between American firms are often longer than 100 pages and include carefully-worded clauses regarding every aspect of the agreement. American lawyers go to great lengths to protect their companies against all circumstances, contingencies, and actions of the other party. In a typical American commercial contract, conditional phrases such as, "If . . . ," "In the event . . . ," and "Should . . . ," are often used more than 50 times. Recognizing that no contract can anticipate every eventuality, still the best contracts are deemed the ones so tightly written that the other party would not think of going to court to challenge any provision. Our adversarial legal system requires such contracts.

In most other countries, legal systems are not depended upon to resolve disputes. Indeed, the term "disputes" doesn't reflect how a business relationship should work. Each side should be concerned about the mutual benefits of the relationship, and therefore should consider the interests of the other. Consequently, in many countries, written contracts are very short—two to three pages—and purposefully loosely written. They primarily contain comments on principles of the relationship. From the foreign point of view, the American emphasis on tight contracts is tantamount to planning the divorce before the marriage. Simply stated, contracts in most other countries do not fulfill the same purposes as they do in the United States.

You can get some measure of the importance of contracts by taking a look at exhibit 9.1. Currently in Japan the government is ramping up legal training and the production of attorneys to better serve global, actually American, standards of commercial law. Our Japanese colleagues say American/Japanese contracts now look like American contracts even in length. But, appearances deceive. Even in Japan the legal system doesn't have the capacity to play the commercial litigation game like it's played in the litigious United States. So, contracts mean less and alternative options to resolve disputes are emphasized.

So what form should a contract between a foreign and an American firm take? There is no simple answer. It may have to be negotiated. It depends somewhat on the size and importance of the agreement and the size and experiences of the firms involved. Generally, larger deals justify the extra expense of including a legal review of the contract by both foreign and American lawyers. Large foreign firms with histories of American contracts will understand the Americans' need for detailed contracts. Some foreign firms, recognizing the increasing frequency of litigation between U.S. and foreign firms, will specify the American approach for their own protection. It is the executives of smaller foreign firms, inexperienced in the ways of Americans, who may become suspicious when faced with lengthy, fully detailed contracts. In these cases, it will be particularly important to explain the necessity of the legal review and detailed contract. However, you should realize that even with the most complete explanation not all foreign executives will understand.

An American-style contract will also cause considerable delays in signing. Foreign lawyers will tediously consider every detail. One rule of thumb suggests that every clause takes an entire day to review. Thus,

Exhibit 9.1   Lawyers per 100,000 People*

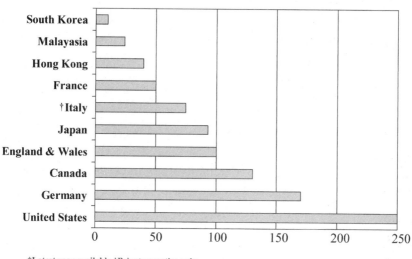

*Latest year available †Private practice only

Source: University of Wisconsin, Institute for Legal Studies

something your legal counsel ordinarily reviews in three days may take three weeks in Bangkok or three months in Lagos.

For example, a California firm was selling training services for executives to First Auto Works, one of China's largest companies. All the prices, content, and other terms and conditions were agreed to and the American firm sent the contract for signatures. However, the Chinese side balked at the "boiler plate" in the contract. The Chinese side simply hadn't seen such standard provisions, and it took another frustrating month before things were finally straightened out.

Thus, it is difficult for us to make general recommendations regarding contracts. Many American executives of even the largest firms have been satisfied with a "compromise" contract when strong, long-standing personal relationships are involved. Ford and Nissan designed and started production of joint-venture cars and the minivans were in customers' garages before the contract was actually signed. That's hundreds of millions of dollars invested without signatures! But each case is different. It is important that you and your firm push for the kind of contract you feel is necessary. And of course, your legal counsel should be consulted on this issue.

The key here is to understand that trust and harmony are more important, particularly to your relationship-oriented counterparts, than any piece of paper. They'll actually be more interested in what James Sebenius and his colleagues call the "spirit of the deal."[1] In many countries, contracts are for reference only and currently mean little, particularly in places like China, Nigeria, Colombia, or Indonesia. Yes, they are becoming increasingly important as countries have joined the WTO, but catching up to the American legal system will take decades. In the meantime, most of your foreign partners will continue to depend on interpersonal harmony.

The Documentation Process

As an overlay to the Fish and as part of open communications, we similarly suggest a simple yet effective legal documentation process.

It has been our experience that relationships and trust must eventually be put down on paper. This usually falls within purview of the legal team. As a general proposition we suggest a documentation process going from a Letter of Intent (LOI) to a Memorandum of Understanding (MOU) to a Definitive Agreement (DA).

The Letter of Intent should normally begin the process. It normally occurs after a sufficient amount of contact and interest has been established. It is usually at this point that legal counsel or someone experienced with such matters drafts the initial concept of the underlying transaction and creates the basis upon which to build the subsequent agreements. It should be noted, however, that the LOI may be binding or non-binding and specific care should be taken to determine what is being drafted in relation to subsequent documents.

Shortly thereafter and depending on the complexity of the transaction, work on the Memorandum of Understanding should begin. In this regard it serves to bridge the gap between the LOI (the initial concepts of the transaction) and the Definitive Agreement (the deal). From an overall perspective, the MOU should serve negotiators well during the various technical (financial, legal, operational, etc.) sidebar negotiations that we refer to within the Fish. In this regard, the MOU should serve as the structural framework upon which to build the underlying transaction and as a checklist that should similarly become the various negotiation points that need to be considered, albeit the "meat and potatoes" of the negotiations.

Finally, and if ideally performed, the Definitive Agreement should be nothing more than a compilation of the concessions and "sub-agreements" reached within the MOU drafting process. Here again, our experience has been such that, if not readily and openly treated up front, as in either the LOI and/or MOU drafting process, unpleasant surprises may surface. From our perspective the DA should be the formalization, the ceremonial culmination, of the deal.

Signing Ceremonies

Informality being a way of life in the United States, even the largest contracts between American firms are often sent through the mail for signature. Here, ceremony is considered a waste of time and money. But when a major agreement is reached with a major foreign client or partner, they will expect the top executives involved to meet and sign the contract with ceremony. We recommend American firms accommodate these expectations.

Headquarters' Assessment of the Agreement

Often U.S. negotiators return to company headquarters with an agreement, only to receive a mixed greeting. Executives at several companies have told us, "The second half of the negotiation begins once I return to the home office." Headquarters, unaware of the requirements of international business negotiations, will ask, "What took so long?" Ordinarily, all compromises and concessions have to be explained and justified in detail. Moreover, commitments requiring specific management actions must be delegated and ordered. All this can slow implementation and performance of the contract. In the worst cases, when negotiator and home office communications have been poor, negotiators have been required to renege and start over. When this occurs, the foreign client or partner will either bypass this executive, who has lost face, or talk to those considered the real decision makers or decline further discussion, thus ending the relationship. Of course, it works this way in the United States as well.

It has been the experience of American firms that once the first deal has been struck with a foreign client or partner, successive negotiations tend to proceed quickly. Therefore, it is generally not necessary to send a complete negotiation team when new issues are to be considered. Clearly, then, it is best to start with a small, relatively simple business proposal. Once the relationship has been established, substantial and complex negotiations will proceed more smoothly. This is the approach used by most foreign firms entering the United States, and it is a sensible strategy when American firms court international business.

FOLLOW-UP COMMUNICATIONS

Just as personal considerations are more important during negotiations with relationship-oriented clients, they are also important after the negotiations are concluded. Obviously, you will be in touch with your overseas clients and partners regarding the business of the relationship. But it will be equally important to keep personal relationships warm.

A formal letter should be sent from your top executive to their top executive expressing happiness that the talks have been concluded successfully and confidence that the new relationship will be prosperous and long-lasting. But even more important will be periodic personal visits with your foreign counterparts. The best way to keep relationships warm in most countries is investing in what Americans call "face time."

One final consideration is crucial when doing business internationally. Avoid switching executives managing your overseas business relationships. In dealing with American clients this is not much of a problem. Here the economics of the business deal are more important than the personal relationships involved. Managers often shift positions within companies and between companies. But in almost all other countries more executives stay with the same company longer. Moreover, foreign executives are given longer-term responsibility for managing intercompany relationships. After all, much was invested in building the personal relations that make business between the companies work smoothly. So when American companies switch key managers, overseas clients get very nervous. Therefore, such shifts should be made with great care, and should be accompanied by new efforts of non-task sounding and rapport building.

DISPUTE RESOLUTION AND MODIFICATIONS TO AGREEMENTS

During the course of almost all business relationships, changes occur in the environment and/or to either partner. In such situations in the United States, the conflicts arising from the changing circumstance would be settled through the use of direct and confrontational legal channels or, as is now more often the case, in arbitration.

In many foreign countries, given the same set of changing circumstances, companies would ordinarily resolve the conflicts through conferral. Thus, local contracts in other countries often include such wording as, "All items not found in this contract will be deliberated and decided upon in a spirit of honesty and trust." When differences can't be ironed out through simple conferral, then the next step is to express concerns through the all-important intermediaries, often the mutual contacts that made the original introductions, who hopefully can mediate a new understanding. Rarely will the confrontational and legal approaches be used in a relationship-oriented culture, for such would destroy the harmony and trust required for continued business dealings, and fledgling legal systems are often plagued by favoritism and inefficiency. Even arbitration is viewed negatively in many countries.

Our recommendation is to include an international arbitration clause in your contract should conflicts arise. For example, "Any controversy or claim arising out of or relating to this contract shall be determined by arbitration in accordance with the rules of the . . ." But even though such measures are included in the contract we suggest a Japanese approach to conflict resolution. That is, approach the dispute from a cooperative standpoint and talk with your international client or partner. Given that you have maintained the harmony and trust, and that you have an honest mutual interest in the deal, then such problems can usually be resolved through simple conferral. The next option is personal mediation with a trusted mutual contact.

The U.S. Department of Commerce provides limited advice and almost no direct help when it comes to dispute resolution in other countries, as is also the case with foreign government bodies. While the Commerce Department of Guatemala offers a few workshops on good business practices, and even huge Russia is working with the Good Governance Program[2] to publish a number of helpful handbooks, assistance in specific situations is rare.

As you might guess, most U.S. government resources are focused on the burgeoning trade with China. Below is pretty much the extent of the help provided for most American companies with commercial disputes in China. Unless your company or industry association has a large lobbying budget significant enough to gain Congressional attention or Executive branch favor, you are pretty much on your own.

There are three primary ways to resolve a commercial dispute in China: *negotiation, arbitration,* and *litigation.* Simple negotiation with your partner is usually the best method of dispute resolution. It is the least expensive and it can preserve the working relationship of the parties involved. In fact, most business contracts in China include a clause stipulating that negotiation should be employed before other dispute settlement mechanisms are pursued. When a foreign firm experiences difficulty in directly negotiating a solution to a dispute with its Chinese partner, companies sometimes seek assistance from Chinese government officials who can encourage the Chinese party to honor the terms of the contract. Companies should specify a time limit for this process. Unfortunately, negotiations do not always lead to resolution.

Arbitration is the next preferred method. Unless the parties can agree on arbitration after the dispute has arisen (which is often difficult), the underlying contract or separate agreement must indicate that disputes will be resolved through arbitration. Agreements to arbitrate usually specify a choice of arbitration body, which may be located in China or abroad, and a choice of law to govern the dispute. There are two Chinese government-sponsored arbitration bodies for handling cases involving at least one foreign party: China International Economic and Trade Arbitration Commission (CIETAC) and, for maritime disputes, China Maritime Arbitration Commission (CMAC). Contracts involving foreign companies doing business in China often provide for CIETAC arbitration. CIETAC distinguishes between two kinds of dispute resolution, foreign-related and domestic. For a dispute to be classified as foreign-related, one of the companies must be a foreign entity without a major production facility or investment in China.

For foreign-related disputes where CIETAC is the selected arbitration body, parties to the contract may specify the nationality of members of the arbitration panel in the contract; CIETAC has implemented contract clauses that stipulate that two of the three arbitrators, including the presiding arbitrator, must be non-Chinese. CIETAC does not have to pre-approve any contractual stipulations on the nationality of the negotiators. CIETAC has published rules which govern the selection of a panel if the contract does not specify how the choice of arbitrators will be handled. CIETAC's list of arbitrators for foreign-related disputes, from which CIETAC's arbitrators must be chosen, includes many non-Chinese arbitrators. Although many foreign experts believe that some aspects of CIETAC need to be improved, it has developed a good reputation.

Companies should be aware when drafting a contract that, as an alternative to CIETAC or CMAC, they can specify an arbitration body outside China, such as Singapore, Stockholm or Geneva. In addition, Hong Kong—under one country, two systems—has a separate and well-regarded international commercial arbitration system. In 1987, China acceded to the United Nations Convention on the Recognition and Enforcement of Foreign Arbitral Awards (the New York Convention).

Under the New York Convention, arbitral awards rendered in other signatory countries are recognized and enforceable in China. By the same token, arbitral awards by Chinese arbitration bodies are enforceable in other countries signatory to the New York Convention.

A final way to resolve a commercial dispute in China is through litigation in Chinese courts. In China, foreign individuals and companies have the same ability to bring action in court as Chinese citizens and companies. There are three levels of courts in China. Every major city has basic courts and intermediate courts. Supervising these courts are the provincial high courts. The Supreme People's Court, located in Beijing, has appellate jurisdiction over all courts in China. Cases involving foreign interests can be filed in either the basic-level courts or intermediate courts, depending on their nature. Most observers agree that Chinese courts are not up to international standards. For instance, most judges have minimal or no legal training and observers have stated those poorly trained court officials are susceptible to corruption and regional protectionism.

In both the arbitration and litigation contexts, mediation represents an early step in the resolution of the dispute. In arbitration before CIETAC or in litigation before the Chinese courts, parties are encouraged to participate in mediation with mediators selected by the arbitral panel or during an in-court session, respectively. The principle of mediation is that the parties may present their proposals to the mediator who suggests a solution based on those proposals. Mediation is by definition non-binding and has achieved great success as a means of settling international commercial disputes between foreign and Chinese parties.

In China, arbitration offers many advantages over litigation. A major advantage is the finality of the rulings. Court rulings are subject to appeal, which means litigation may continue for years. As indicated above, judges in China are often poorly qualified, while arbitration panels are made up of a panel of experts, which improves the quality of the hearing. In addition, the proceedings and rules of arbitration are often more transparent than litigation.

Many observers have noted that it is often difficult for parties to enforce and obtain payment on court judgments and arbitral awards in China. While courts are required to receive approval from the Supreme People's Court prior to refusing to enforce a foreign arbitral award, courts have occasionally circumvented this requirement by employing delaying tactics when local interests are adversely affected by the arbitration rulings. The Supreme People's Court has issued new guidelines to limit the ability of local courts to delay enforcement and this appears to have had a positive effect.

The Role of the U.S. Government in Commercial Disputes

American companies involved in a dispute often approach the Department of Commerce and other U.S. agencies in China or the United States for assistance. The Department can provide companies with assistance in navigating China's legal system, provide a list of local attorneys, and share basic information on potentially applicable trade agreements and relevant Chinese business practices. The Department is not able to provide American companies or individuals with legal advice.

American companies that have disputes with private firms often request U.S. Government intervention with Chinese authorities on their behalf. Such intervention is rarely appropriate unless the company has exhausted all remedies under China's legal system. The Department's efforts in assisting with commercial disputes are aimed at achieving a fair and timely resolution in accordance with Chinese law and advancing both countries' interest in adequate legal and judicial protection for all parties.

When a dispute is in the Chinese court system, Embassy officers will intervene on behalf of an American company only in extremely limited circumstances and in accordance with U. S. government guidelines.

Disputes Involving the Chinese Government

When a U.S. firm has a dispute with the Chinese Government, a Chinese state-owned enterprise, or a government-subsidized project, the most effective initial step is to quietly raise the issue with the entities involved, citing the importance of foreign companies' investment in China. The firm should explain its situation to the Chinese entity, and offer to work with it to resolve the problem amicably. This allows for a more aggressive approach at a later date, if necessary. The Department can work with companies in considering the best strategy.

While China is obligated to fully implement the terms of its trade agreements, including the WTO once it is a member, differences over implementation may arise. In such circumstances, the Department is committed to working with firms and the Chinese Government to ensure full compliance. Generally, U.S. Embassy staff and Washington agencies will work directly with concerned companies, or the industry association, to identify solutions and formulate strategies. If appropriate, the Embassy will advocate on behalf of the American companies with Chinese officials. If the dispute cannot be resolved at this level, and additional U.S. Government support is appropriate, the U.S. involvement will usually involve increasingly senior level officials of the appropriate U.S. Government agencies. If compliance with WTO obligations underlies the dispute, the U.S. Government will examine the possible use of WTO dispute settlement procedures. In reaching a dispute resolution strategy, a firm should consider all possibilities, including negotiation, arbitration, mediation or litigation, and the time and expense that it may take to resolve the problem.[3]

We note that CIETAC has been the busiest commercial arbitration institution on the planet during the last few years. Regarding fairness, in some years foreign firms have won the majority of cases. Still, foreign criticism has been leveled at CIETAC procedures, particularly related to the difficulty of collecting awards. One Hong Kong party that received a $400,000 award by CIETAC so far has only been able to collect a mere $20,000. Most recently, in response to criticism from foreign companies, the Chinese authorities have made two significant changes to CIETAC arbitration rules.[4] First, now arbitrators can be appointed from outside the commission's own panel, including foreigners. Second, the arbitration period has been shortened from nine to six months. These adjustments suggest that Chinese authorities are interested in advancing CIETAC's services to international standards—but work still needs to be done.

CONCLUSIONS

Many experienced Americans report that even with a signed contract negotiations are actually never really completed; and what Americans call "careful follow-up" is really just the continuing maintenance of an ever-evolving business relationship. Indeed, as we recommended in the last chapter, a regularly scheduled (semi-annual or annual) business relationship review will be the best way to positively prevent disputes. Indeed, if the business relationship is evolving and hopefully growing, then changes should be periodically made to contracts, or even more important, to the spirit of the relationship. Such meetings must always begin with "How can we make this relationship better?" and "What haven't we thought of?" Actually, getting your foreign fish to the bank is just half of the job. The other half is keeping it alive and growing.

PART III

COUNTRY/CULTURE SPECIFICS

U p to this point in the book you may be happy with the general advice we've provided about international negotiations, but at the same time you may be thinking it's not quite enough. If you're about to negotiate in Cairo, you will want specific advice on negotiation in Egypt. So far all we've done is teach you about fishing, to use our well-worn metaphor. We haven't gotten down to teaching you the differences between fishing in streams and lakes, or between deep sea and spear fishing!

The Ten Rules for Fishing might be:

1. You can't catch fish unless you have a baited hook in the water.
2. Patience is premium.
3. Keep your mouth shut; fish don't like talk.
4. Once you hook one, keep the tip of your pole up.
5. Keep the line tight, but not too tight.
6. Let the fish exhaust itself.
7. Keep your thumb on the reel to prevent backlash.
8. Keep a baseball bat in the boat for the really big ones.
9. Catch and release unless you're going to eat the thing yourself.
10. Don't catch too many.

The last two would be the "new rules" of twenty-first century fishing. Indeed, we've seen two fisheries collapse out here in California—Monterey Bay sardines and abalone. We're saddest about the latter. But what about fishing for bone fish in Belize, marlins off Baja, or trout in New Zealand? Moreover, the rules above only apply to amateurs. We figure Rule #1 for professionals is "keep a life preserver near"—the deck of a fishing boat is one of the most dangerous places on earth.

Now, in Part III of the book we begin to provide advice about negotiating in specific places—India, Mexico, and China. This covers more than one-third of the planet. We think of these three chapters as a kind of anchovy (bait or *hors d'oeuvre*) to lead you to the website associated with our book—www.GlobalNegotiationBook.com. You will not only be able to view similar passages about many other key countries, but also your fellow readers' comments. Thus, the book you have in your hands becomes the key to this much larger set of dynamic knowledge about international negotiations.

By the way, we chose these three countries not just because of their size, but also because they well represent a cultural progression with respect to distance from the English language and all the other cultural concepts presented in previous chapters. That is, from the American perspective, among these three, India is closest, Mexico is next, and then China is farthest away. Of course, the proximity we're talking about is cultural, since no country is physically closer to the United States than Mexico, and none is further than India. See exhibit 2.3 (page 41) for the numbers. Moreover, it can be argued that American culture has moved closer to Mexican as immigration from Mexico has surged during the last decades. Finally, recall our earlier comments about the substantial cultural differences *within* such large countries in particular. In all three countries it will be crucial that you apply our guidelines, but you must also get to know the people you will be working with. Remember, cultures, countries, and companies don't negotiate. People do.

CHAPTER 10

THE INDIAN NEGOTIATION STYLE

THE FAR SIDE OF THE WORLD

D rill a hole from Omaha through the center of the earth and you won't hit China; you'll actually hit the middle of the Indian Ocean. So, at least in terms of time zones, India is the farthest market from the United States. Of course, we do have democracy and English in common, more or less. But we know from our studies of international trade patterns that time zones are more important determinants of trade between countries than are mere miles or cultural similarities. Consequently, Americans have had little interaction with India over the decades since her independence in 1947. An emphasis on economic self-reliance, well reflected in Gandhi's spinning wheel (*Ashoka Chakra*) on the national flag, and a close political association with the Soviet Union didn't help either. Yes, the internet cures some of the temporal distance problem, but it doesn't alleviate the sleep lost to the worst possible jet lag or late-night conference calls.

Most Americans don't know much about India. We develop impressions from our frequent interactions with the Indian Diaspora, or what Joel Kotkin in his excellent book *Tribes* calls "The Greater India."[1] More than 60,000 Indians legally immigrate to the United States every year, and almost all are well educated, bringing a wealth of creativity to places like Silicon Valley. What Americans generally misunderstand about India is the great cultural diversity of the actual country—a quick look at the ubiquitous 20-rupee note suggests its degree. Fifteen languages are listed:

Hindi, the official national language and the primary native tongue of about 30 percent of the people; 13 other official languages; and English. With its "associate status," English is still the most important language for national, political, and commercial communication. About 80 percent of the people are Hindu, 13 percent Muslim, 2 percent Christian, and 2 percent Sikh. Each of its 26 states and 6 union-territories has its own ethnic culture and often its own language. Most agree that there is more cultural diversity on the subcontinent than among European countries! International negotiations expert Lothar Katz reports, for example, "The business culture can be quite diverse and regional style differences may be significant. While Southern Indian companies, especially those around Bangalore and Hyderabad, tend to be progressive in some ways, southern Indians are often more sober and conservative than the more extroverted Northerners."[2]

While Greater China is also quite culturally diverse, it often has been ruled as one geographical/political entity over the millennia. India's history is very different. Events in one region often had little effect on others, and "Indian history is marked by political fragmentation and regional fiefdoms that nourished wide linguistic, cultural, and religious differences."[3] Of course, all this changed substantially in 1858 when the British won control of the subcontinent, beginning their 89-year *Raj* (Hindi for "rule"). But it will still be worth your while to ask your Indian counterparts how their home region(s) of India differ from the rest of the country. And, by the way, they'll be proud to tell you.

With this caveat about cultural diversity as a backdrop, we now turn to the common threads of Indian culture that will manifest themselves at the international negotiation table.

A RELATIONSHIP-ORIENTED CULTURE WITH A VENEER OF BRITISH INDIVIDUALISM

During the Raj the British delivered the English language, British legal and educational systems, a British-style bureaucracy, and, of course, cricket. The colonials also united the country through guns and trade. So on top of the rough-hewn cultural diversity there now exists a thick veneer of British organization and traditions that has made negotiations simpler in some ways. But the veneer can be deceptive; English-speaking Americans, in particular, can find themselves lulled into an inefficient complacency.

Fundamentally, Indians share a relationship-oriented culture. A quick reference to Geert Hofstede's scale shows India to be a collectivistic (48 compared to America's 91) and hierarchical culture (77 compared to America's 40). See exhibit 2.3 (page 41) for details. Indeed, the literature on the Indian negotiation style is consistent with the implications of the strong relationship orientation Hofstede's numbers predict. Indian culture is high-context, collectivistic, high-power distance, polychromic, linguistically indirect, and background-focused. It achieves efficiency through reduction of transaction costs, and nepotism and bribery are more common. All of these factors hold important implications for negotiations with businesspeople from Greater India.

Rajesh Kumar describes well the consequences of this grand mix of cultural influences in his native country.

> A unique feature of the Indian mindset is that it combines both individualistic and collectivist tendencies. As individualists, Indians are very goal-oriented and aggressive, traits that are not unlike those of the North Americans. At the same time, however, the Indians are a very family-oriented people and confine and ration their loyalties and affections only among those who are close to them. It is the simultaneous presence of individualism and collectivism that distinguishes the Indian manager not only from his North American counterpart but also from his East Asian peer who is unquestioningly collectivist in his or her orientation. Scholars have long debated whether India is part of the East or the West. They have come to the conclusion that the Indians are, on the whole, more Western than Eastern in their way of thinking. This implies that the Indians can behave either in an individualistic or a collectivist manner, depending on the situation. The heightened context sensitivity of the Indian manager may make it difficult for the North American manager to fully understand his counterpart's actions. As a Western manager put it, "I feel that the most difficult thing is that the Indians will tell you one thing, think another, and do a third thing, which is not what a Dane would do." A further implication is that the Indian negotiator is not a good team player. Beyond the confines of the familial in-group, the Indian negotiator does not work well as part of a team due to the ingrained belief that he is right and the other person is wrong. I refer to this tendency as "anarchical individualism."[4]

"Anarchical individualism"—yikes! Let's take a look at the implications of this for the process of negotiating with Indians. The key for you will be to get through the apparently haphazard cultural thicket we have described

Exhibit 10.1   Summary of Differences in American and Indian Negotiation Styles

Category	American	Indian
Basic Cultural Values and Ways of Thinking	Individualism	Collectivism and Individualism
	Egalitarianism	Hierarchy
	Information-Oriented	Relationship-Oriented
	Reductionism	Holism
	Content	Context
	Practical	Idealistic
Negotiation Process		
1. Nontask-Sounding	Short	Can be short
2. Task-related exchange of information	Brief	Tedious
	Directness	Indirectness (face)
	"Cards on the table"	Copious questions
	Proposals first	Explanations first
3. Persuasion	Aggressive, persuasive tactics (threats, promises, arguments, and logic): "You need this."	Thickly padded prices Strategic delays Toughness, shrewdness Opportunities for creativity
4. Concessions and agreement	Sequential	Few, holistic
	Goal = "a good deal"	Goal = very high aspirations, creativity
	Fairness = process, merit-based	Fairness = outcome, need-based

on the path to the *creativity* inherent in the rich cultural soup that is now twenty-first century India.

THE NEGOTIATION PROCESS

Non-Task Sounding

Be careful here. Some advisers suggest that in the beginning not much is invested in non-task sounding, and this will seem comfortable to most Americans. That is, Indians get down to business quickly. But, to make commercial relationships work, to transform commercial relationships into the most valuable, creative kind, strong personal relationships are required in India. Additionally, while you will end up with a well-written contract, reference to the legal system to manage disputes usually isn't a viable alternative in India. Trust and liking are key for preventing and/or managing disputes between business partners. And these crucial criteria of success can only be met by investing time in relationship-building activities *throughout* the negotiation process.

Also representative of a relationship culture is the importance of intermediaries—friends, classmates, consultants, or agents. While cold-calls are described as acceptable, the way to get things going is an introduction to a high-level executive. The intermediary then provides the key conduit of trust upon which you will still need to build throughout the negotiations and implementation of commercial activities.

Business lunches are more traditional, but breakfasts or dinners may also be appropriate (depending on the person, the relationship, and/or the region) for getting to know and trust clients and partners. If you really want to spend some time, ask to see a cricket match! The safest approach is to ask the client or partner what they would prefer or if they have suggestions. An invitation to someone's home means things are going well.

Task-Related Exchange of Information

The folks we have worked with often describe the information exchange with Indians as tedious. While the American approach is to first make the proposal and then ask for questions, the Indian approach is to frontload the presentation with more background information than seems necessary. References are particularly important, such as what other big companies use the product or system. All of this is what you should expect in a relationship-oriented culture vis-à-vis an information-oriented one. The histories of companies and who founded and currently runs them is key information to the big-picture thinking of your Indian counterparts. While Americans value focus, Indians pay more attention to the context of proposals and particularly the people involved.

Americans also complain about the plethora of questions on seemingly unimportant topics and the dearth of information provided by their Indian counterparts on key issues. Typical of relationship-oriented cultures, negative feedback is eschewed in favor of neutral or falsely positive reactions to unacceptable proposals, all in the interest of maintaining interpersonal harmony. Negative hints, delays, simply ignoring issues in the hopes they will fade away, or ambiguous answers such as "we will think about it" are all commonly employed.

The only antidotes to this tedious process are your own patience and a willingness to ask key questions in other ways and in other circumstances. It is also helpful to pay attention to the references, names dropped, and other contextual clues as openings for creative solutions to otherwise intractable problems. Remember, your primary job in a negotiation is to find out what is important to your clients. What may appear inane to you may be important to them. Pay attention. Listen carefully. Take notes.

Persuasion

Everyone agrees that people in India are tough negotiators. Everything is negotiable in India, so bargaining is a daily part of existence. Thick price padding is common, but so are large concessions to move things along. Americans tend to react to "unreasonable" first offers in one of two emotion-laden ways—they get mad or they laugh. Often they walk out of meetings, and perhaps not so politely. Anticipating thickly padded prices, far beyond the typical American approach of "about 20 percent," can lead to a more patient response. Americans must avoid the tendency to let Indian negotiators set a deep anchoring point in their favor when they make aggressive first offers. Americans should instead ask their Indian counterparts how they arrived at that first offer.

Strategic delays are also commonly used. Everyone knows Americans are in a hurry, and making them wait usually yields concessions from them. But Indians are not in a hurry and generally subscribe to what anthropologist Edward T. Hall describes as a polychronic orientation to time. Meetings may be canceled or delayed. Always bring something along to read on your trips to India, plan schedules loosely, and, perhaps most frustrating, expect delays in implementation of agreements and delivery on promises.

Negotiations in India can get heated, just like anywhere else. But this will not happen often. Interpersonal harmony and saving face are important values in Indian culture.

While Americans worry about fair processes, Indians worry about fair outcomes. This difference manifests itself at the negotiation table in the form of Indian requests for fair treatment for all parties in the negotiations. The colonial experience heightens the Indian sensitivity to exploitative agreements. Moreover, as Rajesh Kumar explains, whereas " . . . the perception of equity in North America rests on the norm of proportionality; i.e., the greater the effort the greater the outcome, equity in India is more need based."[5] So, their appeals for fairness will sound particularly odd to American negotiators well-soaked in Adam Smith's economic bath.

Perhaps the greatest opportunity among the cross-cultural differences in persuasion styles is the Indian idealism that results from the combination of their spiritual/philosophical traditions and wonderful analytical skills. When the going gets tough, and things appear to be headed downhill, we recommend application of Rule #1: *Accept only creative outcomes.* Indian negotiators will tend to take this as a worthwhile challenge, one worthy of their vaunted imaginations. It will be the best argument for a creative sidebar negotiation.

Concessions and Agreements

Americans working with Indians often complain about not being able to measure progress. Certainly the aforementioned delays are part of the problem. But the holistic approach of Indian negotiators versus the sequential approach of Americans is often the main cause of the latter's frustrations. To Americans, it appears that Indians aren't willing to make any concessions (until the end) and they keep bringing up what Americans thought were closed issues.

Moreover, decisions tend to be made at the top, based on a combination of extensive research *and* intuition. This allows for personal and/or emotional appeals based on high-quality relationships as well as the usually objective, information-based appeals more typical of Americans. Loyal subordinates do the research, but concessions and decisions won't be made at the negotiation table unless the decision maker is there.

Finally, as mentioned earlier, contracts aren't quite so useful in India. While some investment in well-written contracts is still necessary, their worth is discounted by a legal system that is not quite as efficient as American businessmen are used to and a particularly elastic view about performance commitments. The bottom line is that most Indians view contracts as simply the beginning of a business relationship wherein ultimately flexibility remains a crucial criterion of commerce.

OTHER ISSUES

Nepotism's Role in the Indian Business System

Like almost all relationship-oriented cultures, familial relations are extremely important, and nepotism is an important consideration in the Indian business system. Joel Kotkin explains this well:

> Indian business has followed to a remarkable extent the model of the "joint family company" whose origins lie in India's earliest history, deriving

largely from the economic and social patterns of agricultural village life. Unlike Western societies, where the "rationalist economic order" and the division of property among heirs has dominated, property in this system is held in common, making each son, at least theoretically, an equal co-owner and inheritor.

In the corporate world, the joint family can mean not just sharing in the ownership of the enterprise but living in the same house, with a common kitchen and family worship. Increasingly, however, such family control has been exercised more subtly, through the elaborate use of subsidiaries, with essential control remaining in the hands of family members and kinsmen.

Even into the 1990s, many prominent Indian capitalist enterprises—the Tatas, Hindujah, Reddys, Harilelas, Birlas—continue to follow an essentially family-based model. This pattern has been further accentuated by the importance of particular subgroups, who in their own way may have formed their own well-developed, family-based networks, sometimes on a global scale.

This pattern extends even to the Parsis, arguably the most sophisticated and cosmopolitan of all India's "tribes within tribes." Even the most powerful Parsi group, the Tatas, has remained—despite the increased use of professional managers—largely in family hands, with the disproportionate influence by fellow Parsis in upper management and directors.[6]

At the negotiation table this means that company loyalty will play a key role in negotiation behavior and thinking, particularly when family business is involved. Appeals to individual negotiators' interests on the Indian side of the table will have little effect compared to potential benefits accruing to one's entire "tribe."

Corruption and Bribery

As reported in Exhibit 3.4 (page 63), India flunks the corruption test. It's tied at #70 with Brazil, China, Mexico, and Peru, all with scores of 3.5 on Transparency International's Corruption Perception Index (CPI). America gets a C at #20 and a score of 7.2 on the same scale.

Most of the corruption problem is attributable to the government bureaucracy that so often is involved in business transactions in India. Our favorite scandal regards a police raid on a telecommunications minister's home that found so many rupees tumbling out of plastic bags, suitcases, and bed linens that it took authorities almost two days to count it all![7]

As described in chapter 4, the United States Foreign Corrupt Practices Act (FCPA) forbids paying bribes to government officials in all foreign countries. The Organization for Economic Cooperation and Development (OECD) countries are now following suit in passing comparable prohibitions. The implications for negotiators are clear: when asked for bribes, refusal is the only professional response.

Finally, we do note that India has been improving recently in the CPI with scores improving from 2.9 to 3.3 to 3.5 during the last two years. But the improvement is slow.

There are several lessons for international negotiators in the GECIS story described in exhibit 10.2.

Exhibit 10.2 An Illustrative Case of How Well Things Can Work

GECIS is India's largest and one of the oldest Business Process Outsourcing (BPO) companies, and can safely claim to be the pioneer that triggered the global BPO boom in India that now has every international company of significance establishing similar activities in the country.

When the Indian economy started to grow after the liberalization process was initiated in 1991, GE Capital started operations with its commercial and consumer finance services, the latter as a joint venture with an Indian partner, HDFC. Both these businesses helped GE Capital establish itself in India and set up the base to enter into a major credit card operation as a joint venture with the State Bank of India. With a firm base now in the country, GE Capital was ready to look at other businesses in India.

GECIS actually had an unintended start in 1998. Promod Bhandari, an Indian expatriate chartered accountant working in GE's corporate finance division in Connecticut, was sent out to India to support its appliances business. By then British Airways and American Express had positioned a small portion of their global "backroom" operations to India. Bhandari sensed an opportunity there for GE. With the help of an ex-American Express employee and the full support of the then–vice president of GE Capital, an eight-person team was set up to handle simple address changes. The idea of remote processing services grew out of a company brainstorming session that identified BPO as a possible business, leveraging India's ample supply of well-educated, English-speaking manpower available at highly competitive rates.

With the initial success of this trial activity, the BPO operation, now titled GECIS, was expanded to undertake more work for other divisions of GE. The local workforce was rapidly expanded. Because of the unavailability of adequate numbers of people with BPO experience, bright youngsters from the call center business, hotels, airlines, and courier services were hired at a rate of 50 managers and 500 operators every month.

A group of managers was put together to visit GE operations in many other countries and pitch for new business, highlighting the skill sets and capabilities available with the Indian operations—especially that of remotely handling back-office operations. Senior managers were imparted with thorough voice and skill training, etiquette, as well as process orientation. They were also sent overseas for rigorous advanced training. The team was now ready to deliver the highest possible international standard of business process outsourcing. It was also time to move up the value chain.

Overcoming the initial resistance within GE to outsourcing, and given the backing of then-CEO Jack Welch himself, as many as 700 processes were sent out to India to take advantage of the talent pool available to GECIS at cost advantages of over 50 percent. GECIS was now doing advanced analytics, network security, accounting, claims processing, and customer technical support in addition to basic voice-based call center operations. The combined workforce at Gurgaon, Hyderabad, Jaipur, and Bangalore operations was now a staggering 12,000 employees with an additional 4,000 at backup centers in China, Hungary, and Mexico (but reporting to the Gurgaon Headquarters). The annual turnover of GECIS leaped to US$420 million, which now included revenues from services provided to third parties.

With Jeffrey Immelt replacing Jack Welch at the helm of GE, there was, however, a rethink at headquarters about the positioning of GECIS within the larger framework of GE's global operations, however useful and profitable the company proved to be. As Scott Bayman himself has stated, "GECIS was funny money. We are a technology company and wanted to unleash the capability of GECIS, which is not a strategic fit." On November 9, 2004, GE sold a 60 percent stake in GECIS to two global private equity firms (General Atlantic Partners and Oak Hill Capital Partners) in a whopping $500 million deal.[8]

GE's entry strategy in 1991 when India finally began to open to American enterprise was correctly a joint venture with a local company. They started small and incrementally expanded their ventures in India. Essential to the creation of GECIS was Indian expatriate Promod Bhandari's travel back to his home country to develop business—his knowledge of the local culture and business system was key to laying the negotiating groundwork for the operation. The entire enterprise also demonstrates GE's flexibility and creativity in responding to unforeseen opportunities. We also particularly appreciate the authors' mention of the timely "brainstorming" session in the development of the business. Finally, we note the foundational role to be played in the decades to come by the GECIS employees, thousands of them well trained in language and cultural skills, in building global cooperation, enterprise, and progress. Indeed, their youthful brains and broadened commercial skills will serve them well in the global negotiations of the future, ultimately making the far side of the world not so far away!

Finally, we leave you with the following summary points:

Summary Implications

1. Have patience during information exchange.
2. Have patience during persuasion process.
3. Make no concession until the end.
4. Expect thickly padded prices, and appeals to different kind of fairness.
5. Remain firm and consistent.
6. Don't get mad, save face.
7. Be vigilant for creative options.
8. Contracts have little meaning, so good personal relationships are essential throughout the process.

CHAPTER 11

THE MEXICAN NEGOTIATION STYLE

M any Americans sense that they have an understanding of Mexico and of the Mexican people in general. Mexican culture permeates the U.S. Southwest and for most it is the basis of our knowledge. Considering its proximity to the United States and the long history shared by the two countries, we can most certainly claim a fairly good level of knowledge about our neighbors. That is, we "feel" that we understand them. But, Mexican American culture is not Mexican culture, but rather a hybrid. Perhaps even a culture unto itself. Thus, the comfortable familiarity of Mexican American culture gives way as we travel away from the border. To understand Mexican culture, therefore, it is essential to go deeper into the country.

To understand Mexican culture is to search for an identity that is the product of multiple influences. The more distant from the United States, the more distinct the culture becomes. Here we begin to understand the complexity of Mexican identity and work specifically to integrate its components into the new rules.

THE BEGINNINGS OF MEXICAN CULTURE

Mexican history is a complex mixture of pre-Hispanic Mesoamerican indigenous tribes, U.S., Spanish, and other European influences within a highly diverse geography. And, history is more important to Mexicans than Americans. We strongly advise anyone seeking to work extensively within Mexico to study its history[1] and learn Spanish as well. Current Mexican thought, particularly with reference to Americans, cannot be understood without reference to their history. And to speak Spanish is to interact at a much more sophisticated level.

Mexico can be said to have had five major ancient civilizations: the Olmec, Teotihuacan, the Toltec, the Mexica, and the Maya. The modern name "Mexico" comes from the name of the ruling group of the "Aztec Triple Alliance," the "Mexica." These various tribes formed the foundation upon which the subsequent cultural influence of the Spanish was added.

In 1519, this native culture was invaded by Spain. Two years, later Hernan Cortes conquered the Aztec capital of Tenotichtlan creating "New Spain." The intermingling of the indigenous culture and the Spanish culture led to the creation of "mestizo" culture. That is, the soldiers did not bring women with them. So, most of Mexico is now a product of that mixing of the two cultures. Implicit within this mixture are issues of cultural identity, class distinctions, and national pride.

In many ways, the modern era in Mexico began with the Carlos Salinas de Gotari administration (1988–1994). Although many administrations before had attempted to bring Mexico onto the world stage,[2] it was only during the Salinas administration—in 1994—that the North American Free Trade Agreement (NAFTA) was negotiated. It was NAFTA that catalyzed the most extensive privatization of state-owned enterprises in Mexican history and a huge new flow of foreign direct investment. The country was challenged by the pace of change as evinced by the devaluation of the peso in 1994, the resulting economic crisis, the associated corruption scandals, and the alleged links to the murders of presidential candidate, Luis Donaldo Colosio, and Francisco Ruiz Massieu, another powerful political leader. In this manner, the Salinas administration reflected the underlying yearnings of Mexico as a society: namely, seeking to be within the community of nations evolving toward an interactive economic reality, while being subject to the internal limitations of its history. It was through the Salinas administration, for better or worse, that Mexico became inextricably intertwined within the international economic order. And, in that role, Mexico continues to search for an identity separate from that of Spain and also independent from that of the *Gigante al Norte* (the Giant to the North).

The United States of America is an ever-present force in the socioeconomic as well as the cultural/political life of the United States of Mexico.[3] "Pobre Mexico tan lejos de Dios, tan cerca a los Estados Unidos . . ." (Poor Mexico, so far away from God, so close to the United States) perhaps best reflects this relationship. The United States and Mexico not only share a common border, but also a common history across that border. Mexicans will treat a *"gringo"*[4] differently (at times better, at times worse) because of that common history. To ignore this is to ignore a key point in understanding Mexican culture.

Although you would think that Mexicans have the most conflicted attitudes toward Spain because of its invasion and the corresponding enslavement of the populace, they actually don't. Rather, that position is reserved for the United States. That is, they often view *Norte Americanos* from the United States (Mexico is also part of the Americas), as cold, materialistic, and overbearing. But, they also admire the *"gringo* democracy, prosperity and technological achievements."[5]

In fact, it may be argued that it is precisely because of this proximity that both U.S. and Mexican cultures, especially those along the border regions, are best called hybrid cultures. As we know, Mexican American culture contains its own unique characteristics. As one travels deeper into the country, this hybrid nature tends to fade into more fundamental "national" cultures. And in this regard, each region of Mexico is similarly influenced by the underlying indigenous culture and its geography.

Mexico is a highly polarized society. Power and wealth are limited to a privileged few. Estimates claim 80 percent of the wealth is controlled by 10 percent of the population. Approximately 40 percent of the population lives below the poverty line.[6] Most of the poverty is found within the indigenous populace.

Mexico may be divided into five distinct regions:

El Distrito Federal (D.F.)—Mexico City
El Norte—the Border Area
The Central Part—Guadalajara
The Southeast—Oaxaca and Yucatán
Baja—Tijuana and Cabo San Lucas

As mentioned above, El Norte may be said to have its own cultural attributes as distinct from those of, say, El Distrito Federal, or of the Southeast, Oaxaca and Yucatán. These cultural differences stem largely from the indigenous populations of each region and/or the diverse geography. Whereas Mexico City, D.F., is the capital and most populated city in Mexico, Oaxaca is perhaps the region with the most native people. The first is a large, highly congested, mile-high urban metropolis, and the latter is a rural, poverty-stricken, lush sub-tropical jungle. Any businessperson would be well advised to not only understand Mexico's overall history, but also the particular subtleties of the various regions as well.

With this historical, geographical, and cultural diversity as backdrop, key cultural characteristics can still be delineated. Perhaps most importantly is the concept of time and the "*mañana* phenomenon." Although this concept has been overly used and often abused, it does hold underlying significance that merits closer attention. In saying "*mañana*," literally "tomorrow," the Mexican negotiator is alluding to two distinct concepts. On the one hand, he is saying that the particular task can wait until tomorrow—this is the common interpretation. However, often imbedded a bit deeper in the use of the term is the implication that although the task may be difficult to complete immediately, it is *hoped* that tomorrow may bring about a resolution. In this regard, the fatalistic nature of the Mexican culture is imbued with a sense of *hope,* even optimism, that tomorrow may be better. In many ways, this *mañana* phenomenon has been misinterpreted to mean laziness or procrastination. But, in reality it may also represent an unwillingness to confront a negative or difficult situation immediately because of many other factors. It underscores the role that determinism has within the culture, the more complex socio/philosophical concepts of fatalism.

So the new rules applied in negotiations with Mexicans includes comprehending this nuanced meaning of this most familiar term, *mañana.* Below we describe 11 other elements of Mexican culture that must also be considered by gringo negotiators.

THE ELEVEN ELEMENTS

La Familia

The concept of family is critical and fundamental within Mexican society. It may include a more extended definition than a typical U.S. family. In this regard "family" may include extended family and even close personal friends. Furthermore, within a business environment, nepotism is to be expected. Nepotism is interpreted as "trust-based management structure," and from this perspective who more to trust than your family. Indeed, Mexico is a great example of the bad advice in the iconic *Getting to Yes*—separating the people from the problem is not possible in a family business.

Amigos

Simply stated, Mexicans prefer to do business with people they know. This is a truism applicable to most, if not all, cultures of the world. But, in the concept is the inherent uncertainty that dealing with the unknown conveys. As mentioned above, amigos can become *familia*. Such close friends have *confianza*.

Confianza

The ultimate level of trust and intimacy is characterized in Spanish by the word "*confianza*." Although it comes from the Latin cognate found in "confidence," it means much more in Hispanic culture. It also includes the concepts of reliance and trust. To state that you have "confianza" with someone is to declare a level of trust that clearly entails special consideration and favors. Such *confianza* is reserved only for that small number of people that have such a trusting, reciprocal relationship. You may hear the expression: "*Hay confianza*." (There is trust, reliance, and confidence with this particular individual.) Perhaps the most important aspect of negotiations for Mexicans is *confianza*.

Riesgo

This concept is related to a propensity to take risks. As a general proposition, Mexicans are more inclined to take risks than other cultures. In many ways, such an attitude underlies Mexicans' attitudes toward authority and the rule of law. But, just as important is the deterministic bent, coupled with a certain fatalistic attribute that hopes for *mañana*.

Although Americans are considered risk-takers, the concept of taking a risk is usually with regard to a financial perspective. That is, the level of risk can be quantified. Within Mexican culture, the concept of risk also includes the risk of loss of friendship, family, and/or relationships. Loyalty to the underlying relationship becomes one of the risk factors that must be addressed. And these latter notions usually defy quantification.

La Ley

The concept of rule of law. Adherence to the rule of law is subject to underlying societal predispositions toward history and authority. Understanding the legal/regulatory regime of Mexico can only be accomplished by competent Mexican counsel. But, too much reliance on the rule of law is a typical characteristic of U.S. negotiators working with Mexicans. The latter tend to be more interested in personal relationships than laws. However, as Mexico becomes more interlinked with the global economy, legal considerations are becoming more important. Our story below is a marker of such changes.

Punta Banda, Baja California. A few years back, in Baja, a group of gringo homeowners were in a legal battle to quiet the title to their prospective properties on the coast. Among the other interested parties were Mexican nationals, an *ejido*,[7] and large developers. The latter claimed actual the title, and that the transference of title to the Americans was fraudulent and/or ineffective. Previously, many such disputes had been decided by the depth of the Americans' pockets, that is, their financial clout and political influence with the Mexican authorities. Moreover, there was a more general concern about the bad press of ousting the Americans and the associated negative effects on future investments by foreigners in Mexico.

So, with some confidence, the Americans held fast to a losing proposition, avoiding a compromise when all indications were that, in fact, they had obtained title without the requisite title searches. The legal proceedings lasted more than 16 years. But, apparently gringos had sold to gringos without a good understanding of the underlying legal/regulatory system. And eventually the Supreme Court of Mexico ordered eviction of the American tenants from the land. The press got wind of this and had great fun with the story. Many in the United States viewed the event as just one more example of the risks of working and investing in Mexico. However, the more sophisticated saw Punta Banda, as it came to be known, as an example of the rule of law being applied in an appropriate way, much to the surprise and the chagrin of some very powerful forces.

Convencer

This concept means to convince and it involves persuasive arguments and encompasses any means by which a person is able to persuade another. Thus, the concept is at the core of all negotiations. Whereas we in the United States believe that the most persuasive argument is one based on logic and the use of empirical data, other cultures, Mexico included, do not give as much credence to "the data." In Mexico, personal relationships usually trump smart arguments and even the best evidence. It is not surprising to have U.S. negotiators actively describe a transaction using objective, well-reasoned terms to no avail, only to have the deal work out when the other party views the U.S. negotiator as a trustworthy friend.

We should point out, however, that the importance of logic and empirical data tends to grow when dealing with better-educated Mexicans. In fact, close attention should be given to the educational level of your Mexican counterparts for this and other reasons as well. Simply stated, the more educated your Mexican counterpart is, the more likely he or she will not only speak English, but will understand U.S. culture and its unusual preference for data and analyses that support arguments.

Puntualidad

This involves the concept of time. As mentioned, Americans tend to view time in a linear fashion. When someone arrives ten minutes after the start of a meeting in the United States, that person is said to be late. Alternatively, Mexican society tends to view time in a polychronic manner, focusing on multiple time lines that tend to be interpreted incorrectly, particularly by the punctual ones north of the border. Many things can make a Mexican "late." Although this may be excusable given the concept of polychronic time, it must also be interpreted by the level of experience the Mexican has in the U.S. business system. Sometimes being late can be a "tactical ploy" deployed with a specific purpose in mind.

Mexicans can get to the point quickly. This became quite evident to us recently in a meeting in Irvine with Mexican real estate and development executives. Both of us expected to undergo the traditional formalities of relationship building during a principally non-task sounding sort of lunch. We knew the lead Mexican executive pretty well, but none of the rest of us were acquainted. Much to our surprise however, the Mexican team came to us ready to go. That is to say, they got right down to business. Very little relationship building took place. It was at that point that we came to understand the actual influence of adaptation. The Mexicans, who were well versed in U.S. culture because of their experiences in selling factory space to American firms, were dealing with us using an American approach. We came prepared to build relationships, and they were ready to talk business. The tables had been turned.

Buenos Modales/Etiqueta

This relates to good manners and etiquette and involves direct vs. indirect confrontation. This is associated with the concept of formality and the high-context communication style described in chapters 2 and 3. That is, Mexico is a good example of a relationship-oriented culture as represented in exhibit 3.5 on page 66. Mexicans tend to be less directly confrontational than their U.S. counterparts. At times disagreement is couched in much more "diplomatic"/indirect terms, more padding. Please see exhibits 4.1 and 4.2 on pages 69 and 76 for details. Particular care should be given to subtleties of "no." But *buenos modales* also is at the heart of "getting your way." Politeness and formality go a long way in Mexico.

We in the United States tend to be overly informal in the eyes of most foreigners. At times casual conversation between American men, particularly, can include "friendly disrespect" of what the Mexicans call "*bajar el tratamiento*" ("lower the treatment"). In part, this is based upon the egalitarian nature of U.S. society. This lowering of formality should be done only very carefully and best by invitation. You must listen for their, "Please call me Juan."

The complexity of indirect confrontation is perhaps best exemplified by the use of the *Usted vs. tú* in Spanish.[8] Here, the subtleties of the language manifest themselves clearly. It happens at times that someone asks to lower the treatment (to use "*tú*" in the conversation), and the other person continues to respond in the *Usted*. The implications of this are many. One the one hand, the person that chooses to keep the formality may be doing so because of age, deference, respect or status difference or because they do not have *confianza*. The relationship has not been "seasoned" enough to permit that type of informality. As an example, many children continue to refer to their parents in the *Usted*. Please note that this nuance varies significantly around the Spanish-speaking world.

Patriarquismo/Machismo

This concept involves decision-making authority. Decision-making authority is usually premised on a patriarchic or hierarchical system. The dramatic differences between Mexico and the United States are well represented by Hofstede's scores on Power Distance listed in exhibit 2.3 on page 41—Mexico is high at 81 and the U.S. culture is much more egalitarian at 30. If Mexican culture is highly influenced by the family, then the patriarch, the father, is deemed the leader. While the United States is characterized as an individualistic society and Mexico as more collectivistic, the actual decision-making authority in most situations still resides in the individual, the one at the top of the family. Unlike Japanese culture that clearly maintains a harmonious collective decision-making process, in Mexican negotiations the *patrón* ("boss") will have the ultimate say. All other agreements should be considered preliminary until *the* decision-maker approves.

Outside of the home environment, rarely, if ever, is the ultimate decision-maker a woman. This speaks to the concept of *machismo*.[9] Very much like the concept of *mañana, machismo* is an overly generalized, poorly understood sociological characteristic of Mexican society. While *machismo* most certainly still exists in Mexico, our experience is that it is significantly less of a force now than it was even ten years before. However, in more isolated regions with less international exposure, *machismo* is tolerated much more. And it should be anticipated that gender bias can quickly become an issue in such circumstances.

Formalidad/Lucirse

This relates to the "professional" appearance of everything. Mexicans are much more formal in all aspects of business including appearance. Appearance many times dictates your perceived role in society. Perhaps because of the implicit distinction between the indigenous population and that of the conquering Spaniards, Mexico is a class-conscious society. To be dressed well, to conduct oneself in a more formal manner, elevates the ranking within that class. Although somewhat strained, a comparison may be made to the use of jewelry and ostentatious exhibitions of wealth within U.S. society. It is a means of communicating one's place within society. This professional "look" is also a crucial aspect of all business presentations.

El Acuerdo/El Contrato

This aspect has to do with the role of the written agreement or contract. The handshake is more important than the contract for all the reasons listed above. It is irrelevant how well-written the agreement is. No agreement can incorporate every eventuality, and in Mexico, it will be natural to resort to the relationship of the principals to resolve a dispute. Only when the principals are incapable of working out their differences will the other dispute resolution mechanisms come into play. Unlike most U.S. agreements, Mexican transactional agreements tend to be shorter and less subject to litigation. Particular care should be given, however, to potential dispute resolution mechanisms within the final definitive agreement. Experience has shown that a carefully drafted dispute resolution clause that contemplates informal creative solutions works well.

Despite some of the xenophobic suggestions of the day, the old American bromide, "good fences make good neighbors" is just plain wrong. What makes a good neighbor is a sophisticated recognition of our interdependence, and the associated need for cross-border understanding driven by commercial contact. In no place is this truer than in the multicultural North America of the twenty-first century. The history of our two nations is so intertwined that we must appreciate our similarities and our differences as we seek to live side by side.

SUMMARY IMPLICATIONS

1. Build relationships—eat, drink, and be merry. It's the best investment.
2. Dress up, be formal until friendships are well established.
3. As in poker, don't come out too strong or too bold.
4. Learn the culture and history. Buy a good history book.
5. Be patient. Bring the history book in your brief case. You may get a chance to read it.
6. A "no" may be hidden in a "yes." Explore seemingly simple answers.
7. Adapt, yet "To thine own self be true."
8. Work in a team environment.

Exhibit 11.1 The View from Both Sides

Here we present key differences between the cultures.

U.S. Culture	Mexican Culture
Manifest Destiny, masters of our fate	Deterministic, fatalistic, subject to resignation
Emotion seen as weakness	Tends towards more emotionalism, not to be confused with the *machismo* tendency
Change is a constant, including values	Values tradition
Inductive reasoning, pragmatism	Deductive reasoning, ends justify means
Truth is absolute	Truth is relative
Direct, bold, specific communications favored	Indirect, ambiguous communication, subtlety favored
Values analytical, linear problem solving	Values intuitive, lateral problem solving
Individualism, places emphasis on individual performance	*Personalismo,* more toward collectivism, especially if viewed within family and friends, places emphasis on group performance
Considers verbal communication most important	Considers context & nonverbal communications most important
Focuses on task and product	Focuses on relationship and process.
Places emphasis on promoting differing views	Places emphasis on harmony and consensus
Prefers informal tone	Prefers formal tone
Emphasizes rigid adherence to schedules	Is flexible about schedules

CHAPTER 12

THE CHINESE NEGOTIATION STYLE

THE ROOTS OF THE CHINESE STYLE OF BUSINESS NEGOTIATION

Land, not Islands

As we said before, culture starts with geography. China is a continental country surrounded by the Gobi desert, Siberia, the Tibetan Plateau, and the seas. Even with their long coastline, the Chinese had no maritime tradition of exploration and trade.[1] Instead, their closed harbors were opened only with European cannon during the nineteenth century. Their love was and is their land. Pearl S. Buck's 1930s classic, *The Good Earth*,[2] recognized the salience of their soil for Chinese.

Chinese philosophers have historically distinguished between "the root" (agriculture) and "the branch" (commerce). In such an agrarian society as China, social and economic theories and policies have always tended to favor the root and slight the branch. The people who deal with "the branch"—the merchants—were therefore looked down upon. They were the lowest of the four traditional classes of society, the other three being scholars, farmers, and artisans. A family tradition of "studying and farming" was something of which to be proud.[3]

For the last 1,000 years, the economic center of China has been the great alluvial plain between the last 300 miles of the Huanghe (also called the Yellow River) and the Changjiang (Yangtze River), particularly that portion between Nanjing and Shanghai. Certainly other cities have been capitals, Xi'an and Beijing are examples, but the population center of the empire has been here. The rich soil left by eons of flooding and the humid, subtropical climate combine to make rice cultivation ideal. Indeed, this region has always been one of the most densely populated areas of the world because of the productivity of the land. The Chinese refer to the region as the *Yu Mi Zhi Xiang* (the land of rice and fish). And, historically most of the fish have come from the rivers, not the seas.

Despite the burgeoning modern cities that represent the Westerners' views of modern China, some 70 percent of the Chinese workforce is still involved in the production of food and live in rural areas. More than half the food produced in China today is rice. Of course, historically rice was much more important than it is today; and this central activity of the people has left an indelible mark on the Chinese culture. Rice production requires community effort and cooperation. Irrigation, planting, and harvesting are most efficiently accomplished with the participation of small groups of people. In China, these salient social units are primarily comprised of members of extended families. Individual needs and desires were and still are de-emphasized in favor of one's family. Loyalty and obedience to hierarchy are key elements that bind such groups together.

The crowding in "the land of rice and fish" made necessary a social system that promoted harmony and order. Living in close quarters with neighbors does not permit the aggressive individualism and egalitarianism so characteristic in the United States, or in ancient Greece for that matter.

The Sages

There was King Kong, the great ape that held Fay Wray, Jessica Lang, and most recently Naomi Watts in the palm of his hand. Remember Kung Fu fighters? How about the old TV show of the same name with David Carradine as "Little Grasshopper"—cowboys meet Confucius. And then there's Confucius, who says, "A picture is worth a thousand words." All of this pop cultural lore is derived from the name, life, and teachings of a Chinese philosopher who lived some 2,500 years ago. Born Kong Qiu or Kong Zhongni, he was known to his disciples by the honorific term Kong Fuzi[4] (no, not meaning "furry ape," but rather "Master Kong"). The Latinized version is Confucius, in common usage in the West today.

The wandering scholar of the Yellow River valley offered a moral code based on benevolence roughly represented by the notion, "Do not impose on others what you yourself do not desire." Sound familiar? He maintained that a society organized under this moral code would be both prosperous and politically stable (that is, safe from attack). Reverence for scholarship and kinship were fundamental lessons as well. His writings, as preserved by his disciples, served as the foundation for Chinese education for some 2,000 years. During those two millennia, knowledge of the Confucian texts was the primary requisite for appointment to the offices of government.

Roughly contemporary with Confucius was Lao Tzu, the founder of Taoism. Pronounced "Dowism," it provided a more religious view of the world. Fundamental to Taoism were the notions of Yin (the feminine, dark, and passive) and Yang (the masculine, light, and active). The two forces oppose and complement one another simultaneously. They cannot be separated, but must be considered as a whole. The implications of this collision and collusion of Yin and Yang are seen to be pervasive, affecting every aspect of life from traditional medicine to economic cycles. According to Lao Tzu, the key to life was not synthesizing the two forces (in the Hegelian sense), rather it was to find "the Way" between them, the middle ground, a compromise. This philosophy allows that two people (negotiators) disagreeing can both be right. Different from their Greek contemporaries, both Lao Tzu and Confucius were less concerned about finding the Truth and more concerned about finding the Tao, the Way. Indeed, as China evolves away from the influences of Lenin and Marx, these older philosophers are holding new sway today.

The Language

The values of harmony and hierarchy are further promoted in Chinese classrooms. Highly respected teachers deliver lectures. Students ask few questions and don't disagree. Memorization is the key pedagogy leading to the best scores on the historically all-important national exams. Moreover, students spend a lot of time learning to write the thousands of Chinese characters. Because these characters are pictorial in nature, the written language promotes an unusual concreteness in thinking. It's easier to represent pictorially flowers than philosophies. And, because words are pictures rather than sequences of letters, Chinese thinking tends toward a more holistic, big-picture processing of information rather than the Western reductionism that breaks down problems into presumably solvable parts. Also, recall from chapter 2 that Chinese is very distant from English, reflecting substantial cultural differences in general.

Political History

Finally, the history that Chinese students read teaches a wariness of foreigners. The Middle Kingdom has been attacked from all points of the compass—Chinese have died from Hun and Mongol arrows, and Manchurian, Japanese, Russian, American, Vietnamese, and British bullets. But, the disruptions caused by these "barbarians at the gates" have been more than matched by internal squabbling, civil wars, and the ebb and flow of empires. The combination of famine, unstable political systems, and aggressive foreigners yields a cynicism about the rule of law and rules in general. Chinese invest trust only in family and a big bank account.

ELEMENTS OF THE CHINESE STYLE OF BUSINESS NEGOTIATION

Guanxi (Personal Connections)

The English "personal connections" doesn't do justice for this fundamental concept of business negotiations with Chinese. Everyone knows about the importance of networking in the United States. But, we also trust information and institutions; by comparison, the Chinese do not. For the Chinese, nothing is more important than one's place within his or her social network. The importance of *guanxi* has its roots in filial piety, but the notion is extended to include friends, friends of friends, former classmates, relatives, and associates with shared interests.

The medium of *guanxi* is reciprocity, or what the Chinese call *hui bao*. But, it's reciprocity of a sort different than most Americans are used to. Americans expect immediate reciprocity—"I make a concession and I expect one in return at the table that day." For Chinese, there's no hurry. Favors are almost always remembered and returned, the latter often not right away. This long-term reciprocity works well in the context of long-term personal relationships. In China, ignoring such reciprocity is not just bad manners, it's immoral. To be labeled *wang en fu yi* (one who forgets favors and fails on righteousness and loyalty) poisons the well for all future business.

Further, cold calls and cold contacts with the Chinese do not work. Potential Chinese business partners must be approached through their network, making use of *guanxi*. Even then it takes time to be accepted and treated as an insider, but the introduction by a mutually connected third party is requisite.

Guanxi also provides a source of influence during negotiations. Impasses can be addressed by consultation with influential connections. Indeed, mere references to one's *guanxi* bolster a negotiation position better than a mountain of technical information. Given the centrality of *guanxi* in the Chinese business culture you should expect your Chinese counterparts to display their own connections. Where Americans value expertise, Chinese value *guanxi*. What some Americans might deride as "name dropping" isn't a matter of personal puffery for Chinese negotiators, it's a matter of necessity. And, it's also a matter of important information for you, so pay attention.

Mianzi (Face or Social Capital)

It seems all Asian cultures have some notion of face: in Japan it is called *omoiyari;* in the Philippines, *pakikisama;* in Korea, *kibun;* and in Thailand, *krengchai*. The notion of face for the Chinese is closely associated with American concepts of dignity and prestige. *Mianzi* defines one's place in his or her social network. It is the most important measure of social worth. Sources of face can be wealth, intelligence, attractiveness, skills, position, and, of course, good *guanxi*. But, while Americans think in absolute terms—s/he has dignity or prestige, or not—the Chinese think of face in quantitative terms. Face can be gained, lost, given, earned, or taken away.

Breaking promises, displays of anger, or other disreputable behaviors at the negotiation table can all cause you, or, more importantly, your client or business partner, to lose face. Public praise and social recognition are the means for giving a business partner face. However, going too far or praising too frequently can suggest insincerity. Care must be taken. You can also save your Chinese counterpart's face by helping him or her avoid an embarrassing situation, ignoring a gross technical error until a moment of privacy, for example. But, causing a Chinese business partner to lose *mianzi* is in no mere faux pas. It's a disaster. It marks the end of negotiations. The only way to recover is to replace the "barbarian" on your side of the table. There are several ways to cause a loss of face. Casual kidding may do it. Insults, criticism, or a lack of respect for status will subtract substantially from your partner's *mianzi*. None are a good idea.

Shehui Dengji (Social Hierarchy)

The crowding and collectivism of Chinese culture provide fertile ground for hierarchy. Add in a little Confucian advice and status relationships become central for understanding Chinese business systems. Confucius defined five cardinal relationships: between ruler and ruled, husband and wife, parents and children, older and younger brothers, and between friends. Except for the last, all relationships were hierarchical. The ruled, wives, children, and younger brothers were all counseled to trade obedience and loyalty for the benevolence of their ruler, husband, parents, and older brothers, respectively. Strict adherence to these vertical relations yielded social harmony, that being the antidote for the violence and civil war of Confucius's time.

Recall that in chapter 2 we listed Americans as being the most individualistic folks on the planet at least according the Geert Hofstede's studies of work values at IBM. Hofstede also studied the importance of social hierarchy across cultures measuring a dimension he called Power Distance Index (PDI). PDI scores tend to indicate a perception of differences between superior and subordinate and a belief that those who hold power are entitled to privileges. A low score reflects more egalitarian views. As might be expected, Hofstede reports high PDI scores for Chinese (PRC at 80, Singapore at 74, Hong Kong at 68, and Taiwan at 58) and a low score for Americans (40).

So by all accounts, status is no joke among Chinese people. The point is that age and rank of executives and other status markers must be taken into account during business negotiations with the Chinese. Chinese tend to address others by their official titles plus their family names, such as Director Li, Manager Zhang, or President Chen. American informality and egalitarianism and "just call me Mary" will not play well on the western side of the Pacific.

When the Communists took over on the Mainland, one of their first actions was to give women legal rights equal to those of men. Officially, women have equal pay and equal status in the workplace. Women hold important positions in factories, offices, ministries, and the military. However, old hierarchies die hard. Confucian male chauvinism lingers in the People's Republic of China and certainly in other areas among Chinese. The good news for foreign businesswomen is that they will be considered foreigners first and will not be subject to the same discrimination as Chinese women.

Finally, the requisite benevolence of the superior in the Confucian social system opens up a negotiation tactic not so available among Americans. Begging can work in the context of the right kind of relationship and the right circumstances in China. So-called appeals to the heart (*ren qing*) can play an important role in commercial relationships with Chinese businesspeople.

Renji Hexie (Interpersonal Harmony)

The Confucian grassroots approach to peace preached interpersonal harmony as key. The saying goes, "A man without a smile should not open a shop." Harmonious relations between business partners are essential for successful commercial negotiations and relationships with Chinese. While respect and responsibility are the glue that binds hierarchical relationships, friendships and positive feelings hold horizontal relationships together. Thus, politeness and indirect communication are king—direct refusals are rare. Rather than saying "no," Chinese negotiators are more likely to change the subject, turn silent, ask another question, or respond by using ambiguously and vaguely positive expressions with subtle negative implications, such as *hai bu cuo* (seems not wrong), *hai hao* (seems fairly alright), and *hai xing/hai ke yi* (appears fairly passable), etc. The subtlety of these expressions, however, is hard to translate and explain in English. Usually only native Chinese speakers can tell the differences during a formal negotiation session, through consideration of their moods and intonations, facial expressions, and body language. Hearing what one wants to hear may not promote efficiency in communications, but it does promote harmony at least in the immediate context. Ambiguity is preferred to confrontation.

Expressions of negative emotions are most inappropriate in negotiations with the Chinese. "Getting mad" may work with Americans, but it most often ends talks with Chinese. The notion of venting anger and emotions makes no sense to Chinese businesspeople. We know. We've tried to explain it many times with little success to our business associates in Beijing and Hong Kong. American arguments and aggressiveness not only cause a loss of face (for both the angered American and the chagrined Chinese), but such outbursts will also most certainly destroy *renji hexie* and the potential for creative commercial negotiations.

Qundai Guanxi (Nepotism)

Qundai guanxi is really an innate in-group collectivism, which is a key part of the Chinese cultural traits. We've already made reference to the importance of family in Chinese society. The extended family is the basic social unit. This is as true today as it has been historically. Indeed, China expert Gordon Redding in his excellent book *The Spirit of Chinese Capitalism* suggests that Chinese-owned companies seldom grow beyond the bonds and bounds of the extended family. This explains the fundamental distinction of what he calls a fourth kind of capitalism—different from those in the United States, Japan, and Europe.

Family businesses are autocratic, with the father usually in charge. Squabbles can break out in family boardroom meetings, but a united front will always be presented to outsiders. Moreover, persuasive appeals composed of benefits targeting individual negotiators will be of little or perhaps negative consequence. Benefits offered should be directed toward the welfare of the company/family.

All of this sounds strange to Americans who often work in companies that have rules against nepotism. Our point here is that things are different among Chinese, indeed, very different. And negotiation strategies must take into account these strong social and family ties prevalent in the Chinese business system.

The social leveling of Communism reduced the importance of *qundai guanxi* in the Peoples' Republic. In fact, it must be noted that since the Communist revolution in 1949, most of the wealth and resources in China have been controlled by the Communist Party. As such, powerful party members, princelings of the ruling elites, classmates at outstanding universities such as Tsinghua and Peking University, and colleagues have been often more important than family relations. But, everywhere else— Hong Kong, Singapore, Taiwan, the United States, even Europe, and so on—the concept is key for understanding Chinese. And, as Communism continues to dissipate on the mainland, the salience of this concept of *qundai guanxi* burgeons anew.

Zhengti Guannian (Holistic Thinking)

Michael Harris Bond, a cross-cultural psychologist at Chinese University of Hong Kong, has written perhaps the most important book on Chinese thinking, *Beyond the Chinese Face*. In it, he describes a fundamental cultural difference in thinking patterns. In a variety of psychological tests, Chinese children are better at seeing the big picture, and American children are better at seeing the details of the parts. He states, "Apparently the stimulus as a whole has more salience for Chinese; the parts of the whole for Americans."[5] Surely this holistic thinking of the Chinese comes from the years of learning the thousands of ideographs or characters. Words for them are more like pictures rather than the sequences of letters learned by Westerners. Thus, people themselves must be evaluated in the context of their overall social relations or *guanxi* in China. Americans' identities are more defined by individual accomplishments. Indeed, had Socrates been Chinese, rather than "know thyself," his motto may have been "know thy place!"

The implications of these differences in thinking patterns hold significant salience for international business negotiations. Americans tend to take a sequential approach to problem solving, breaking up complex negotiation tasks into a series of smaller issues—price, quantity, warranty, delivery, etc.—settling them one at a time and the final agreement is the sum of the parts so to speak. Alternatively, Chinese negotiators tend to talk about all issues together, skipping around the issues, and seemingly never settling anything. This difference in style presents two major problems for Americans bargaining with Chinese. First, Americans get frustrated because discussions seem quite disorganized. Second, Americans cannot measure progress in negotiations because nothing ever seems to get settled. In the United States, you're halfway through when you've discussed half the issues. But with the Chinese, "settled" issues keep coming up again. Americans are getting ready to call it quits and get on the airplane home when the Chinese side may be about ready to settle. Indeed, in our current studies of Americans bargaining with businesspeople in Hong Kong, this difference is the source of the greatest tension between negotiation teams.

Chiku Nailao (Endurance or "Eating Bitterness and Enduring Labor")

The Americans and Chinese are famous for their work ethic. More than 100 years ago, missionary Arthur Smith listed "industry" as the number three trait behind only "face" and "economy" in his guidebook of *Chinese Characteristics*. But, the Chinese take diligence one step farther—to endurance. Hard work, even in the worst conditions, is the ideal. Indeed, because Chairman Mao's 18-month Long March was endured, he was endeared to the Chinese people. And, while communism ultimately did do damage to motivation on the Mainland, the innate industriousness of the Chinese people is showing through bright and shiny as the planned economy evolves toward free enterprise. The hard work begins in school.

Long hours, long weeks, and long school years are prevalent in Chinese cultures, although this is changing some recently. This early socialization yields a work ethic admired around the world today. Where Americans place high value on talent as a key to success, Chinese see endurance as much more important and more honorable.

Our own studies of businesspeople in Guangzhou, Hong Kong, Tianjin, and Taiwan confirm such differences. Where American managers list analytical skills as most important for bargainers, Chinese list persistence, determination, and preparation as key traits. And we see Chinese diligence primarily reflected in two ways at the negotiation table. First, the Chinese will have worked harder in their preparations for the negotiations. Much midnight oil gets burnt in Hong Kong, Shanghai, Singapore, and Taipei. Second, your Chinese counterparts will have expectations about longer bargaining sessions than you. Combine jetlag and late-night business entertainment with long hours in negotiations and trips to the cities listed above can prove exhausting experiences. Your Chinese counterparts know to take advantage of the circumstances.

Jiejian (Thrift)

China hands have been marveling over Chinese thrift for more than two centuries. Today saving rates in China exceed those in both Japan and the United States. Of course, it's no accomplishment to beat the U.S. savings rate since recently it's been negative. However, the Japanese are famous for their high savings rate at over 30 percent and the Chinese rate has consistently exceeded that. Such thrift is encouraged by the long history of economic and political instability. In the United States, we haven't experienced real economic "rainy days" since the 1930s. Alternatively, in China, disruptions of the magnitude of our "great depression" have gripped the country about once a decade during the last century.

Price will often be the crucial issue. We see this quite directly in our work with Americans negotiating with managers in Hong Kong. Among all the issues involved including quantity, product options, service contracts, terms of payment, warranty, and so on, price ends up being the central point of disagreement. You should know that your Chinese counterparts will pad their offers with more room to maneuver than most Americans are used to. And the Chinese will make concessions on price with great reluctance and only after lengthy discussions. Moreover, the combination of American impatience and Chinese patience further strengthens their strongly defended price positions. Finally, Americans should not be put off by aggressive first offers by the Chinese. Chinese negotiators do expect concession to be made by both sides, particularly on prices. Indeed, they expect that everyone pads prices as they do. This is a case where American negotiators will do well to meet Chinese expectations.

Linghe Tanpan (Zero-Sum Negotiations)

In Chinese cultures, cooperation and trust among family members is standard procedure. Reciprocity and creative business negotiations among friends and acquaintances result from the degree of interdependence that has been established and the face invested in them. However, business negotiations with outsiders and foreigners take on a very different character, one more akin to the notion of zero-sum negotiations. All who write about the Chinese comment on this clear East–West difference. The Chinese distrust outsiders and expect competitive negotiations with them. The fundamental notion of expanding the pie before dividing it up common in the West is not shared by them. Indeed, they expect to be distrusted and they expect competitive behavior from you.

To carry this notion further, negotiations with outsiders can be seen as a kind of warfare where all the tools of the trade introduced by Suntsu's *The Art of War* can come into play. And warfare is a familiar theme for the student of Chinese history. The Chinese aphorism, "s*hang chang ru shan chang*," literally translates as "the market place is a battlefield." And battlefields have spies, offensives, maneuvering, etc., and are generally places of destruction, not creativity.

The management implication here is simple. Only well-managed, long-term relationships with Chinese partners will result in anything resembling creative, mutually beneficial business negotiations. Since initial negotiations are apt to be zero-sum, they should involve relatively small numbers of dollars. Once trust is established and insider status is confirmed then, and only then, can the best kinds of substantial commercial relationships be negotiated.

Jiao Ta Liangshi Chuan (Threatening to Do Business Elsewhere)

When the persuasion starts in your negotiations with Chinese businesspeople, you can depend on hearing about your competitors. Everyone commenting on the Chinese negotiation style mentions this particular tactic—threatening to do business elsewhere.

The Chinese version of displaying one's BATNA is a bit more aggressive and carries the additional implication that their talks with your competitors have already begun. That is, a good alternative by definition is one already inside one's network where *guanxi* can be brought to bear.

Chinese seem to use this tactic with little regard for its aggressiveness as perceived by most Americans. Because American negotiators tend to be in a hurry and tend focus on "one thing at a time," the development of a symmetrical set of alternatives begins only when troubles crop up with the focal business deal. So most Americans feel like they're being "two timed" when the "there's-more-than-one-game-in-town" threat is delivered. Americans get mad when the Chinese are just pointing out what they believe should be obvious to everyone.

CONCLUSIONS

The differences we have described between the American and Chinese cultures and styles of business negotiations are large. We have summarized them in exhibit 12.1. Indeed, in many ways the Western approach and the Eastern approach are simply incompatible. Languages, values and negotiation processes are about as different as they can get. However, business still gets done and commercial relationships thrive across the Pacific because the opportunities and economics of cooperation are great. Moreover, when both sides take into account the many predictable differences in expectations, values, and behaviors, business can be conducted more efficiently and with more creativity and more mutual gain.

SUMMARY RECOMMENDATIONS

1. Use intermediaries (for introductions and during impasses).
2. Let them bring up business when the relationship is established.
3. Reflect their team composition.
4. Provide explanations first with copious information.
5. Expect to hear about your competition.
6. Persuade with questions.
7. Don't get mad, preserve their face.
8. Make no concessions until the end.

Exhibit 12.1 Summary of Differences in American and Chinese Negotiation Styles

Category	American	Chinese
Basic Cultural Values and Ways of Thinking	Individualism	Collectivism
	Egalitarianism	Hierarchy
	Information-Oriented	Relationship-Oriented
	Focus, foreground, object	Big Picture, background, environment
	Reductionism	Holism
	Content	Context
	The Truth	The Way, compromise
Negotiation Process		
1. Non-task Sounding	Short	Long, expensive
	Informal	Formal
	Cold calls	Intermediaries
2. Task-related exchange of information	Full authority	Limited authority
	Directness	Indirectness
	"Cards on the table"	Intermediaries
	Proposals first	Explanations first
3. Persuasion	Aggressive, persuasive tactics (threats, promises, arguments, and logic: "You need this.")	Questions, competing offers, delays
4. Concessions and agreement	Sequential	Holistic
	Goal = "a good deal"	Goal = long-term relationship

PART IV

LOOKING TO THE FUTURE

W e hope by now you're much better prepared for your next business negotiation, whether it's in St. Petersburg, San Salvador, St. Croix, or St. Louis. In this last part of the book, we turn to the larger future. We're promoting a revolutionary style of global negotiation—one that goes beyond competition, past problem-solving, all the way to collaborative creativity. We provide this last chapter to help you spread the revolution, the new rules, to your own organization and the people and the organizations you will be working with all around the world.

CHAPTER 13

GLOBALIZATION x NEGOTIATION = INNOVATION^2

I can always come in on the glow from Havana.

—Ernest Hemingway,
The Old Man and the Sea

Human progress has always depended on the innovations yielded by international trade. Politicians and political scientists often lose sight of this fundamental truth. Their emphases on power, using it or studying it, have almost always interfered with the grassroots, trade-based creativity that leads to better lives for us all. In this closing chapter, we first address how high-level politics most often block human creativity. Next, we explain how unfettered globalization combined with efficient and creative negotiations delivers innovation "on steroids." Then we present three short stories about firms that have committed resources to maximize their innovativeness and therefore their success in the continuously faster-changing global environment. That is, we document how Philips, Shell, and Toyota go about exploiting their self-recognized global interdependencies for the sake of profit and progress. Finally, we make specific recommendations for building innovative organizations by applying the new rules for global negotiation to company practices, human resources management, and corporate strategies.

POWER POLITICS USUALLY PARALYZE PROGRESS

We start this section with a quick international relations quiz—just two questions: Who invented the political tool of trade sanctions? Who was U.S. Secretary of State when Richard Nixon and Henry Kissinger visited Mao Zedong and Zhou Enlai in Beijing in 1972? The answers follow shortly.

The stated goal of the field of international relations is world peace. Most folks on the planet would agree that starting a war doesn't lead to peace. That is, power can't produce peace. We would argue that politicians can't produce peace either. Take the United States for example. No war we've ever won, no trade sanction we've ever applied, and no treaty we've ever signed has caused an improvement in international relations. What causes real, long-term peace is the aggregation of creative international business relationships that comprise trade. Trade also creates human progress.

Think of the wars the United States has fought: Two against the British, then Mexico, Spain, Germany, Germany again, Italy, Japan, the Soviet Union (sort of), North Korea (with help from China), Cuba, Vietnam, Grenada, Panama, Iraq, Afghanistan, Iraq again. Nobody won those wars—one side just lost less than the other. We fought two wars with Germany because the treaty between them was stupid. Likewise, we're in a second round with Iraq because the first one ended with a set of trade sanctions. Many of the countries listed above are now among our best friends internationally. It wasn't the wars or the treaties; rather, it was the commerce that followed the wars and treaties that built the peace. Indeed, the Danes that complain loudly about European unity are loudly demonstrating their ignorance of history. The purpose of the European economic union wasn't commerce, it was peace. The EU's produced on that goal for 50 years.

It was 1807 when Thomas Jefferson came up with trade sanctions as an innovation in diplomacy. The countries he endeavored to persuade then were quite big and quite stubborn, England and France. The goal was to get these warring nations to leave American ships alone on the high seas. Lacking a competitive Navy, our third president dreamed up the trade embargo—rather than using trade as a carrot he planned to withhold trade and use it as a stick. However, instead of changing French or English policies and behaviors, Jefferson's policy actually endangered New England traders. They complained:

Our ships all in motion, once whiten'd the ocean;
They sail'd and return'd with a Cargo;
Now doom'd to decay, they are fallen a prey,
To Jefferson, worms, and EMBARGO.[1]

Jefferson's embargo fell apart in just 15 months. Only the War of 1812 settled the problems with English aggression at sea.

Consider the track record of trade sanctions in the last century. In 1940, the United States told the Japanese to get out of China—the ensuing embargo of gasoline and scrap metal led directly to the Pearl Harbor attack. Since 1948, Arab countries have boycotted Israel. Given that countries trade most with their closest neighbors, you have to wonder how much this lack of trade has promoted the continuing conflicts in the area. Israel is still there. In 1959, Castro took over Cuba. For almost 50 years the United States has boycotted sugar and cigars, and Castro is still there. OPEC's (Organization of Petroleum Exporting Countries) 1973 oil flow slowdown was intended to get America to stop supporting Israel. However, the dollars still flow fast to Israel and now to Egypt as well.

In 1979, the United States told the Soviets to get out of Afghanistan. They refused. America boycotted the 1980 Moscow Olympics and stopped selling them grain and technology. The Soviet response—they continued to kill Afghans (and, by the way, Soviet soldiers) for another ten years. Moreover, in 1984, they and their allies' athletes stayed away from the Olympics in Los Angeles. And the high-tech embargo didn't work anyway. A San Diego division of Caterpillar lost millions of dollars in service contracts for Soviet natural gas pipelines. These revenues were lost permanently, because the Soviets taught themselves how to do the maintenance and overhauls. In 1989, we walked through a Moscow weapons research facility—they had every brand of computer then available in the West, IBMs, Apples, and the best from Taiwan and Japan, as well.

Perhaps the 1980s multilateral trade sanctions imposed on South Africa hastened Apartheid's demise? But, look how well the world's ten-year embargo of Iraq changed policy there. Using trade as a weapon killed kids while Saddam celebrated at $12 million birthday parties. Indeed, the best prescription for Middle East peace (and American taxpayers' wallets, by the way) is for all sides to drop all embargoes.

The end of the last century witnessed great strides in the elimination of ill-conceived trade sanctions. Perhaps most important was the U.S.

Senate's and president's approvals of permanently normalized trade relations (PNTR) with China. However, other important steps were the relaxation of some of the trade restrictions on Vietnam, North Korea, Iran, and Cuba. Indeed, as a result of President Clinton's diplomacy, North and South Koreans marched together at the Sydney Olympics; Americans could then buy pistachio nuts and carpets from Tehran; and U.S. firms can sell medical supplies and services in Havana.

A SHORT STORY ABOUT THE GOOD, THE BAD, AND THE UGLY OF DIPLOMACY

Historian Margaret MacMillan in her wonderful book, *Nixon and Mao*,[2] tells the story of "the week that changed the world." It's the single best account of a major international negotiation we've come across. The detail and insight are extraordinary. She makes one mistake, though. She gives credit to two American statesmen for this history-making accomplishment, Nixon and Kissinger. But, the real hero of her story was the third "good" statesman, U.S. Secretary of State at the time, William P. Rogers. Nixon, Kissinger, and MacMillan all assign Rogers second-class accord. But, actually he was the true genius there. He pushed for opening up trade between the two countries.

Trade was low on the list of international relations objectives agreed to in advance by Nixon and Kissinger. Both were brilliant political strategists, but only in a narrow and ultimately irresponsible sense—they both eschewed commercial considerations as boring. Indeed, Kissinger's book, *Diplomacy*,[3] still displays his dangerous disregard for commerce—we don't recommend it. So, it's not surprising that the 1972 political negotiations between the United States and China accomplished nothing for either side. Nixon and Kissinger's goal at the top of their list was to get Mao to lean on the North Vietnamese to seriously negotiate a peace in Paris. Mao and Zhou's purpose was to get Taiwan back. Indeed, the only win, so to speak, for Nixon was John Haldeman's orchestration of the TV crews that produced spectacular pictures of "world leader" Nixon for prime time at home. Despite the tragic quagmire in Vietnam, Nixon looked good in China. Good for him, ultimately bad for America, and other innocent peoples and places like Laos and Cambodia. Nobody there except William Rogers understood the subtle, creative power of international commerce.

THE BASES OF CREATIVITY

So wars and trade sanctions kill creativity. But, what causes it? As we said earlier, the key to human progress is innovation; and innovation has always been mostly a consequence of trade and indeed, international negotiation. Jared Diamond makes this point most eloquently and convincingly in his Pulitzer Prize-winning book, *Guns, Germs and Steel*.[4] Therein he argues that historically, Western and Eastern civilizations dominated American and African civilizations because of the continuous innovation stimulated by trade and interaction along the Silk Road. Alternatively, travel and trade along the North/South axes of the latter two continents were limited by climatic variation, thus blocking cultural and technological exchange and development. With the exception of some of the former British colonies there, these lands still lag their Eurasian cousins even after 600 years of oceanic trade. Perhaps the new electronic commerce will speed the leveling. Let's hope so.

Everyone agrees that the key to global competitiveness for companies is also innovation; but not all American companies have yet grasped the crucial connections among innovation and trade and international negotiation. Even though the term "innovation" is trumpeted in corporate mission statements, by the American business press, and by CEOs of our largest companies, most of the words haven't been followed by fundamental changes in corporate structures and cultures. This is our national mistake. But, we complete our book here with a remedy.

INNOVATION PROCESSES "ON STEROIDS"

We now turn to the newest thinking on the causes of innovation, those beyond simple exhortation. There are two innovation processes—*creativity* and *diffusion*. The latter recognizes that good ideas are not enough. Marketing them is essential as well. But, we'll start here with the good ideas.

Everyone agrees that *creativity* thrives in egalitarian environments. Think Silicon Valley. Everyone agrees that creativity is enhanced by diversity. Think Silicon Valley. Why Silicon Valley? Why not on the East Coast of the United States? Why not in the middle of the country? Indeed, why the United States?

Perhaps the most important book ever written on creativity is *Whack on the Side of the Head*, by Roger von Oech.[5] It's such a simple, quirky, and fun read. But it's based on his Stanford dissertation on the *History of Ideas*. It's very deep thinking disguised in a lightweight package. Genius! First published in 1983, we haven't yet been able to find a book on the topic of innovation and/or creativity that doesn't depend on this seminal research-based work.

Some of von Oech's basic ideas include:

1. Creativity is blocked by routinized thinking. For example, generals are trained to think the solution to all problems is a war. Financial analysts are trained to see all problems as a matter of measuring risk.
2. A whack on the side of the head is one way to get people to think differently. When wars don't work, other options must be considered—even by generals.
3. Creativity is maximized first by putting the largest possible number of ideas on the table from which to choose, and second by getting the maximum number of different perspectives on those options.
4. Egalitarian social settings allow everyone to table ideas, thus their numbers are maximized.
5. Diverse social settings yield more ideas and more different perspectives on them.

The United States was born an egalitarian place—" . . . all men are created equal." Compared to our European forefathers with their histories of feudalism, more here[6] had the then unusual "freedom of speech" to begin with. This is the ultimate freedom to put ideas on the table, and we continue to do so even two hundred years later. Thus, creativity has thrived in the United States.

Silicon Valley dominates the creativity game in the United States because the West coast is more egalitarian than the East and more diverse than the middle of the country. East Coast culture is dominated by the Ivy League—private schools where it often makes a difference who your parents are. Hierarchy hurts creativity. The rest of the country's culture is dominated by public university systems; and the admission standards to the best public schools are based on merit, not family. More ideas are tabled in these egalitarian cultures. Both East and West coasts have rich mixes of international immigration, but not so much in the center of the country. Only the West coast has both positive traits, a fundamentally egalitarian culture and an immigration-driven diversity. Throw in the close proximity of Berkeley and Stanford and you get Silicon Valley. And, oh by the way, you also get Roger von Oech.

Now we know by this point in the chapter we've angered everyone east of the Mohave Desert (including our editor and particularly Henry Kissinger) by our California ethnocentrism. But, there is a solution to your geographical handicap besides moving west. So, please read on.

The Midwesterners will like our story better here. The seminal thinking on the topic of the *diffusion* of innovations comes from one Everett Rogers. He was born on an Iowa corn farm and eventually received his PhD from Iowa State University after serving in the Korean War. For his dissertation, he studied the diffusion of innovations among farmers in Iowa. Soon after his dissertation was filed on the shelf at the Iowa State library, he wandered over to admire the tome. It occurred to him to do a little test of the diffusion of his own ideas—so he put a $20 bill in it as a book mark. When he checked 20 years later, it was still there!

But his ideas on how ideas diffuse did eventually expand far beyond the university library in Ames, primarily in his five-edition *Diffusion of Innovations*.[7] Malcolm Gladwell's *The Tipping Point*[8] is an easier to read version of Rogers' original ideas. Rogers tells us that diversity also helps in the diffusion of ideas. That is, he reports in his arcane academic prose, "Heterophilous network links often connect two cliques, thus spanning two sets of socially dissimilar individuals in a system." His point is that while similar folks have an easier time communicating with one another, interactions between dissimilar people are more powerful in broadly diffusing ideas. Such views have been echoed in a plethora of more recent academic studies. So now we see a second value for diversity. Diverse organizations, as long as they can "negotiate" the communication problems that accompany their diversity, are better at both creating ideas *and* spreading them around!

OPEN INNOVATION

Henry Chesbrough's[9] book concisely describes the new model for innovation. He distinguishes between the old "Closed Innovation" and the new "Open Innovation." The old way was to hire the smartest people you could find in your industry, put them to work in a stimulating and modern R&D facility, patent the technologies you develop, and quickly deliver the related products directly to the market ahead of your competitors. Certainly this sounds familiar. Open innovation involves working with partners and collaborators in both developing new technologies and taking them to market. Research ideas may be bought from others (or at least invested in), and your homegrown ideas might be sold to other firms to take to market. The latter assumes that you cannot possibly hire all the smartest people in your industry. The latter approach is fast being adopted by firms like Proctor & Gamble, Intel, Cisco, and those in Hollywood. Actually, for the last, open innovation is an old practice involving a fast mix of talent, writers, studios, agencies, etc.

The odd thing about Chesbrough's excellent book is that it's almost mute on the globalization of innovation. Of the dozens of companies he mentions, only Bayer AG is a foreign company. He is describing this "new" interdependence among companies as if it were something new. We suppose it is new among independence-burdened American commerce. Control and independence have always been powerful values among American executives and their boards of directors. American firms have never been much good at interdependence, and as a business culture, the idea of sharing control is an anathema. Anti-trust laws also worked to keep American firms from collaborating in creative ways. Up until the end of the last century these values served American firms pretty well. But, as we've entered the twenty-first century, American firms are noticing another approach, one long used in Europe and Asia. Thus, circa 2006 we had just seen Chesbrough's announcement of *Open Innovation*. The book is important as it becomes the new rallying cry, a new catalyst for change for American CEOs. Meanwhile, the Europeans and Asians we compete with are wondering about all the fuss.

John Seely Brown is one of the planet's experts on innovation. He has been the Chief Scientist for Xerox Corporation and served as director of the Xerox Palo Alto Research Center. In his presentations and new book with John Hagel, *The Only Sustainable Edge*,[10] he pushes the notion of open innovation a bit further. That is, he explains why it works. He uses racy new terms like dynamic specialization, process networks, productive friction, and performance fabrics. He argues that successful firms will specialize based on their competitive strengths and their abilities to collaborate with complementary firms in process networks. These collaborations will naturally yield new, mutually advantageous ideas, but it won't be easy. In fact, Brown comments that "When people with diverse backgrounds, experience, and skill sets engage with each other on real problems, the exchange usually generates friction—that is, misunderstandings and arguments—before resolution and learning occur." This is where the international negotiation skills we have been talking about in this book are most crucial. Innovation can result if, and only if, the cross-cultural communication problems can be overcome. This is particularly so in international alliances.

Hagel and Brown emphasize that this approach works only when companies and executives have been able to build long-term, trusting commercial relationships. To their credit, they provide metrics for measuring the usefulness of such collaborations. Their ultimate bottom line requires that all partners must be more capable after the collaboration than before. Everyone must have benefited. Penultimate is testing the performance fabric. They advise:

> Identify the five most innovative business partners of your company. Use an independent third party to assess the degree of trust that you have established with these business partners, particularly in creating a foundation for capability building. [Then ask:]
>
> - How willing are these business partners to discuss some of their most creative ideas with you?
> - What would these business partners expect to happen if they did discuss some of their most creative ideas with you?
> - Have these business partners learned from you anything that makes them better at what they do?
> - Have you learned from these business partners anything that makes you better at what you do?
> - What could be done to strengthen incentive structures on both sides of the relationship to motivate better performance against expectations?
> - What are the specific opportunities to deepen capabilities on both sides of the relationship, and to what extent are these opportunities effectively addressed?

Leaders at America's largest companies are beginning to see the importance of a new approach. Specifically Larry Burns, Vice President of R&D and Planning at General Motors, is responsible for seeing the future of the firm. In our recent meeting with him, he clearly articulated the necessity for the company to "leverage its global workforce and alliances." But previously successful, large American firms aren't built to collaborate internationally. Most simply stated, we suffer a geographical/cultural handicap that must be overcome before our firms can compete anew in the dynamic global landscape. Because we've suffered the wealth of the largest home market on the planet, our international ventures have always been ancillary to our business systems.

We've been able to live the unreasonable dream of our founding fathers. Ah, independence.

It's now time to recognize the fundamental condition of global enterprise—*interdependence*—and behave accordingly. It won't be an easy transformation, and the Detroit analogy applies: "It's like trying to change your fan belt with the engine running." But, actually this instructive metaphor understates the problem. It's actually more like converting from a gasoline engine to nuclear power while the car is hurtling down the autobahn at 200 kph.

PHILIPS AND OPEN INNOVATION

The Dutch have all kinds of advantages vis-à-vis large companies in larger countries like the United States or even neighboring Germany. We already talked about both their fishing and trading heritages. They also enjoy the luxury of living in a small country. The head of Philips R&D Laboratory in Aachen, Germany, put it most succinctly: "We have very smart people here at Philips, but we don't have all the smart people." And actually their country is getting smaller as the water from global warming subtracts from their land literally. Thus, there's an urgency to their commerce. They're also renowned for their thrift. You'll recall the story about the invention of copper wire.

Dutch people know foreign languages better than most. It seems to us that the Dutch businesspeople we run into all over the world all speak about five each. The Netherlands also sits on the north/south divide in Europe. In the north you have Protestant Europe; in the south you have Catholic Europe. Going back even further in history, in the North you also had the "barbarians" yet unconquered by the Romans. The three rivers flowing east/west that the Romans had trouble crossing make and mark the divide—the Maas, Waals, and Rhine. Thus, it's no accident that the foremost international business scholar is Dutch—Geert Hofstede as mentioned in chapter 1. Professor Hofstede also reports another Dutch advantage for creative interactions—high scores for both individualism and egalitarianism.

But, the fundamental advantage of the Dutch is that they have always clearly recognized their international interdependence as a competitive advantage. And, Philips' corporate culture and strategic structure represents this realization. You can see the differences reflected in a simple comparison of the websites of Philips and General Electric in exhibit

Exhibit 13.1   "About Us" Page Menus of Corporate Web sites

Philips "Company Profile"	*General Electric "Our Company"*
Mission and vision/values and strategy	Investor Communications
Businesses	Business Directory
Participations	Company Information
Alliances	News
Management	GE Foundation
Key inventions	GE Volunteers
Corporate governance and business	Careers
principles	Features Archive
Business excellence	
History	
Businesses & Suppliers	
Our Brand	
Design	
Research	
Sustainability	
News Center	
Investor Relations	
Careers	

Sources: www.philips.com/about/company/index.html and www.ge.com/en/company/; both accessed March 2007.

13.1. Philips celebrates its "participations and alliances" toward the top of its menu. Finding GE's international alliance structure takes substantial searching. GE has "investor communications" at the top of its menu, while that topic resides near the bottom of the Philips list. Perhaps the American emphasis on investors reflects the actual users of the website— the millions of stock traders in the population. The executives at Philips don't have to kowtow to Wall Street, just their various boards including a fully independent (by Dutch law) Supervisory Board of non-employee, leaders of commerce from around the world including Europeans, North Americans, and an Asian. Alternatively, the GE directors are all Americans. Finally, Philips' mission statement emphasizes its customers: "We improve the quality of people's lives through the timely introduction of meaningful technological innovations." Alternatively, GE has no mission statement, but the comparable verbiage in their annual report suggests different constituencies: "reliable growth company," "winning in the future," and "imagination at work." Indeed, we actually like best the 1960s expression of their corporate goals so frequently announced then by company spokesman, actor Ronald Reagan: "At General Electric, progress is our most important product."

Thus, Philips is one of the originators of "open innovation." Thirty years ago, they pioneered the concept of partnering to develop new ideas and partnering to market new ideas. Open innovation for Philips also means that they buy ideas from R&D partners and they sell ideas to marketing partners, rather than developing and marketing all their own. One current project exemplifies their innovative approach to developing innovations and intellectual property in China:

> The PHENIX Initiative is a commercial, industrial, and R&D coopera-
> tion launched by a consortium of Chinese and European partners, led by
> France Telecom. It received the support of the EU-China Working
> Group on Digital Olympics, of the MOST (Chinese Ministry of Science
> and Technology), the BOCOG (Beijing Organizing Committee for the
> Games of the XXIX Olympiad), and was co-financed by the European
> Union. Philips Research (Europe and East Asia in Shanghai) partici-
> pated in the project, which aimed at studying the commercial potential
> in China for mobile interactive services, analyzing the DVB-H position-
> ing in China, and developing innovative concepts in the area of mobile
> services, particularly targeting the upcoming Olympic Games.[11]

Philips engages in dozens of major and minor business partnerships around the world like the Phenix Initiative. Surprising to us, company executives admit they might do better at their international negotiations. But, the company culture and structure are most well suited to take advantage of "smart people everywhere" in the dynamic global marketplace of the twenty-first century.

SHELL, A NEW EMPHASIS ON NEGOTIATION

Royal Dutch Shell, now referred to as the Shell Group is a global company that shares many of the advantages ascribed to its Dutch half-sister above. Most of the key executives are Dutch or British, reflecting its heritage of dual ownership and stock listings in both the Netherlands and the UK. Many top executives are from the American oil patch as well. Historically, the firm has been run by engineers, excellent on technology and weak on people skills.

But things are changing now. In 2004, the CEO, COO, and the head of Shell's Exploration and Production operations resigned in a scandal regarding overstated reserves. As a consequence, the company was reorganized under a new CEO, Jeroen van der Veer, a long-time Shell executive, and most recently a new Chairman, Jorma Olilla, the Finnish former CEO of Nokia.

Recognizing its competitors' greater successes in negotiating large international project contracts, the new CEO has launched a push to improve Shell's project capture rate and management skills. He's hired 3,000 new technical staff and is training them in the finer points of procurement, cost estimation, and reserve classification. This new push is reflected in part of Shell's statement of General Business Principles, "We aim to work closely with our customers, partners, and policymakers to advance more efficient and sustainable use of energy and natural resources."

Thus, the firm is investing millions of dollars in developing and delivering international negotiation training programs. A new cadre of international negotiators includes members from all levels of management, ranging from those involved in million dollar partnerships to those heading multibillion dollar mega-projects. And the key aspect of this new initiative flowing from the top of the company is its goal to change the culture of the company through engagement with foreign partners at all levels of the company. We expect this new focus on integration of its traditional technological expertise with a new open-innovation culture will prove to be a growing competitive advantage.

THE JAPANESE APPROACH HOLDING SWAY

Shortly after his retirement in 1989 as one of Ford Motor Company's most successful CEOs ever, Donald Petersen warned that Toyota was coming on strong. He was right. Toyota has finally weathered the ten-year SUV mania in the United States and their lineup of fuel-efficient cars is taking over again, very much reminiscent of their 1980s competitive surge. Yet, when you juxtapose the circumstances of Philips and Toyota, you have to wonder how they're doing it again. Japan is a populous country with a collectivistic/hierarchical cultural values system—all these traits add up to a low innovation home environment. The board of Toyota has been 100 percent Japanese men, so no diversity there. However, we must mention that just in 2007 they did add their first *gaijin* board member, one James E. Press, also president of their North American operations. It will be interesting to see who they add from China. But, we begin to see some of the seeds of their success in their statement of Corporate Philosophy from their 2006 Annual Report:

#5. Foster a corporate culture that enhances individual creativity and teamwork value, while honoring mutual trust and respect between labor and management.

#7. Work with business partners in research and creation to achieve stable, long-term growth and mutual benefits, while keeping ourselves open to new partnerships.

They add: "We respect our business partners such as suppliers and dealers and work with them through long-term relationships to realize mutual growth based on mutual trust."

Their primary American competitor, General Motors, has always grown mainly through acquisitions, including international ones. Alternatively, Toyota has grown from within, building green-field plants in other countries rather than acquiring other companies. So from where does their vaunted innovativeness emanate?

Of course, books have been written on this question. Our reading of them boils down to two things: (1) Despite the hierarchical nature of Japanese society, Toyota has successfully created an egalitarian work environment where "anyone can stop the production line" in the name of quality improvement. New ideas are solicited from shop floor to board room. New ideas are welcomed from everyone in the company because of the high values placed on continuous improvement. (2) Toyota has also maximized its learning from other countries. As we said earlier, the Japanese are the world's greatest listeners. Dutch international negotiations expert, Samfrits LePoole, agreed, " . . . they spend days getting to know their opponents." Tom Kelley at IDEO, the innovation champion in Silicon Valley says, " . . . the anthropologist role is the single biggest source of innovation at IDEO."[12] Japan is the anthropologist culture. They are information vacuums. They keep their mouths shut and carefully observe.

The analysts also echo these themes. Indeed, Jeffrey Liker describes in *The Toyota Way* how the firm seeks to "find solid partners and grow together to mutual benefit in the long term."[13] We particularly notice this approach by Toyota as they are "listening" here in innovation-rich California. They have an important design center in Newport Beach. They collaborate with UC Irvine's National Fuel-Cell Research Center in a variety of ways. John Graham finished his dissertation comparing Japanese and American negotiation styles in 1980 supported by a grant from Toyota Motor Sales, USA, to the University of Southern California. And perhaps most impressive is their joint venture with General Motors.

The GM/Toyota joint venture plant in Fremont, California, remains one of the most successful international alliances in corporate history after more than 20 years. The New United Motor Manufacturing, Inc. (NUMMI) plant itself continues to win quality awards both for the cars it produces, but most recently for energy savings—the U.S. Environmental Protection Agency granted its ENERGY STAR Sustained Excellence 2006 Award to the Fremont plant. It is also interesting to note that the Toyota Corolla is the best-selling passenger car in the history of the planet. Of the 31 million Corollas produced over the last four decades, 2.5 million were built at the NUMMI facility. The plant has some 5,700 employees and is represented by the United Auto Workers, Local 2244. Almost 70 percent of the workforce are minorities. General Motors has adopted many of Toyota's manufacturing processes in its plants all over the world. Toyota has expanded its international manufacturing operations from the NUMMI experiment to seven new countries including five additional plants in the United States.

Perhaps most interesting is Jeffrey Liker's relationship-oriented explanation of Toyota's fundamental motivation for joining GM in NUMMI:

> . . . But at least one consideration was that Toyota realized GM was the world's largest carmaker and was struggling in its manufacturing operations. By helping to raise the level of manufacturing at GM, they were helping American society and the community, as well as creating high-paying manufacturing jobs for Americans. The senior executives at Toyota speak of giving back something to the U.S. for the help they provided Japan to rebuild its industry after World War II. This is not mere lip service or pie-in-the-sky idealism. They really believe it.[14]

The two firms are now engaged in a new five-year partnership to develop and possibly jointly produce advanced-technology vehicles, including those powered by fuel cells.

It's interesting to look back and see how the companies got together in the first place. Steven Weiss,[15] a professor of International Business at York University in Canada and one of the most prolific writers on the subject of international business negotiations, comments at length on the original negotiations between the two companies:

Creating an international joint venture is neither an easy nor certain process. Like other negotiations, joint venture negotiations may at worst fail completely. Undertaking negotiations in an international context, moreover, adds obstacles as well as opportunities. Before its talks with GM for example, Toyota negotiated with Ford (unsuccessfully as it turned out) for 13 months. Even the GM-Toyota talks were in participants' words, "long," "hard" and "frustrating." So the agreement leading to the establishment of the joint venture now known as New United Motor Manufacturing, Inc. (NUMMI) represents an important accomplishment . . .

GM's decision to enter joint venture negotiations, like Toyota's, appears to follow naturally from the two companies' interests and complementary resources and skills. Through collaboration GM could learn production and management techniques from a company renowned for them, and Toyota could gain low-cost entry to the U.S. auto industry with the assistance of the industry leader. Other concerns and motivations are also worth noting . . .

On the skeptical side, one could speculate that each company could gain merely from the act of negotiating, regardless of the result. During the Toyota-Ford talks, after all, several American observers opined that Toyota was simply trying to demonstrate responsiveness to the Ministry of International Trade and Industry (MITI) and the U.S. government without intending to reach an agreement. The same motivation coupled with gathering information about GM is conceivable here. GM too could benefit from "side effects" such as learning more about its competitor and delaying Toyota's move to produce and to sell without restraints in the U.S. The delays, expressed "worries," and actions that came up during the negotiations are consistent with these possibilities.

One GM participant who was interviewed mentioned that the possibility of Toyota's simply "buying time" did occur to the GM team and concerned them enough to ask Toyota about it. Toyota responded that they were negotiating in good faith and would go into the joint venture with an "open mind." GM itself had no desire to learn just from negotiating, according to another GM interviewee.

Communication was difficult due to culturally based factors. For example, Japanese negotiators for Toyota addressed issues in ways that appeared "oblique" to the GM team. Some silences and affirmations at the negotiating table were mistaken for agreement. Translation also slowed the negotiation process considerably.

Negotiating and decision-making styles also contrasted. According to the participants interviewed, the Japanese tended to start talks with statements of general principles and usually did not respond to proposals before checking with their headquarters. The Americans preferred specific proposals and responses at the table. In fact, the GM team received so few proposals from Toyota initially that they wondered where they stood. Further, Toyota was struck by GM negotiators' ability to source information quickly from particular individuals within their organization; GM saw the Toyota team's ability as less clear cut . . .

The agreement reached . . . stipulated:

1. Limited production of a car derived from Toyota's "new front wheel drive Sprinter" for sale directly to GM.
2. Equal shares of capital from the parent companies (as it turned out, $100 million cash from Toyota; from GM, $11 million cash and the Fremont plant ($89 million); and another $250 million was later raised.
3. Equal ownership by the parents.
4. Design of the Fremont manufacturing layout by Toyota, construction of a stamping plant.
5. A "reasonable royalty" to Toyota for the license to manufacture the car.
6. Technical assistance from GM and Toyota on a cost-plus basis.
7. Nominal annual production capacity of 200,000 cars.
8. Pricing joint venture cars on a market-basket standard.
9. Startup for the 1985 Model Year.

Some American observers complained in the American press that Toyota out-negotiated GM. Toyota did gain operational control of the venture, although that could have been seen by GM as necessary for creating an accurate and didactic model of Toyota's system. Most of the components were to be Japanese. Toyota also had a built-in client and royalties and other fees that considerably lowered its risk. Toyota clearly gained a great deal. But the achievement of each company's primary goal, learning from the other, depended on yet to be designed mechanisms and on experiences of the joint venture well after startup.

At least based on John Seely Brown's criterion, "mutual long-term increases in capabilities" have been dramatically achieved in the NUMMI joint venture.

PRESCRIPTIONS AND CONCLUSIONS

The first step toward this new kind of commerce we've described is recognizing that business negotiations are not a competitive activity, nor are they a problem-solving activity. Rather, they are opportunities for innovation and mutual gain through long-term relationships. Anything less than a creative outcome is leaving money on the table. Anything less than a creative outcome is a primitive way of doing business. Anything less than a creative outcome is a bad outcome.

The second step is building international negotiation skills in your company. All of the new ideas about open innovation and such don't work internationally unless managers and engineers from different companies and cultures are able to communicate efficiently with one another. This book is meant to serve as an outline for an international negotiations training program. It combines our ideas about both negotiation processes and creativity. So, follow the fish: Knowledge ➔ Communication ➔ Creativity.

#1. Accept only creative outcomes
#2. Understand cultures, especially your own.
#3. Don't just adjust to cultural differences, exploit them as well.
#4. Gather intelligence and reconnoiter the terrain.
#5. Design the information flow.
#6. Invest in personal relationships.
#7. Persuade with questions.
#8. Make no concessions until the end.
#9. Use techniques of creativity.
#10. Continue creativity after negotiations.

The third step is beginning to build these skills into job descriptions and HR strategies in your company. Training and experience in international negotiations and creative processes should be important criteria for hiring new employees.

The fourth step involves developing a cadre of what we will call "relationship managers." In concept, these roles are similar to other boundary spanning job titles such as account managers or project managers. They become the relationship-building glue between international business partners. Their jobs are to promote trust and creativity within the partnerships similar to that described by John Seely Brown and the others.

The fifth, and perhaps the final, step is to create and manage strategic relationships in which boundaries between companies, countries, and cultures begin to dissolve. Such commercial relationships replace fences and serve as bridges that stimulate innovation and human progress.

Herein we haven't just given you a fish. Instead, we hope we've actually taught you how to fish—taught you to take a new, creative approach to your international negotiations. And if we've done a really good job with the book, you now can see ways to use it to teach your colleagues and organizations how to fish as well. Indeed, we hope what we've taught you will actually serve you well even if your metaphorical fishery collapses (think Monterey Bay sardines), that is, when the economic or ecological seas are their roughest. That will be the time when we need new ideas the most, and those spawned from *Global Negotiation* will be among the most useful.

NOTES

INTRODUCTION

1. All cases are based on actual events. Specific effort is given to being as faithful as possible to the underlying facts while presenting the multitude of issues as clearly and comprehensively as possible. Similar care has been given to the confidential and sensitive nature of some of the information included. Throughout this book, we adhere as closely as possible to this stated policy.

CHAPTER 1

1. In addition to our subsequent work, two earlier articles have served as a foundation for this chapter: "Negotiators Abroad—Don't Shoot from the Hip" by John L. Graham and Roy A. Herberger, *Harvard Business Review,* July-August 1983, pp. 160–168; and John L. Graham's, "Vis-à-vis International Business Negotiations," Chapter 9 in Pervez N. Ghauri and Jean-Claude Usunier (eds.), *International Business Negotiations* (Oxford: Pergamon, 1996), pp. 69–90.
2. *Expansion,* November 29, 1991, p. 41.
3. There are two hugely important books on this topic well worth the read on your next overseas flight: Jared Diamond's *Guns, Germs, and Steel: The Fates of Human Societies* (New York: Norton, 1999) won a Pulitzer Prize. Richard E. Nisbett's *The Geography of Thought: How Asians and Westerners Think Differently . . . and Why* (New York: Free Press, 2003) is essential reading for anyone doing business in Asia. Use your jet-lag recovery days to read your reports, etc.
4. Actually, we may have all been better off if Thomas Jefferson and the Founding Fathers had used the more accurate terms, *Declaration of Political Sovereignty.* Globalization has taught us that nations, even the "most powerful country on the planet," are still *inter*dependent.
5. We think this is the most often forgotten word in his sentence. He says "frequently," not "always" or even "most of the time." Through his use of the term "frequently," Smith granted that competitive behavior can have negative consequences for society and organizations, and cooperative behavior can be a good thing. This subtlety in his lesson is most often missed (ignored?) by our colleagues in the finance departments of our business schools and on Wall Street. Gordon Gecko actually should have said, "Greed is *frequently* good."
6. We note that many U.S. medical schools have gone to a pass/fail grading system because the competition between the high-achieving students over grades did damage to the learning process.
7. We laud James Sebenius and his colleagues at the Harvard Business School for making a course on Negotiations a requirement in their MBA program. Most schools offer negotiations as a popular elective, but Harvard has rightly recognized that negotiations are a fundamental aspect of commercial activity by giving it prominence in their curriculum.
8. We do get arguments from Australians on this. They often describe Americans as stuffy and hierarchical. Indeed, as will be seen in Chapter 3, they as a group score lower on the power distance index (PDI), 36 to the American 40.
9. *The McNeil Lehrer News Hour,* April 4, 1991.
10. W. H. Newman, "Cultural Assumptions Underlying U.S. Management Concepts," in *Management in the International Context,* James L. Massie, Jan Luytjons, and N. William Hazen, eds. (New York: Harper&Row, 1972), p. 75.

CHAPTER 2

1. Geert Hofstede, *Culture's Consequences,* 2nd edition (Thousand Oaks, CA: Sage, 2001); Susan P. Douglas, "Exploring New Worlds: The Challenge of Global Marketing," *Journal of Marketing,* January 2001, pp. 103–109.

2. Edward T. Hall, *The Silent Language* (New York: Doubleday, 1959), p. 26.

3. James D. Hodgson, Yoshihiro Sano, and John L. Graham, *Doing Business with the New Japan* (Boulder, CO: Rowman & Littlefield, 2008).

4. Deborah Tannen, *The Argument Culture: Stopping America's War of Words* (New York: Ballentine, 1999).

5. Harry C. Triandis, *Individualism and Collectivism* (Boulder, CO: Westview Press, 1995).

6. Edward T. Hall, "The Silent in Overseas Business," *Harvard Business Review*, May–June, 1960, pp. 87–96. A discussion of the salience of Hall's work appears in John L. Graham, "Culture and Human Resources Management," Alan M. Rugman and Thomas L. Brewer (eds.), *The Oxford Handbook of International Business* (Oxford: Oxford University Press, 2001) pp. 503–536.

7. The spices a nursing mother consumes actually affect the flavor of the milk she produces.

8. Joel West and John L. Graham, "A Linguistics-Based Measure of Cultural Distance and Its Relationship to Managerial Values," *Management International Review*, 2004, 44(3), pp. 239–260.

9. In English, there were historically two second-person forms. That is, "thee" was the informal form up until the last century. Even in some Spanish speaking countries such as Costa Rica "tu" is being dropped in a similar manner.

10. Martin J. Gannon, *Understanding Global Cultures: Metaphorical Journeys through 23 Nations* (Thousand Oaks, CA: Sage, 2001).

11. Richard Nisbett, *The Gergraphy of Thought* (Nicholas Brealey Publishing Ltd., 2005).

12. Lawrence I. Harrison and Samuel P. Huntington (eds.), *Culture Matters* (New York: Basic Books, 2000).

CHAPTER 3

1. Max Weber, *The Protestant Ethic and Spirit of Capitalism* (London: George Allen & Unwin, 1930, 1976).

2. David C. McClelland, *The Achieving Society* (New York: Free Press, 1985).

3. Edward T. Hall, "Learning the Arabs' Silent Language," *Psychology Today*, August 1979, pp. 45–53. Hall has several books that should be read by everyone involved in international business: *The Silent Language* (New York: Doubleday, 1959), *The Hidden Dimension* (New York: Doubleday, 1966), and *Beyond Culture* (New York: Anchor Press-Doubleday, 1976).

4. Interestingly, the etymology of the term "frankness" has to do with the Franks, an ancient Germanic tribe that settled along the Rhine. This is not mere coincidence, it's history influencing symbols (that is, language).

5. Robert Levine, *The Geography of Time* (New York: Basic Books, 1998).

6. Lester Thurow, *Head to Head* (New York: William Morrow, 1992).

7. Cathy Anterasian, John L. Graham, and R. Bruce Money, "Are U.S. Managers Superstitious about Market Share?" *Sloan Management Review*, 37(4), pp. 67–77.

8. Don Y. Lee and Philip L. Dawes, "Guanxi, Trust, and Long-Term Orientation in Chinese Business Markets," *Journal of International Marketing*, 2005, 13(2), pp. 28–56.

9. Mark Lam and John L. Graham, *China Now* (New York: McGraw-Hill, 2007).

10. This continuum has also been labeled "social context salience" in H. Rika Houston and John L. Graham, 2000.

11. Richard E. Nisbett, *The Geography of Thought* (New York: Free Press, 2003).

CHAPTER 4

1. Several excellent books have been published on the topic of international business negotiations. Among them are Lothar Katz, *Negotiating International Business* (Booksurge LLC, 2006); Jeanne M. Brett, *Negotiating Globally* (San Francisco: Josey-Bass, 2007); Michelle Gelford and Jeanne Brett (eds.), *The Handbook of Negotiation and Culture* (Stanford, CA: Stanford Business Books, 2004); Camille Schuster and Michael Copeland, *Global Business Practices, Adapting for Success* (Mason, OH: Thompson, 2006); Robert T. Moran and William G. Stripp, *Dynamics of Successful International Business Negotiations* (Houston: Gulf, 1991); Pervez Ghauri and Jean-Claude Usunier (eds.), *International Business Negotiations* (Oxford: Pergamon, 1996); Donald W. Hendon, Rebecca Angeles Hendon, and Paul Herbig, *Cross-Cultural Business Negotiations* (Westport, CT: Quorum, 1996); Sheida Hodge, *Global Smarts* (New York: Wiley, 2000); and Jeanne M. Brett, *Negotiating Globally* (San Francisco: Jossey-Bass, 2001). Additionally, Roy J. Lewicki, David M. Saunders, and John W. Minton's *Negotiation: Readings, Exercises, and Cases*, 3rd edition (Boston: Irwin/McGraw-Hill, 1999) is an important book on

the broader topic of business negotiations. The material from this chapter draws extensively on John L. Graham, "Vis-à-Vis International Business Negotiations," Chapter 3, pp. 69–91, in the Ghauri and Usunier book; James Day Hodgson, Yoshihiro Sano, and John L. Graham, *Doing Business with the New Japan* (Boulder, CO: Rowman & Littlefield, 2008); and John L. Graham, "Culture and Human Resources Management," in Alan M. Rugman and Thomas L. Brewer (eds.), *The Oxford Handbook of International Business* (Oxford: Oxford University Press, 2001), pp. 503–536 .

2. Suein L. Hwang, "Some Type A Staffers Dress for Success with a Shot of Botox," *Wall Street Journal,* June 31, 2002, pages B1.

3. The following institutions and people have provided crucial support for the research upon which this material is based: U.S. Department of Education; Toyota Motor Sales USA, Inc.; Solar Turbines, Inc. (a division of Caterpillar Tractors Co.); the Faculty Research and Innovation Fund and the International Business Educational Research (IBEAR) Program at the University of Southern California; Ford Motor Company; The Marketing Science Institute; Madrid Business School; and Professors Nancy J. Adler (McGill University), Nigel Campbell (Manchester Business School), A. Gabriel Esteban (University of Houston, Victoria), Leonid I. Evenko (Russian Academy of the National Economy), Richard H. Holton (University of California, Berkeley), Alain Jolibert (Université des Sciences Sociales de Grenoble), Dong Ki Kim (Korea University), C. Y. Lin (National Sun-Yat Sen University), Hans-Gunther Meissner (Dortmund University), Alena Ockova (Czech Management Center), Sara Tang (Mass Transit Railway Corporation, Hong Kong), Kam-hon Lee (The Chinese University of Hong Kong), and Theodore Schwarz (Monterrey Institute of Technology).

4. For additional details see John L. Graham, "Culture and Human Resources Management," in Alan M. Rugman and Thomas L. Brewer (eds.), *The Oxford Handbook of International Business* (Oxford: Oxford University Press, 2001), pp. 503–536.

5. "A Global Generation Gap," Pew Research Center report, February 24, 2004.

6. Roger O. Crockett, "The 21st Century Meeting," *BusinessWeek,* February 26, 2007, pp. 72–80.

7. Albert Mehrabian, *Silent Messages; Implicit Communication of Emotions and Attitudes* (2nd edition, Belmont, CA: Wadsworth, 1980).

8. As quoted in Walter Iasaacson's *Einstein* (New York: Simon and Schuster, 2007). The story about the "little tramp's" love for a beautiful blind girl was doubly ironic—she could neither see the city lights nor his facial movements. Thanks Lionel!

9. Donald D. Hoffman, *Visual Intelligence: How We Created What We See* (New York: Norton, 1998).

10. Roger Fisher, William Ury, and Bruce Patton, *Getting to Yes: Negotiating Agreement without Giving In* (New York: Penguin, 1991).

11. Geert Hofstede, *Cultures Consequences* (2nd edition, Thousand Oaks, CA: Sage, 2001).

CHAPTER 5

1. Richard E. Davis, "Compatibility in Corporate Marriages," *Harvard Business Review,* July-August 1968, pp. 87–93.

2. Scarlet Pruitt, "AOLTW Board May Attempt to Oust Case," *InfoWorld Daily News,* September 17, 2002.

3. Ron S. Fortgang, David A. Lax, and James K. Sebenius, "Negotiating the Spirit of the Deal," *Harvard Business Review,* February 2003, pp. 66–75.

4. "Survey Uncovers Generation Gap in Attitudes to Industry," sponsored by The Work Foundation, October 1, 2006, www.prneswire.co.uk.

5. "A Global Generation Gap," Pew Research Center report, February 24, 2004.

6. Joel Garreau, *The Nine Nations of North America* (New York: Avon, 1989).

7. N. Mark Lam and John L. Graham, *China Now: Doing Business in the World's Most Dynamic Market* (New York: McGraw-Hill, 2007).

8. Joel Kotkin, *Tribes: How Race, Religion, and Identity Determine Success in the New Global Economy* (New York: Random House, 1992).

9. Ibid., from the back cover.

10. Deborah Tannen, *You Just Don't Understand: Men and Women in Conversation* (New York: William Morrow, 1990).

11. Hodgson, et al., *Doing Business with the New Japan,* 2008.

12. Nancy J. Adler, "Pacific Basin Managers: A Gaijin, Not a Woman," *Human Resource Management,* 26(2), summer 1987 pp. 169–191; and Nancy J. Adler, *International Dimensions of Organizational Behavior,* 4th edition (Mason, OH: Southwestern College Publishing, 2001).

CHAPTER 6

1. Peter Drucker, "Management by Walking Around, Outside," *Wall Street Journal*, May 11, 1990, p. A15.
2. AAP–6 (2004)—NATO Glossary of Terms and Definitions, p. 96
3. As defined in Sec. 931 of Public Law 109–163, entitled, "National Defense Authorization Act for Fiscal Year 2006." Open-source intelligence (OSINT) is intelligence that is produced from publicly available information and is collected, exploited, and disseminated in a timely manner to an appropriate audience for the purpose of addressing a specific intelligence requirement.
4. www.eiu.com (accessed April 15, 2007).
5. www.oxan.com (accessed April 15, 2007.
6. Moon Ihlwan and Kenji Hall, "New Tech, Old Habits," *BusinessWeek*, March 26, 2007, pp. 48–49.
7. Edward Iwata, "More U.S. Trade Secrets Walk out Door with Foreign Spies," *USA Today*, February 13, 2003, p. 5A.

CHAPTER 7

1. Daniel Goleman, *Social Intelligence: The New Science of Human Relationships* (New York: Bantam, 2006), p. 84.
2. The Harvard Program on Negotiations provides a range of negotiations courses (www.pon.harvard.edu). Also, negotiations courses are the most popular in MBA programs around the country: see Leigh Thompson and Geoffrey J. Leonardelli, "Why Negotiation Is the Most Popular Business Course," *Ivey Business Journal Online*, July/August 2004, p. 1.
3. See Karrass's website for information regarding his programs: www.karrass.com. Other websites providing information about publically offered training programs and information on international negotiation styles are www.pon.harvard.edu, www.usip.org, www.iimcr.org, www.executiveplanet.com, www.etiquetteintl.com. See Marisa Mohd Isa, "Learning the Art of Refined Behavior," *New Straits Times*, March 17, 2003, p. 23.
4. Lee Edison provides an interesting description of what he calls "The Negotiation Industry," in an article he wrote in *Across the Board*, April 2000, 37(4), pp. 14–20. Other commentators on training for international business negotiators are Yeang Soo Ching, "Putting a Human Face on Globalization," *New Straits Times*, January 16, 2000, p. 10; A. J. Vogl, "Negotiation: The Advanced Course," *Across the Board*, April 1, 2000, p. 21; and R. V. Veera, "MIT Preparing Students for New Millennium," *New Straits Times*, July 21, 2002, p. 5.
5. Daniel Michaels, "Boeing and Airbus in Dogfight to Meet Stringent Terms of Iberia's Executives," *Wall Street Journal*, March 10, 2003, pp. A1 and A5.
6. David A. Lax and James K. Sebenius, "3-D Negotiations Playing the Whole Game," *Harvard Business Review*, November 2003; and their book, *3-D Negotiations: Powerful Tools to Change the Game in Your Most Important Deals* (Boston: Harvard Business School Press, 2006).

CHAPTER 8

1. James K. Sebenius, "The Hidden Challenge of Cross-Border Negotiations," *Harvard Business Review*, March 2002, pp. 76–82.
2. Richard H. Solomon, *Chinese Negotiating Behavior* (Washington, DC: USIP Press, 1999), p. 9.
3. Howard Raiffa with John Richardson and David Metcalfe, *Negotiation Analysis* (Cambridge, MA: Belknap, 2002), p. 196.
4. Roger Fisher and William Ury, *Getting to Yes* (New York: Penguin, 1981).
5. David J. Lax and James K. Sebenius, *3-D Negotiations: Powerful Tools to Change the Game in Your Most Important Deals* (Boston: Harvard Business School Press, 2006).
6. Lawrence Susskind, Sarah McKearnan, and Jennifer Thomas-Larmer, *The Consensus-Building Handbook: A Comprehensive Guide to Reaching Agreement* (Thousand Oaks, CA: Sage, 1999).
7. Ann Hulbert, "Re-Education," *New York Times Magazine*, April 1, 2007, pp. 36–43.

CHAPTER 9

1. Ron S. Fortgang, David A. Lax, and James K. Sebenius, "Negotiating the Spirit of the Deal," *Harvard Business Review*, February 2003, pp. 66–73.
2. See www.ita.doc.gov/goodgovernance/regions/index.asp.

3. Susan Hamrock and Fewick Yu, "Dispute Avoidance and Dispute Resolution in China," *Export America*, U.S. Department of Commerce, April 2003.
4. Toh Han Shih, "Reforms of China's Trade Arbitration System Welcomed," *South China Morning Post*, May 2, 2005, p. 3.

CHAPTER 10

1. Joel Kotkin, *Tribes* (New York: Random House, 1993).
2. Lothar Katz, *Negotiating International Business* (Booksurge, LLC, 2006), p. 226.
3. Sanjoynt P. Dunung, *Doing Business in Asia* (New York: Lexington Books, 1995), p. 358.
4. Rajesh Kumar, "Negotiating with the Complex, Imaginative Indian," *Ivey Business Journal* (April 2005): 3. Also see Professor Kumar's book with Anand Kumar Sethi, *Doing Business in India: A Guide for the Western Expatriate Manager* (New York: Palgrave Macmillan, 2005).
5. Kumar, "Negotiating with the Complex, Imaginative Indian," p. 5.
6. Kotkin, pp. 214–215.
7. Manoj Joshi, *Passport India* (San Rafael, CA: World Trade Press, 1997).
8. Kumar and Sethi, 2005.

CHAPTER 11

1. For an abbreviated history, we found useful *The Mexico Reader: History, Culture, Politics (The Latin America Readers)* by Gilbert M. Joseph and Timothy J. Henderson, eds. (Duke University Press, 2003).
2. The 1968 Olympics in Mexico City during the Gustavo Diaz Ordaz administration, the Jose Lopez Portillo era and the Harvard-educated Miguel de la Madrid government as the most recent.
3. The official name of Mexico is "Estados Unidos Mexicanos."
4. *Gringo* (feminine, *gringa*) is a term in the Spanish and Portuguese languages used to refer to foreigners, especially those from the United States. Although its original meaning was perhaps derogatory, its usage today is not necessarily pejorative, even though it may be considered offensive by English speakers. The American Heritage Dictionary does however classify the term as offensive slang. In informal Spanish speech, *gringo* offers a convenient shorthand to refer to a person from the United States, since the term "American" is used to refer to anyone from the entire American continent (North, Central, and South), while the more specific term "estadounidense" ("one from the United States") is somewhat cumbersome to pronounce. www.wikipedia.com.
5. Randy Malat, *Passport Mexico*, World Trade Press, San Rafael, California, 1996, p. 19.
6. Malat, p. 34.
7. Trans.: "farming cooperative that squatted on the land"
8. Very much like German, Spanish has a formal and informal variation of "you." In referring to another, the variation used is critical to understanding the underlying relationship. In the acquisition of the language, even in learning catch phrases, one would do well in first learning the formal. It is always easier to lower the treatment rather than attempt to raise it.
9. *Machismo* is a noun of Spanish origin, and refers to a prominently exhibited or excessive masculinity. The word *machismo*—and its derivatives *machista* and *macho*, "he who espouses *machismo*"—comes from the Spanish word *macho*, meaning "male" or "manly." (The word *macho* literally translates as "male," but is applied primarily to animals in this sense.) In Spanish *macho* can sometimes mean "courageous" or "valorous," although *machista* rarely has such positive connotations. As an attitude, machismo ranges from a personal sense of virility to a more extreme masculinism. Most *machistas* believe in conservative gender roles. Generally speaking, *machistas* oppose a woman's right to work, participate in sports, or pursue other traditionally male roles in society. Many *machistas* also believe it is their right as men to seek extramarital adventures, although women are to remain faithful. *Machistas* believe that women were created to stay home and be mothers and wives. Thus, most *machistas* believe firmly in the superiority of men over women. www.wikipedia.com.

CHAPTER 12

1. There is an exception to this rule. Huge Chinese trading junks plied the oceans about 70 years before Columbus, and some argue they visited the Americas at the time. See Gavin Menzies" *1421: The Year China Discovered America* (New York: Morrow, 2003) if you enjoy historical controversies.

2. The classic portrayal of the life of Chinese peasants Wang-Lung and O-Lan. Awarded the Pulitzer Prize for fiction in 1932 and the William Dean Howells Medal for the most distinguished work of American fiction published in the period 1930–35 in 1935.

3. Fung Yu-Lan, *A Short History of Chinese Philosophy: A Systematic Account of Chinese Thought From Its Origins to the Present Day* (New York: Free Press, Reissue edition, 1997), pp. 17–19.

4. Also often spelled K'ung-fu-tzu.

5. Michael Harris Bond, *Beyond the Chinese Face* (Oxford: Oxford University Press, 1991).

CHAPTER 13

1. Excerpted from "The Embargo," Hunry Mullen. See Jerry W. Knudson, *Jefferson and the Press: Crucible of Liberty* (University of South Carolina Press, 2006).

2. Margaret MacMillan, *Nixon and Mao: The Week that Changed the World* (New York: Random House, 2007).

3. Henry Kissinger, *Diplomacy* (New York: Simon and Schuster, 1995). Perhaps in his more recent books and based on his current international business dealings he's wised up on the importance of trade, but we haven't seen value in reading them.

4. Jared Diamond, *Guns, Germs, and Steel: The Fates of Human Societies* (New York: Norton, 2005).

5. Roger von Oech, *A Whack on the Side of the Head: How You Can Be More Creative* (3rd edition, New York: Warner Books, 1998). Also see John Kao, *Innovation Nation: How America Is Losing Its Innovation Edge* (New York: Free Press, 2007). He defines " . . . creative arbitrage . . . taking advantage of cultural, market, and technological differences" (page 245).

6. We recognize that slaves brought from Africa, native Americans, women, and others haven't always enjoyed freedom of speech, even in the United States.

7. Everett M. Rogers, *Diffusion of Innovations* (5th edition, New York: Free Press, 2003).

8. Malcolm Gladwell, *The Tipping Point* (New York: Back Bay Books, 2002), p. 306.

9. Henry Chesbrough, *Open Innovation: The New Imperative for Creating and Profiting from Technology* (Boston: Harvard Business School Press, 2006).

10. John Hagel III and John Seely Brown, *The Only Sustainable Edge* (Boston: Harvard Business School Press, 2005), pp. 100, 116–117.

11. Philips Research, *Password,* Issue 26, February 2006, p. 14.

12. Tom Kelley with Jonathan Littman, *The Ten Faces of Innovation* (New York: Currency-Doubleday, 2005).

13. Jeffrey K. Liker, *The Toyota Way* (New York: McGraw-Hill, 2004), pp. 75, 202.

14. Ibid., page[0] 75.

15. Stephen E. Weiss, "Creating the GM-Toyota Joint Venture: A Case in Complex Negotiation," *Columbia Journal of World Business,* Summer 1987, pp. 23–37.

INDEX